Sea Venture

WEST'S
FORT
• Orapaks
• Powhatan

Chickahominy River

Pamunkey (York) River

• Werowocomoco

Henrico
• Weyanock
• Chickahominy

Paspahegh

Powhatan (James) River

JAMES
FORT

• Kiskiack

Appomattoc

Chesapeake Bay

JAMESTOWN ISLAND

HOG ISLAND

Kecoughtan
• FORT
ALGERNON

SCALE
0   5   10   15
in Miles

Nansemond

ENGLISH SETTLEMENTS
AND
NATIVE VILLAGES
IN VIRGINIA

Map by David Cain

Sea Venture

Shipwreck, Survival, and the
Salvation of the First English Colony
in the New World

KIERAN DOHERTY

ST. MARTIN'S PRESS
New York

www.stmartins.com

Design by Kathryn Parise
Frontispiece map by David Cain

LIBRARY OF CONGRESS CATALOGING-IN-PUBLICATION DATA

Doherty, Kieran.
    Sea venture : shipwreck, survival, and the salvation of the first English colony in the New World / by Kieran Doherty.—1st ed.
        p. cm.
    Includes bibliographical references.
    ISBN-13: 978-0-312-35453-4
    ISBN-10: 0-312-35453-3
    1. Jamestown (Va.)—History—17th century.   2. Sea venture (Ship).
3. Seafaring life—History—17th century.   4. Shipwrecks—Bermuda Islands—History—17th century.   5. Bermuda Islands—History—17th century.   6. Virginia—History—Colonial period, ca. 1600–1775.
7. Great Britain—Colonies—America—History—17th century.   I. Title.

F234.J3D64   2007
973.2'1—dc22

                                                          2007005488

First Edition: May 2007

10   9   8   7   6   5   4   3   2   1

To my wife, Lynne

CONTENTS

ACKNOWLEDGMENTS

My deepest thanks go:

To James Fitzgerald, my agent, who took me on when I needed guidance and help. To Michael Flamini at St. Martin's Press, who was ready with encouragement and guidance; I hope I have lived up to his expectations.

To the people of Bermuda for making me feel welcome during my brief sojourn to do research. To William Kelso and his staff on the Jamestown Rediscovery Team for their hard work and dedication in bringing Jamestown back to life. To my friends and family in Richmond, Virginia, for hospitality and support.

To Mark Ford, mentor and loyal friend for many years, for all his support. To Sylvia Andrews and Peter Hawkins and the other members of my writing circle for critiques of the work in progress. To Jack Nordloh for his words of encouragement. To Jack Furet for all his help over the years. To John and Vicky Manley for their assistance in solving a particularly vexing problem.

Special thanks to that overlooked group of professionals, the librarians, who give unstintingly of their time to help writers like me find the materials we need. And to my mother, Mary Doherty, herself a librarian, for instilling in me a love of books and history.

Very special thanks to my wife, Lynne, for taking the time to lend her editing skills to the effort, for listening to my talk about the *Sea Venture* and her passengers, and, of course, for all her loving pep talks in the dark days.

Any mistakes in this volume are mine and mine alone.

Sea Venture

I

"Preparations Most Urgent"

In the spring of 1609, all London was filled with talk of Virginia. Businessmen who gathered in the nave of old St. Paul's and in the vast courtyard of the Royal Exchange spoke excitedly of the profits that might be theirs if they invested in a new scheme to settle the rich lands named in honor of the Virgin Queen. Sailors on the docks and boatmen on the Thames traded in wild tales of the riches that waited in the lands of the Chesapeake. Gentlemen and poets who met in the Mermaid Tavern and other London watering holes mused late into the night, night after night, of Virginia, nothing but Virginia. Preachers spoke of the chance to do God's work while finding opportunity in that far-off country the Almighty had set aside for England. The unemployed and desperate, whose minds raced at the thought of owning their own land, made hurried plans to leave crowded, dirty, smoky London for a better life, no matter what the dangers.

Profits, freedom from want, and the possibility of escape from desperate lives, all these things and more seemed possible in this place called Virginia. Though most who dreamed of emigrating knew as little of the distant lands across the Atlantic as they knew of the moon, they were willing to believe the lines that had been written by the poet Michael Drayton, giving voice to the hopes and dreams of the first Virginia settlers who had left England for the New World in late 1606:

Virginia,
Earth's only paradise!
Where nature has in store
Fowl, venison, and fish,
And the fruitful'st soil
Without your toil,
Three harvests more,
All greater than your wish.[1]

It mattered little to these westward-looking Englishmen that many of those who had already made the journey from England to the lands they called Virginia found death instead of opportunity. It mattered little that in the two years since a group of English settlers struggled ashore in Virginia to establish a settlement they called Jamestown no fortunes had been made, no gold or pearls or silver had been discovered. This was a new day, a new opportunity for all to gamble their money (or their very lives) in the hopes that England would finally, after a long history of failure, establish a profitable, secure, and lasting presence in that far-off land most could not even begin to imagine, a settlement where dreams could come true.

One Londoner who saw Virginia as a place he might find financial salvation was William Strachey, a failed civil servant, poetaster, and sometime playwright. The son of a successful gentleman with landholdings in rural Essex, Strachey had studied law at Gray's Inn, but cut his training short to spend his time scratching out mostly unpublished verse and socializing with London's literary set.[2] Strachey particularly enjoyed London's lively and rambunctious playhouses. He was a stockholder in Blackfriars Theatre and a regular playgoer who was almost certainly friendly with the company's actors, including William Shakespeare. Strachey was also acquainted with other well-known dramatists and poets of his time. In a letter, the poet John Donne called Strachey "allways my good friend."[3] He was close enough to Ben Jonson, the poet and playwright, to write a dedicatory verse included in the quarto version of Jonson's play *Sejanus*, performed by Shakespeare's company in 1603 and published in 1605. Strachey's circle of friends almost certainly also included George Chapman, a collaborator with Jonson in the writing of *Eastward Ho!*, a somewhat scandalous play about the Virginia colony.

Living a literary gentleman-poet's lifestyle took so much of Strachey's time in the early 1600s that he seems not to have had many hours to devote to the business of making money. And what with evenings at the theater and afternoons spent in Southwark watching cockfights and bearbaitings and hours spent drinking and swapping lies with his friends, Strachey found himself forced to borrow heavily from London's moneylenders. In 1606, in an attempt to claw his way free from the morass of debt in which he found himself, he used family connections to land a job as secretary to the ambassador to Constantinople and traveled with his employer to the Turkish capital.[4] His hopes of recouping his fortunes in the foreign service ended in near disgrace and even deeper indebtedness, however, when he had a falling out with the ambassador and was forced to borrow money to return to London.

By the spring of 1609, Strachey—he was aged thirty-six or thirty-seven by then—was so deep in debt that he feared imprisonment. Sometime that spring, a friend who had been jailed as a debtor wrote a letter to Strachey pleading with him for aid. Strachey replied that he was "haretly sorrie" he was unable to help, adding that he was himself in danger of being sent to prison "for want of present money."[5] In fact, Strachey's situation was perilous. As the weather warmed that spring and the Thames thawed and began flowing again after one of the coldest winters ever, he knew that each time he dared to quit his lodgings for even a brief foray into the street, he ran the risk of an unpleasant scene with a creditor or—worse—arrest and a stint in the Clink or one of London's other infamous gaols.

Still, it is safe to assume that Strachey managed to sneak from his lodgings to meet with friends, probably to try to borrow funds or simply to escape the tedium of his rented rooms. It would be surprising if he did not, on occasion, make his way along Cheapside, London's main market street, to the turning that led to the door of the Mermaid Tavern, where his friends Jonson and Donne were frequent visitors. Perhaps it was there that Jonson told him—it was advice he gave to others—that the only hope for any man in debt was to flee "to Constantinople, Ireland, or Virginia" if he wanted to rebuild his life and repair his credit.[6] Strachey had already tried his luck in Turkey, and failed. Now, while Ireland may have beckoned, it must have seemed to the impoverished poet that Virginia offered a better chance to escape his creditors and perhaps, just perhaps, his best opportunity, if not for riches, then for security and freedom.

And in 1609, he was ready to risk all to find blessed freedom from the financial woes that threatened to send him to the prison he called "that place of dead men . . . that Golgotha."[7] Of course, he had heard of Virginia. He was

obviously fond of the theater, fond enough to put some of his money at risk
as a shareholder of the Blackfriars Theatre Company. He said, in a court deposition, he visited the theater "sometymes once, twyce and thrice in a week."[8]
Given his love of theater, it would have been remarkable if he had not been in
the audience at least once when *Eastward Ho!*, coauthored by his friends Chapman and Jonson, was staged in 1605.[9] He would have heard Captain Seagull,
one of the characters in the play, cozen two young men not unlike himself
into signing on for a voyage to Virginia where Indians, in Seagull's words,
were so in love with the English "that all the treasure they have they lay at
their feet." Like the other Londoners in the audience, Strachey would have
been enthralled by the description of the land across the sea. And he must
have gasped when Seagull went on to describe the treasure that waited. "I tell
thee," Seagull said, "gold is more plentiful there than copper is with us; and
for as much red copper as I can bring, I'll have thrice the weight in gold. Why,
man, all their dripping pans and their chamber pots are pure gold; . . . and for
rubies and diamonds, they go forth on holidays and gather them on the sea
shore, to hang on their children's coats."[10]

By 1609 Strachey, like other Englishmen, knew that Seagull's words were
not true. He knew that no diamonds had been found on Virginia's beaches,
that no golden chamber pots had been discovered. But he also knew that the
land across the Atlantic still held hope for men like himself who wanted to
flee their problems in search of a new opportunity. And so, in the spring of
1609, William Strachey decided that Virginia was the answer to his troubles.

———◦•◦◦•◦———

Virginia—the Americas—had not always beckoned to England and Englishmen. Though an English ship under the command of Genoese mariner
John Cabot visited Newfoundland in 1497, just five years after Columbus
stumbled across the New World, there had been no serious attempt to establish an English presence in the Americas until 1583. In that year, Sir
Humphrey Gilbert, a brilliant navigator and explorer, led a fleet of ships to
Newfoundland in what proved to be an ill-fated attempt to build a settlement. The settlers soon found the weather too harsh and cold for their liking
and, after the flagship of Gilbert's fleet was lost with most of the expedition's
supplies, turned tail for home. During the voyage back to Plymouth, the fleet
ran into a fierce North Atlantic gale. Gilbert and his vessel, *Squirrel*, were lost
at sea with all hands.[11]

Following Gilbert's death, his patents to establish a settlement were transferred to his half brother, Sir Walter Ralegh. Ralegh (sometimes spelled Raleigh) was an avid backer of colonization who never visited the New World. Instead, he put his considerable fortune to work trying to establish a settlement in the vast territory he named Virginia in honor of the queen who had made him powerful and wealthy. His efforts to colonize Roanoke Island in what is now North Carolina ended tragically when what is now the famous "Lost Colony" vanished without a trace.

Following Ralegh's failure to establish a colony on Roanoke Island, no real attempt to settle the region known as Virginia was made for almost two decades. As Ralegh and Gilbert proved, it was a difficult matter for a private individual to finance the creation of a settlement. And Ralegh's beloved Virgin Queen was far too cautious with her funds to finance a colonial venture, even if England's long-running war with Spain had left enough coin in the royal treasury to cover the expense. Then, in 1603, everything changed.

Early in the morning of March 24 of that year, Elizabeth I, the queen whose reign was expected to outlast the moon and sun, died in her private chamber in Richmond Palace. The queen's death and the accession of James VI of Scotland as James I of England brought quick peace between England and Spain; freed private capital that could be used to finance foreign settlements; and made soldiers and sailors available, indeed desperate, for employment. Suddenly, English capitalists were looking hungrily at Virginia as a potential outlet for English woven goods, as a possible source of gold and other riches, and, it was hoped, as a shortcut to the Spice Islands of the Indies. By that time, English merchants had experience taking profits from foreign trade through the formation of joint stock companies like the Muscovy Company. Now they hoped to do the same in Virginia.

These merchants were achingly aware of the tragedies that had befallen Cabot and Gilbert and all the settlers of the Lost Colony. Some of them had backed Gilbert's ventures and Ralegh's, too. But, they told themselves, this was a new age. With ample financing and with the right men at the helm, Virginia would be settled and profits would be theirs for the taking.

In 1606 Sir Ferdinando Gorges, an accomplished soldier and the military governor of Plymouth, the city that was home to many of the Elizabethan sea dogs who had spent decades harassing Spanish ships, put together a consortium of merchant-investors who were willing to sign on to his idea to colonize the New World. These investors, along with some of their fellows in

London, asked King James I for government approval for their plans to establish colonies in Virginia—then considered to be the entire swath of land running roughly between Spanish Florida and the French colonies in Canada. Backers of the plan included Gorges; Sir John Popham, lord chief justice of England; Sir John and Raleigh Gilbert, sons of the same Sir Humphrey Gilbert who vanished when the *Squirrel* sank in 1583; Richard Hakluyt, the compiler of the massive *Principal Navigations, Voiages and Discoveries of the English Nation*, a history of English seafaring and exploration that helped kindle interest in New World colonization; the Earl of Southampton (William Shakespeare's patron); and other notables whose names made up a veritable who's who of Early Stuart England.

Those who invested in the Virginia Company were primarily motivated by a desire for profits. There was little of the religious idealism or of the search for personal freedom that motivated the Pilgrims in 1620 and none of the search to create a "City on a Hill" that spurred the Puritans to take ships for Boston in 1630. To these financial backers, the settlement of Virginia was primarily about trade and money.

In April 1606, the king granted a royal charter that created two separate joint stock companies. The Virginia Company of Plymouth (also known as the Plymouth Company) had the right to colonize lands above thirty-eight degrees north latitude (roughly the position of Delaware Bay.). The Virginia Company of London (also known as the London Company) was granted the right to establish colonies between thirty-four and forty-one degrees north latitude (roughly between Cape Fear, North Carolina, and Long Island Sound).

The Plymouth Company's designs soon came to nothing and were to remain dormant until 1620, when a group of religious separatists would establish Plymouth Colony in what would become Massachusetts. The London Company, however, immediately put into action its plan to erect a settlement on the Chesapeake Bay in the southern region of "Virginia." Men were recruited—no women, for this initial attempt at colonization—and ships and supplies were obtained. In December of that year, a fleet of three vessels dropped down the Thames from London. For long weeks, the ships lay anchored in the Downs, just off the southeast coast of England, battered by terrible storms, waiting for favorable weather. Finally, in February 1607, the three ships set out across the wintry Atlantic. After crossing from England to the West Indies and then north along the Atlantic coast, the ships—the *Susan Constant*, the *Discovery*, and the *Godspeed*—dropped anchor in the Chesapeake on April 26, 1607. On board were 104 settlers who had no idea what awaited them in the wilds of Virginia.

Before leaving England, the expedition's leaders had been given specific instructions by the Virginia Company about what to look for when searching for a spot to "plant" their settlement. Among other things, these instructions urged the settlers to look for a site on a river one hundred miles from the sea, to make it difficult for an enemy to attack; to settle on the banks of a river that "bendeth most to the Northwest," to make it easier to find a route to the Pacific Ocean; and to avoid settling "in a low and moist place" that would "prove unhealthful."[12] After exploring for about a month, the English decided to build on a roughly comma-shaped peninsula on the north bank of a river they called the James, in honor of the king.[13] This site met two of the company's criteria—it was located about eighty miles from the river's mouth and was easily defensible—but it failed to meet the third. It was low lying, swampy, insect infested, unhealthy. But to the settlers it seemed ideal, at least at first glance. Landing their supplies, the English set about the business of erecting a triangular, palisaded fort they christened Jamestown.[14]

In the ensuing months, support for the fledgling settlement was haphazard at best. Settlers were dispatched in a slow trickle—a few score at a time—when in fact a torrent of carpenters, husbandmen, fishermen, hunters, and laborers was needed. Many of those who were sent to establish the settlement were unfit, either by breeding or experience, for the trials they would face. About half of those sent to establish the colony were gentlemen unused to hard work, more suited to the drawing rooms of London than a harsh life in the wilds of North America. Captain John Smith, the "president" of the colony during much of its earliest history, regularly complained of the quality of those sent to establish the settlement. The colony, he said, would have been better off if the company in London had sent "one hundred good labourers (in place of) a thousand such Gallants as were sent me, that would doe nothing but complaine, curse, and despaire."[15]

There were other problems in Jamestown. Supplies were lacking. Tents sent to provide shelter for the settlers while they were building permanent dwellings had been used by English soldiers who fought against the Spanish in the long-running wars in the Netherlands two decades earlier. They were rotten, in tatters even before they were raised on the banks of the James River. Settlers were supplied with equipment needed to refine gold and silver but no farm implements. Nobody thought to send lines or hooks or nets to catch the fish that swam thick in the waters near Jamestown and even thicker in the Chesapeake not far away.

The lack of willing, experienced laborers and supplies meant that hunger was a constant in Jamestown's early days. The dark cloud of famine always loomed on the horizon. But even if the settlers had been better suited to the task of establishing a colony in the wild, even if they had been given supplies and needed tools, even if they had had ample food, they still would have found rough going in Jamestown. Given that they chose to erect their settlement on a low-lying, marshy peninsula, a spot surrounded by a mosquito-infested marsh, without an adequate supply of fresh water, it was inevitable that disease soon began to take a terrible toll on the settlers, killing scores.

Then there were the people the Virginia Company called the "naturals"— the roughly nine thousand Indians gathered into a loose-knit confederation of disparate groups ruled by the paramount chief, Wahunsonacock, who was known to the English as Powhatan. Trouble between the Indians and the settlers started on the first day the English stepped ashore on the banks of the Chesapeake. Late that day, as an exploring party of about two dozen armed settlers returned to the safety of the three ships anchored off a spot of land they called Point Comfort, a group of natives crept from the woods "like Beares," in the words of settler George Percy, "with their Bowes in their mouths." When the Indians—there were only five or six—got close enough, they loosed a volley of arrows. Gabriel Archer, one of the colonists, was wounded in the hands and a sailor, Matthew Morton, "in two places of the body very dangerously."[16] The English responded with a volley of musket fire that drove the Indians back into the woods.

This episode on the first day of the English "occupation" of Virginia foreshadowed what was to come in the years that followed. The native people, the Powhatans, and the English would clash again and again, seeming to try to outdo each other in terms of their bloodthirsty behavior as they battled for dominance in Tidewater Virginia, the region the natives called *Tsenacommacah*, believed to mean "our place."

In the midst of all these adversities, good leadership was in even shorter supply than tools and fishing gear in Jamestown. Under the terms of the royal charter signed by King James I in 1606, Jamestown was under the immediate control of a seven-man council of settlers, settlers chosen by the Virginia Company in London. This seven-man group, in turn, elected one of its number the president (governor) of the colony. Experience would prove that this arrangement was a recipe for failure. The leaders plotted against each other and haggled and jockeyed for favor with their backers in London. As a consequence, there was no real leadership even as famine and illness and Indian arrows and clubs wreaked a terrible toll on the English.

George Percy, a highborn settler and a bit of a snob, took quill in hand and wrote a detailed and moving account of the devastating trials faced by the 104 English settlers in their fort on the banks of the James River. "There were never Englishmen left in a forreigne Countrey in such miserie as wee were in this new discovered Virginia," he wrote. In fact, the men he called "feeble wretches" had only a handful of water-soaked barley to eat each day. Their only drink was water dipped from the James, salty at high tide and filthy at low. So many were sick that only six men were able to keep watch at night; so many died that the survivors dragged the dead from their tents each morning, "many times three or foure in a night," to be buried "like dogges," out of sight of spying Indian eyes. Within a matter of months, the settlement's population plummeted from 104 to fewer than 40.[17]

In all likelihood, the Jamestown Settlement would have failed had it not been for the efforts of an unlikely duo: Captain John Smith and Pocahontas, the daughter of Wahunsonacock (Powhatan). But these two—the barely pubescent Indian maid and the battle-scarred soldier—formed a partnership that ultimately saved the English colony.

Smith, the son of a yeoman farmer who was given a coat of arms—and status as a gentleman—while serving as a mercenary soldier in Transylvania, became Jamestown's president in September 1608. Even before that, he'd had a famous (some say fictional) brush with death at the hands of Wahunsonacock, only to be saved by the chief's young daughter, Pocahontas.[18] Eventually, under Smith's leadership, life in the colony started to improve at least in part because the feisty Smith imposed a he-who-does-not-work-will-not-eat rule. Though settlers kept dying at an alarming pace, Jamestown's population increased, thanks to the slow infusion of new settlers, including two women.

By early 1609, corn had been planted and the colony boasted a healthy supply of both pigs and chickens. Twenty rough homes were built inside the triangular "fort" on Jamestown Island and a well was dug. It seemed the colony was finally on the cusp of success. Clapboard and wainscoting, in short supply in England, were shipped from Virginia in late 1608, along with samples of pitch, tar, glass, and soap ash that could, it was hoped, put Jamestown on a profitable footing.

In England, the backers of the Jamestown colony were heartened by these signs of potential profits in the goods sent from Virginia. Boards and ash and glass weren't precious metals or pearls, to be sure, but they were better than nothing. At the same time, there were still hopes that Virginia would eventually yield gold or silver ore or perhaps the much-hoped-for quick passage to the wealth of the Spice Islands of the Pacific Ocean. And these investors were determined to succeed where Gilbert and Ralegh had failed.

The merchant-capitalists knew, though, that changes would have to be made if the English colony was ever to be anything other than a wilderness that devoured men and money with equal ease. Determined to make Jamestown successful, the rich and powerful men who comprised the leadership of the Virginia Company decided to send a large fleet of ships and several hundred settlers—more than had ever been sent before—to Virginia with adequate supplies to place the settlement on a firm footing at last. Of course, sending enough supplies and settlers to guarantee—as much as possible—success in Virginia was an expensive proposition. To cover the costs of the venture, it was proposed that the original stock company with its small handful of investors be restructured to give the colony the support it needed. A new corporation, named the Treseror and Companie of Adventurers and Planters of the Citty of London for the Firste Collonie in Virginia, would be headed by Sir Thomas Smythe, a wealthy London merchant, who would be designated the company treasurer. And, like a modern-day public company, the new Virginia Company would be open to any investor, large or small, who wanted to become an "adventurer" by "venturing" money for profits.

Even as the Virginia Company presented its plans to the king—through his privy council—for royal approval, Smythe set out to promote the company's new venture. Sir Thomas (he was knighted by James I soon after the king took the throne) was one of England's wealthiest and most powerful merchants. He had long been involved in foreign trade with Russia, through the Muscovy Company, and he was the head of the East India Company. He was also a marketing genius. In late January or early February 1609, Smythe opened the company's books to investors and began aggressively promoting the venture. He enlisted the aid of clergymen as propagandists. In late May, the Reverend Daniel Price, chaplain to Prince Henry, the king's eldest son, spoke from the open-air Paul Cross pulpit at St. Paul's Church, praising the

Virginia Company's plans to bring the Christian faith to heathen natives of Virginia.[19] Other divines sermonized directly to leading lights of the company. One who preached and prayed was the Reverend William Crashaw, a minister who addressed the original Virginia settlers before their departure from London in 1606. Now he praised Smythe and the adventurers for again backing the Virginia Company, and he ended his sermon with a fervent prayer that the company would be successful in its goals.[20] Other promoters rushed to print pamphlets lauding the company's plans. One such tract, *A Good Speed to Virginia*, penned by a clergyman named Robert Gray, explained in simple terms why English men and women should risk their money—or their lives—in Virginia.

> Seeing there is neither preferment nor employment for all within the (limits) of our country, we might justly be accounted . . . both imprudent and improvident, if we yet sit with our armes foulded in our bosomes, and not rather seeke after such adventures whereby the glory of God may be advanced, the territories of our kingdome inlarged, our people both preferred and employed abroad, our wants supplied at home, his Majesties . . . customes wonderfully augmented, and the honor and renown of our Nation spred and propogated to the ends of the world.

Gray went on to paint a benign picture of what awaited those who went to Jamestown. The Powhatan people, who were native to the Chesapeake region, were "loving and gentle, and desirous to imbrace a better condition." And, of course, that was what the English would bring to the natives since there was, Gray promised, no "intendment" on the part of the Company to take from the natives by "force that rightfull inheritance which they have in that countrey."[21]

An investor named Robert Johnson seconded Gray's argument in a tract he called *Nova Britannia*. Dedicated to Sir Thomas Smythe, this pamphlet started with the somewhat dubious claim that Virginia had belonged to England since the days of King Henry VII, when John Cabot sailed along the coast of North America. It called the new land on the Chesapeake a paradise and praised Virginia for its ready supply of game and fish, its rich soil, and its woods thick with oak and elm and cedar and fir trees. Like Gray, Johnson praised Virginia for its uncivilized yet friendly natives and argued that the

English settlers' goals included the betterment of the savages. Of course, the truth was different, as Johnson and Gray might have known had they visited the land they praised so lavishly. The English had high enough purposes, to be sure, but they were all too ready to take by force any land they wished. The Powhatan people, of course, were just as ready to fight to protect their way of life.

Still, the promotional schemes worked. The plan to send a large fleet of ships and hundreds of settlers to Jamestown quickly became the hottest topic in London. Four months after the company opened its books, its reorganization was complete, funds were raised, the needed number of settlers had signed on for the venture, and ships were obtained. Investors of all classes lined up to back the Virginia Company's new plan. More than 650 individuals became shareholders along with fifty-six city companies and guilds, including the Company of Drapers, the Company of Grocers, the Company of Brewers, and the Company of Poulterers.

One who invested was Sir Stephen Powle, clerk of Chancery Court, and hence one of the most important legal officers in the kingdom. At midmorning on May 6, 1609, Powle made his way to Smythe's spacious house on narrow, cobblestoned Philpott Lane, not far from the Tower of London. The large, two-story dwelling is long gone. It was lost—left "all in dust" according to Samuel Pepys—by the Great Fire of 1666 that destroyed the homes and shops on the lane, along with most of the center of the old capital.[22] In 1609, though, the imposing, half-timbered mansion with its narrow windows was not just Smythe's dwelling, it was also the headquarters of the Virginia Company of London.

Sir Stephen Powle and Sir Thomas Smythe (like Smythe, Powle had been knighted in 1604 when James I, new to the throne, curried favor by handing out knighthoods to almost any taker) were old acquaintances. Both were friends of Sir Walter Ralegh and both were interested in English attempts to settle the New World of Virginia. When the two men met in March 1609, they embraced as good friends.[23] Soon, though, they got down to business. "I delivered to Sir Thomas Smythe Treasorer of the viage to Virginia the summe of fifty powndes in money," Sir Stephen wrote in his journal soon after his visit to Smythe's mansion. In exchange, he was given a note "with the armes of Englande testifying the receipt therof."[24] Because of the size of his investment—£50, or roughly $10,000 in modern money, compared with the single share price of £12 10s (12 pounds, 10 shillings), or about $2,500 in modern terms—and because of his legal background, he was also appointed to the Virginia Council, the group of men whose job it would be to oversee operations of the colony from London.

At about the same time that Sir Stephen visited Smythe, William Strachey formalized his intention to go to Virginia by agreeing to buy two company shares for £25. Given his financial problems, Strachey almost certainly had to borrow the money to make his investment, perhaps from his brother-in-law, Edmund Bowyer, who invested in the company a year later. In any case, Strachey's name appears on the list of investors included in the charter—investors King James called his "trustie and welbeloved subjects." Sir Stephen's name is also listed in the charter, as a member of the "Counsell for the said Companie of Adventurers and Planters in Virginia," though he is misidentified in the document as "Sir Stephen Poole."[25]

The lengthy list of financial backers includes the names of twenty-one peers, including Henry, the earl of Southampton, Shakespeare's patron; Thomas, the earl of Suffolk; and Robert, the earl of Salisbury. Sir Oliver Cromwell, the uncle of the future lord protector who would be instrumental in the overthrow of Charles I, invested in the venture. So did the archbishop of Canterbury, the bishop of Bath and Wells, the preacher William Crashaw, and both the sheriff and lord mayor of London. Powle was one of 96 knights of the realm who invested along with 28 esquires, 58 gentlemen, 110 merchants, and several hundred other men and women, including yeoman farmers, landholders, and landlords who had managed to save a few pounds.

In addition to those who risked money, more than six hundred men and women—those who dreamed of a new life in a new land—"invested" themselves in the venture, signing on to make the voyage to Virginia and to work in the colony for seven years. In return, each of these "planters" would receive free passage, one share of stock, and, at the end of their seven-year term of service, a grant of land, as well as a share of any profits earned by the Virginia Company from its New World venture.

Many of those who signed on for the voyage were what the gentlemen and peers considered the "lesser sort" of people, but that was fine with the organizers of the venture. Johnson, in *Nova Britannia*, said the colony provided an opportunity for England to see the backs of "swarmes of idle persons, which having no meanes of labour to releeve their misery, do likewise swarme in lewd and naughtie practices." The alternative to sending them off to the

Chesapeake, he added, was providing "more prisons and corrections for their bad conditions." [26] It had always been thus. From its inception, Virginia was seen as a convenient place to send the poor and unemployed and to dump some of the criminals who infested London's crowded streets and alleyways.

Of course, all this frantic activity did not go unremarked by the Spanish, who had staked what they thought was an unassailable claim to the lands ranging from Florida all the way to Newfoundland and who had, in 1570, sent a group of Jesuit missionaries to the Chesapeake Bay region in an unsuccessful attempt to start a mission. By late February 1609, three months before the new charter was signed by King James I, Pedro de Zúñiga, a savvy Spanish spy on the lookout for unusual activity in the capital, knew of England's plans to strengthen and resupply the Jamestown settlement. He sent a series of frantic warnings to his monarch, King Philip III.

In mid-March 1609, Zúñiga advised Philip that the Virginia Company had floated an idea that all English pirates might be pardoned if they agreed to move to Virginia. While that was a bit paranoid, and apparently untrue, there was validity to Zúñiga's claim that the Chesapeake was "so perfect (as they say) for piratical excursions that Your Majesty will not be able to bring silver from the Indies without finding a very great obstacle there."[27]

The spy also warned his monarch that the English would set about converting the Indians not to the Roman Catholic faith, but to the hated Protestant faith. "The preparations they are making here are the most urgent they know how to make, for they have seen to it that the ministers, in their sermons, stress the importance of filling the world with their religion. . . . In this way a good sum of money is being collected."[28]

By mid-April, Zúñiga's warnings were growing shrill. He told the king that the English planned to quickly establish a presence so large that by the time "they open their eyes in Spain" it will be too late to take action. "Your Majesty will appreciate how important this is to your royal interests, and so I hope [you] will quickly command the extirpation of these insolents."[29]

If the king's father, Philip II, had still been on the throne, the "insolents" might indeed have been "extirpated" without much delay. This was the man, after all, who sent his fearsome armada to destroy England. But his son, Philip III, delayed, pondered, and took no action.

While Zúñiga fretted and his monarch fiddled around, the English moved full speed ahead with their plans to resupply Jamestown. According to the terms of the second charter, Thomas West, Lord De La Warre, was appointed captain general and governor for life of the colony. About thirty-two years of age when he was given his appointment, West, an enthusiastic colonizer, had already led a full and exciting life. Like most of the men who would be appointed to positions of authority in Virginia, he had served (in his case with distinction, under the Earl of Essex) in the Netherlands, where the Protestant English battled Catholic Spain for a generation. The grandson of a first cousin to Queen Elizabeth, West was knighted for his service in Ireland, where he had proved himself an able leader of men. His connections and high standing did him little good, however, when he was implicated in the Essex Rebellion in 1601 and imprisoned. Luckily for West, Essex cleared West's name, or he, like Essex, might well have lost his head. His reputation restored, he became a member of Elizabeth's privy council, a position he also held under James I. Most important, he was a fervid backer of English Protestant colonies and devoted to Jamestown's success.

De La Warre, however, was not to be sent to Virginia with the fleet that was already gathering. Instead, he was to follow at a later date, with several hundred additional settlers. Sir Thomas Gates, named the colony's deputy governor, was to accompany the fleet and to serve as interim governor until West's arrival. Like West, Gates was an accomplished military man. About fifty years of age in 1609, he had been knighted for his service against the Spanish at Cádiz in 1596 and had served with distinction in the Netherlands. He was also an avid colonizer, having been one of the original grantees in the 1606 London Company Charter.

Sir George Somers, an experienced mariner, was put in charge of the fleet. Roughly sixty years of age, Somers, from the town of Lyme on England's southwest coast, had a resume that included service under Essex, Sir Francis Drake, and the privateering Sir John Hawkins.[30] A member of parliament, he was an accomplished mariner and navigator. His second in command as master of the fleet's flagship was Captain Christopher Newport, whose maritime pedigree was every bit as impressive as Somers's. About forty-nine years of age in 1609, Newport had gone to sea as a young man, sailing to South America and the Caribbean as a privateer. In 1590, when he was about thirty years of age, Newport had been in a sea battle with two Spanish treasure ships off the coast of Cuba. In that battle, Newport lost his right arm but persevered. For the next thirteen years, he was an active Caribbean privateer and was a leading participant in the capture, in 1592, of the Spanish treasure ship the *Madre de Dios,* a prize that carried about half a million pounds in gems, spices, silks, and other goods. Newport's long experience as a privateer helped him establish strong links with English merchants. He was also known to King James I, having presented the monarch with two live crocodiles and a wild boar following one of his New World voyages. In 1606, he was named commander of the first Virginia expedition and sailed as captain of the *Susan Constant,* flagship of the first Virginia fleet.[31] By the time he was named sailing master of the flagship of the 1609 fleet, he had made three crossings between England and Jamestown.

The company also set about the business of gathering vessels to carry the settlers across the Atlantic. Eventually, the company obtained nine ships considered seaworthy; some were purchased outright, others leased. The largest vessel, called the "admiral" of the fleet because she would carry Sir George Somers, was the *Sea Venture* (or more rarely, *Sea Adventure*). Believed to have been built in East Anglia in about 1603, the *Sea Venture* was a three-masted vessel roughly a hundred feet long from the end of her bowsprit to her stern post. The vice admiral, or second-largest ship in the fleet, was the *Diamond,* probably just a little smaller than the *Sea Venture.* She was captained by Vice Admiral John Ratcliffe, who had served as captain of the *Discovery,* one of the three ships of the first Virginia fleet. The third-largest vessel, the *Falcon,* was called the rear admiral. She was under the command of John Martin, one of the original Virginia settlers who had returned to England in 1608 and who was now on his way back to Jamestown. Sailing master of the *Falcon* was Francis Nelson, a veteran of one ocean crossing, having made a voyage to the New World as captain of the *Phoenix,* a pinnace that brought forty settlers to Virginia in 1608. Other ships in the fleet were the *Blessing,* the *Unity,* the *Lion,* and the *Swallow.* In addition, the fleet included a pinnace named the *Virginia,* and an unnamed ketch, a two-masted vessel not much larger than a modern family cruising sailboat. The *Virginia* had been built in Maine in 1606 by settlers who made an unsuccessful attempt to establish an English colony in the cold northeast, then sailed back to England late that year. This ship was under the command of Captain James Davies, a mariner who had accompanied the expedition to Maine. His brother, Robert Davies, served as sailing master.

Since the days of the earliest English voyages to the New World, ships crossing the Atlantic had typically followed a course that took them first to the Canary Islands, off the coast of Africa, and then across the southern reaches of the ocean to the Spanish territories in the West Indies before swinging north to use the Gulf Stream to carry them to the coast of what they knew as Virginia. Now the Virginia Company was determined to find a faster course from England to the Chesapeake. At the same time, fearful of Spanish privateers, despite the formal peace between England and Spain, the company wanted to keep its ships out of the Spanish territories of the Caribbean. In early 1609, soon after announcing plans to send a huge fleet to the Chesapeake, the company ordered Captain Samuel Argall, an experienced mariner who would later loom large in the story of Virginia, to put to sea to find this faster, safer course across the Atlantic.

Argall's life, from the time of his birth in Kent in far southeastern England, was remarkably similar—if markedly less romantic and adventure-filled—to the life of John Smith, who was his elder by about eight months. Like Smith, Argall had limited prospects at birth. In Smith's case, it was the relative poverty of his father, and in Argall's, it was the fact that he was the eighth son, so far down the family line that he could expect little in the way of inheritance from his rather prosperous father. Like Smith, Argall sought his fortune as a soldier in the Dutch wars against the Spanish.

Sometime before 1608, it seems that Argall contacted Sir Thomas Smythe—the treasurer of the Virginia Company who happened also to be distantly related to Argall by marriage—to wrangle some sort of promising job aboard a ship. Though it is not certain exactly where Argall got his shipboard experience, there is no doubt he spent a few years learning the arts of the sea, perhaps in the service of the East India or Muscovy Company, where Sir Thomas had a lot of power and many friends. No matter what kind of connection Argall had to Sir Thomas, the company would not have entrusted such an important task to an inexperienced mariner. His commission, as printed later, made it clear that the officers of the company fully expected him to put his experience to good use:

> For the discovery, Captain Argoll received our commission under our seal, with instruction—to avoid all danger of quarrel with the subjects of the King of Spain—not to touch upon any of his dominions...and to shape his course free from the road of pirates...and to attempt a direct and clear passage by leaving the Canaries to the east, and from thence to run in a straight western course or some point near thereunto; and so to make an experience of the winds and currents which have affrighted all undertakers [explorers] by the north [the more northern route].[32]

On May 5, 1609, Argall set sail from Portsmouth, following the company's orders. Shaping his course to the south-southwest, he dropped the Canaries about three hundred miles to his east, found the winds favorable, and reached the anchorage off Jamestown on July 13. His time across the ocean was credible, about nine weeks, or half as long as the voyage of the first Virginia settlers on board the *Susan Constant,* the *Discovery,* and the *Godspeed.* Perhaps more important, he had followed the company's instructions to avoid any of the king of Spain's dominions and ships.

Meanwhile, in England, the fleet bound to resupply the struggling Jamestown Settlement had gathered. Passengers were making their final preparations, crew was being recruited and signed on. Soon the ships would lade and make ready for the voyage itself. First, though, the second Virginia Charter had to be signed by King James I. Finally, then, the great venture could get under way.

2

Sailing in Friendly Consort

By May 1609, even though the charter authorizing the reorganization of the Virginia Company and the resupply of Virginia Colony was not signed by King James I, the ships of the Virginia-bound fleet began gathering. The *Sea Venture*, the "admiral" of the fleet, docked at Woolwich, the bustling royal dockyards about eight miles down the Thames from central London. There she and six other ships of the fleet—the *Diamond*, the *Falcon*, the *Blessing*, the *Unity*, the *Lion*, and the *Virginia*—anchored just off the noisy, bustling warren of storehouses and dry docks and sailmakers' lofts and ropeworks and carpenters' works that had been built in the days of King Henry VIII. At the same time, the tiny unnamed ketch and the pinnace *Virginia*, the two smallest ships in the fleet, came to anchor in Plymouth Harbour, on England's far southwest coast, to wait for the bulk of the fleet to arrive from London. Over the next few weeks, as the charter languished unsigned, the ships began loading passengers and supplies.

Sir Thomas Gates and Sir George Somers and one-armed Captain Newport were certainly among the first to board the *Sea Venture*, followed by mariners hauling the officers' sea chests, heavy with clothes, books, charts, weapons, nautical instruments, and, it is safe to say, special food to supplement the shipboard diet as well as some aqua vitae and wines to liven the table and conversation in the admiral's quarters. Gates also brought on board some fruit and vegetable seeds he hoped to plant in Jamestown.

While no record exists to tell us exactly how the *Sea Venture* was laid out or what the accommodations were, it is safe to say that the three leaders—the most important men sailing with the fleet—appropriated the best quarters for themselves. This would have been the great cabin, the largest "private" space on the vessel, running the width of the ship, well aft beneath the ship's tiny poop deck. While Gates, who had little experience at sea, tried to acquaint himself with his new surroundings, Somers and Newport, the two sea dogs, would have surveyed the vessel that would carry them and about 150 other men and women across the Atlantic to Virginia. No doubt they went below and checked the hold with its ballast of stones. They would have rapped ship's timbers with the hafts of the kidney daggers they carried at their belts and inspected ribs and knees and planking and crossbeams for signs of rot or weakness. They would have walked through the main deck area, where most of the passengers were to be housed and wondered how on earth more than one hundred Virginia-bound settlers would squeeze themselves into a space not much larger than a middling-sized English cottage. By that time, carpenters would almost certainly have built crude partitions dividing the already small space into a maze of tiny compartments designed to provide some privacy for the passengers who would soon be jammed on board. From below, the three would have climbed a ladder to the mate's cabin, situated just below the great cabin aft and now turned into a crowded dormitory for a few of the gentlemen settlers who were making the voyage to Virginia. They would have inspected the bread room, which would soon be filled with casks of flour and biscuits; the gunner's room, where powder and shot were stored; and the steerage area and tiller room. Making their way topside, the ship's officers would have checked the rigging and eyed ropes and lines and masts and spars and surveyed the ship's boat, turned turtle on the upper deck.

Though the *Sea Venture* was the largest vessel in the fleet, she was small compared with all but the most modest, modern oceangoing vessels. Described as a galleon, she was in reality a merchant ship, properly called a carrack. The ship's provenance is uncertain. It is believed that she was about six years old and that she was owned by a group of businessmen known as the Company of Merchant Adventurers, for whom she made trading voyages between London and Holland, carrying mostly wool and cloth. In 1609 she was purchased or chartered by the Virginia Company as the flagship of the Virginia-bound fleet. Like other ships of her type, she had a high sterncastle and forecastle and a wide, well-rounded hull that allowed her to carry large amounts of cargo. Because of her short, chubby hull shape and high profile, the *Sea Venture*, like other vessels of this kind, had a tendency to wallow and roll alarmingly in high seas and was not well able to sail into the wind.

Like many other merchant vessels, the *Sea Venture* was armed. Though England and Spain had signed a peace treaty in 1604, soon after James took the English throne, there were still scores of Spanish vessels sailing the Atlantic and the Caribbean just waiting to fall on ships like the *Sea Venture*. And since the Spanish continued their claim to the lands the English knew as Virginia, the company had every reason to fear Spanish attempts to keep it from re-supplying Jamestown. The "admiral" herself carried sixteen cannon and at least one small swivel gun that could be used to repel boarders. To save space below, where passengers and stores would be jam-packed for the voyage, these heavy guns were mounted on the *Sea Venture*'s upper deck instead of on the main deck, or in the 'tween deck area, their usual location. As Newport and Somers looked at the heavy cannon—minions that weighed 1,500 pounds each, sakers that weighed 3,500 pounds, and demi-culverins that tipped the scales at 4,500 pounds each, as well as the smallest of the guns, falconers, that weighed as much as two large men—their eyes would have narrowed with concern as they imagined how all that weight topside would unbalance the vessel in strong seas and high winds.[1]

By the time the ship's officers were surveying the vessel, the *Sea Venture*'s crew would have reported for duty. There had been no difficulty recruiting sailors willing, even anxious, to sign on for the voyage to the Chesapeake. Since the end of the war with Spain and the end of privateering, out-of-work sailors thronged every port looking for any work that would put a few shillings in their pockets. Taverns near the London waterfront and inns and all along the docks must have been filled with talk of how a fleet headed for Virginia was taking on able-bodied men. To these men, work—any work—would have been attractive, but an opportunity to sail with salts like Somers and Newport, men who were known to be as fair and brave as Sir Francis Drake himself, would have been as welcome as a clear sky after weeks of rain.

Admiral Somers and Captain Newport and the old soldier Sir Thomas Gates would have been satisfied as they looked over the men who signed on for the dangerous voyage, for the crew was no better or worse than the typical company that did the harsh work on board any merchant vessel that sailed from London or Plymouth or Bristol in those days. Many in the crew—a surprising number—were almost certainly teenagers, still boys, but boys who were expected to do the work of grown men.[2] Others in the crew were "old men"—probably in their twenties or thirties—men with salt in their veins, veterans of earlier transocean voyages who knew their way around a ship like *Sea Venture*. These hard men were middle-aged in their twenties and ancient if they saw their thirties, made old by poor diet and lives filled with dangerous work performed under terribly harsh conditions. Many were scarred, missing fingers or ears or eyes. Most were nearly toothless, their skin wrinkled from constant exposure to the elements. They knew of the hazards they faced at sea, knew of the brutal conditions, yet they would have rushed to sign on for the voyage, at least in part because living and working conditions for the working poor on land in England were hardly better than those at sea.

Some of these men, it is safe to say, had sailed with Newport or Somers before. The ship's company included good men, among them Henry Ravens, the master's mate and an accomplished navigator, and Richard Frobisher, a well-regarded shipwright who hailed from Limehouse, Captain Newport's birthplace. But the crew also included its share of rascals, such as seamen John Want, Christopher Carter, William Martin, Francis Pearepoint, William Brian, and Richard Knowles, all of whom would eventually turn mutinous. And then there was Robert Waters, a mutineer who added murder to his résumé before the colonists reached Jamestown.

Sometime in early May, the *Sea Venture* and the other vessels were warped or towed to the shoreside mole so passengers could begin boarding. Some, those with a few shillings to spare, made their way from London to Woolwich by private carriage or in one of the Thames wherries that served as water taxis on the great river that was London's main street. There, they said their farewells to friends and climbed on board with sea chests and ditty bags and a few treasured personal items. Soon they were joined by men and women who trekked from London on foot or perhaps on one of the open carts that made more or less regular trips from the city center to outlying areas. Rough-handed coopers and joiners and farmers and unemployed seamen clambered aboard, along with a good number of soldiers who had served with Gates in the Dutch wars. There were also a few women—settlers' wives mostly, along with a tavern maid and a serving girl or two. And, of course, as with the crew, the passengers also included a few troublemakers, men and women who had been freed from debtors' prison on their promise to emigrate, perhaps a cutpurse or two, and maybe worse.

Sylvester Jourdain, a merchant from Lyme on England's west coast and, it seems, an acquaintance of Sir George, who was himself from Lyme, boarded. So did John Rolfe, a gentleman-farmer who hoped to introduce West Indian tobacco as a paying crop in Virginia and who climbed the gangplank to the ship's deck with his pregnant wife. Master Richard Bucke, an Anglican minister whose services would be welcomed many times as the *Sea Venture* passengers made their way across the lonely ocean, made his way to the ship's deck carrying his Anglican prayer books while George Yeardley, a veteran of the Dutch wars and probably a friend or at least an acquaintance of Sir Thomas, climbed on the vessel, almost certainly without a hint that he would find wealth and fame in the wilds of Virginia. Stephen Hopkins, a self-important, preachy Puritan who would gain a measure of infamy as a *Sea Venture* passenger and enjoy a taste of fame later in the Plymouth Colony, boarded with his wife and children. And troublemaking Henry Paine, a down-at-the-heels gentleman, came aboard accompanied by a manservant. The highest born of the women to make the journey, a Mistress Horton, was ushered aboard by her maid, Elizabeth Persons. These, the "better sort" among the passengers, would have made their way to the deck dressed in the bright clothes and lace and finery that marked them as people of quality, and they would have brought along sea chests filled with clothes and books and drink as well as some small pieces of furniture, a few weapons, seeds that might be useful in the New World, Bibles, prayer books, practical handbooks, and keepsakes.

It is safe to say that at sometime in this period William Strachey, the impoverished gentleman-poet, would have risked arrest to leave his rooms so that he could drop in to the Mermaid Tavern to say good-bye to Ben Jonson and his other friends who made up the Mermaid Club. It isn't likely that Shakespeare was there since he seems not to have been fond of drink himself, but perhaps some of his fellow actors bought Strachey a farewell drink, then raised a glass to him as they wished him good fortune in Virginia. Then, his farewells out of the way, Strachey would have turned his back on London and started the short journey to the docks at Woolwich. Given the slenderness of his purse, he likely made the journey on foot, carrying a few of his most treasured belongings—a book or two, a journal or a few sheets of blank paper and quills and ink, and perhaps a change of clothing—in a ditty bag. As he walked the eight miles to where the *Sea Venture* lay docked, passing from his old life to his new, it would have been perfectly natural for him to wonder if he would ever again see the bustling, civilized city of London with its crowds and theaters and taverns and good food and, of course, his friends at the Mermaid and his family. At the same time, his mind must have been filled with doubts and questions. What would the voyage to the Chesapeake be like? What would he find in Virginia? Was he making the right choice in fleeing London?

In mid-1608, or at about the time that Strachey started thinking of emigrating, Captain John Smith, the Virginia settler, had written a long letter to a friend about conditions in Jamestown. This letter, hastily edited and rushed into print, was published in August of that year as *A True Relation*.[3] It is a safe bet that at some point before the voyage the book-loving Strachey skulked from his rooms to visit the stall of John Tappe, a bookseller, at the sign of the Greyhound in St. Paul's Church. Strachey, no doubt hungry for firsthand information about the colony, would have passed the bookseller a few coins, snapped up a copy of Smith's brief report, and hurried home to read it voraciously as he searched for clues about what he could expect in Virginia. He would have learned of the Indian attacks that started soon after the English landed on the banks of the Chesapeake. He would have read of "such famin and sicknes, that the living were scarce able to bury the dead," a time when settlers died one or sometimes two or even three at a time until more in the colony were dead than were alive.[4] He would have read of all the struggles to survive in the colony's early days. What he read would naturally enough have made him think carefully about his decision to leave the safety of London for the dangers of Virginia. After all, debtors' prison in London, though terrible, was better than death in Virginia.

Finally, though, Strachey would have found comfort in the fact that Smith ended his letter on an optimistic note, a note so sanguine that he made Virginia sound like a paradise on earth.

> Wee now . . . being in good health, all our men wel contented, free from mutinies, in love one with another, and as we hope in a continuall peace with the Indians: where we doubt not but by Gods gracious assistance, and the adventurers willing minds . . . in after times to see our Nation to enjoy a Country, not onely exceeding pleasant for habitation, but also very profitable for comerce in generall; no doubt pleasing to almightie God, honourable to our gracious Soveraigne, and commodious generally to the whole Kingdome.[5]

And so, no doubt holding those words in his mind like a talisman against bad fortune, Strachey would have climbed aboard the Virginia-bound *Sea Venture* to stand on the vessel's deck, surrounded by the smells of the sea and of tar and the sounds of wheeling, crying gulls and the shouts of dockworkers and sailors as they rushed to make the ship ready. From that vantage point, he might have looked north to London and hoped that Virginia would indeed be the answer to his financial woes.

Most who boarded the *Sea Venture* as passengers were men like Strachey who had fallen on hard times. These were men—there were probably fewer than a dozen women on board—who were turning their backs on debt and hunger and toil and hoping for better times in Virginia. And as they boarded the vessel and settled themselves for the long voyage, Somers and Gates and Newport would have observed them all, the rich and well dressed in their finery as well as the more common people in their rough-made clothes and shoes, looking for any signs of potential trouble and knowing as they looked that a long ocean voyage with passengers and crew thrown together in danger and fear and discomfort could bring out the worst in people, as well as the best.

A sea voyage in 1609 was, even under the best of circumstances, a miserable affair. On deck or below, passengers were cold and damp in the winter and fall and beastly hot and damp in the spring and summer. Seasickness was endemic. Passengers were crowded together, forced to live and sleep and eat in intolerably cramped conditions. There was almost no privacy, no water for washing, no break in the tedium as the ship rolled and pitched, hour after hour, day after day, even in fine weather. It did not take long for food and drink to turn bad, so passengers as well as crew were forced to drink foul water or flat beer, eat weevil-infested biscuits, and try to choke down green salt meat. Ships teemed with vermin: roaches and fleas and lice and rats beyond counting. In addition, those who were lubbers—and that was most—had entered a world that was overwhelmingly strange and confusing. The deck appeared to be nothing more than a jumble of ropes and lines. The vessel was filled with objects that seemed to have no discernible purpose. Even the sailors appeared like aliens. They dressed their scarred, often disfigured bodies in strange clothing, ran around the deck barefoot, or scampered aloft like monkeys as they mouthed words that might as well have been Greek: talk of luffs and cringles and futtocks and grommets and buntlines and so on. And then there was the fear, for even those who had never seen a body of water larger than a millpond knew that ocean voyages were dangerous, that the sea killed hundreds, even thousands, of men each year.

Given the dangers inherent in a sea voyage, it is surprising that the Virginia Company allowed Somers and Gates, the most important men to travel with the fleet, to sail together on *Sea Venture*. It seems likely, though, that neither Lieutenant Governor Gates nor Admiral Somers was willing to cede the privilege of sailing aboard the fleet's flagship to the other. John Smith, writing after the fact, said that because the "Captaines could not agree for place, it was concluded they should goe all in one ship."[6] And so it was that the Virginia Company made its decision to allow Somers and Gates to sail as shipmates, for better or for worse.

Sometime in early May, Sir Thomas Gates must had been given a copy of the new Virginia Charter along with some positive word—perhaps delivered by Jamestown's appointed governor for life, Lord De La Warre, who served the king on the privy council—that the charter would soon be signed and sealed by the king. On May 15, Sir Stephen Powle, the knight who had invested £50 in the venture and who was named to the advisory council in London, noted in his diary, "Our . . . shippes lying at Blacke wall wayed Anker and fell downe to begeinne ther viage toward Virginia. . . . Capitayne Neweport captayne Sir George Sommers and 800 people of all sortes went in these 6 shippes . . . god blesse them and guide them to his glory and our goode: Amen."[7] Over the next few days, the *Sea Venture*, the *Falcon*, the *Blessing*, the *Unity*, the *Lion*, and the *Virginia* made slow progress down the Thames and then south and west past the Downs and the Isle of Wight and into Plymouth Harbor.

By May 20, the entire fleet was gathered at Plymouth. Over the next ten days, passengers fretted as sweating sailors and dockworkers packed the vessels full of food and other supplies needed for the voyage and in Jamestown. Men swarmed over the ship, storing supplies, bending on sails, readying the rigging, hauling cables on board, making last-minute repairs, and doing the countless jobs necessary to prepare a wooden sailing vessel for an open-ocean voyage of some three thousand miles.

As the flagship and the largest vessel in the fleet, the *Sea Venture* carried the lion's share of the supplies. The English in the time of James I were hearty eaters, ashore or at sea. Huge hogsheads filled with five tons of salt beef were packed into the ship's deep hold, along with casks of salt pork and salt cod. Tons of biscuits—hard as stone even when they were fresh and destined to be so filled with weevils before the end of the voyage that the biscuits themselves seemed to writhe like living things—were packed below along with "pease" and oatmeal and flour and butter and cheese. There was beer for the mariners and Canary Sack and aqua vitae along with other spirits packed aboard by individual gentlemen passengers.

There are no records that tell exactly what was carried in the vessel's hold. However, an idea can be gotten from the records of Martin Frobisher's 1577 voyage in search of the Northwest Passage. For that voyage, Frobisher packed one pound of biscuit and one gallon of beer per man per day, one pound of salt meat (beef or pork) per man for each "flesh" day, as well as one dried codfish for every four men on fast days. Each man was supplied with a quarter pound of butter daily, along with a half pound of cheese, as well as four bushels of peas (pease) per man during the voyage.

John Smith, for one, knew the value of good food during an ocean voyage. The want of good food, he said, "occasions the losse of more men, then in any English fleet hath bin slaine in any fight since 1588."[8] Smith was not exaggerating. Scurvy, a terrible wasting disease caused by a lack of vitamin C, wreaked havoc on crews during long ocean voyages. Symptoms often appeared within weeks of leaving port as men complained of weakness and a feeling of general malaise. Soon bleeding was seen around hair follicles on the arms and legs and around rapidly loosening teeth. As the illness progressed, skin was discolored by large purple bruises that often became open sores. In the worst cases, old wounds that seemed to be healed reopened. Eventually sufferers died screaming in agony.

While no one in 1609 had certain knowledge about how to prevent or treat scurvy, it was obvious to many mariners that diet played some role in keeping sailors and passengers healthy. In addition to the stored foods, livestock—chickens and pigs and probably a few goats and geese—were penned on *Sea Venture's* deck, both to provide fresh meat during the voyage and to help stock Jamestown's farms. Along with the livestock, there was at least one ship's dog on board and, no doubt, several cats, good hunters that might keep the ship's voracious rats at bay. In addition, the flagship carried powder and shot for the cannon on deck along with muskets, wheel-lock or flintlock pistols, sabers, and other weapons for use in Virginia or in case of an attack at sea.

At the end of May, all the supplies were laded and stowed. Those bound for Virginia had boarded their assigned ships, found their quarters—in most cases a cramped area belowdeck—and made ready for the voyage that lay ahead. On June 2, as friends and family members of the future settlers waved from Plymouth's quay and cheering crowds bid the fleet good luck, the nine ships "brake ground out of the sound of Plymouth," in the words of William Strachey, and turned their bows to the west.[9]

The fleet ran into difficulty almost as soon as it left the security of Plymouth Harbour. Heading south and west along the English coast, the nine ships were soon beset by strong, contrary winds that made it necessary for the captains to order a course for Falmouth on the Cornish coast. For the next several days, until the wind moderated, the fleet remained secure and battened down in Falmouth.

On June 8, the ships set their sails again, hoisted anchor, and headed into the open waters of the Eastern Atlantic. Before leaving Plymouth, Gates had been given a set of instructions by the Virginia Company. Along with advice about conditions in Jamestown and guidance about how to deal with the settlers already in Virginia and with the natives were directions about the course that the fleet was to take from England to the Chesapeake. Gates was advised to "hold Counsell with the Masters and Pilottes and men of the best experience" to determine "what way is safest and fittest for you to take, because we hold it daungerous that you should keep ye old Course of Dominico and [Nevis] lest you fall into ye hand of the Spaniard."[10] Gates certainly shared this advice with Somers, Newport, and the other ships' masters. He also told the masters that if they were separated, they should repair to the West Indies, to the island of Barbuda, where they should wait for seven days before continuing on to Virginia.[11] In keeping with the company's instructions, the fleet, led by the *Sea Venture*, avoided the course that had been followed by earlier expeditions, including the *Susan Comfort,* the *Discovery,* and the *Godspeed* on their 1607 Jamestown voyage. These earlier expeditions had, without fail, headed south to the Canaries, then across the Atlantic to the West Indies before turning to follow the north-setting current of the Gulf Stream to the Chesapeake Bay. The new course, followed by the 1609 fleet, called for the ships to sail a straighter, more northerly path across the Atlantic.

Sailing in formation for safety, the nine ships in the fleet found the winds on this northerly course steady and easy. For long, easy days after their departure from Falmouth on June 8, the vessels sailed in what Strachey described as "friendly consort."[12] These benevolent winds slowly pushed the ships—nine tiny specks in the midst of the vast, open ocean—from the Cornish coast of England south and west to the latitude of the Azores Islands and then north of west on a track that would carry them to their landfall in the New World. Day after day for almost two months, the daytime sky remained clear of storm clouds, the wind moderate and steady, the blue waters of the Atlantic stretching peaceful as far as the eye could see. At night, the sky was thick with stars, millions of stars splashed across the darkness like spilled milk.

As peaceful and beautiful as the natural surroundings were, life on board the *Sea Venture* was anything but pleasant. Despite the steady wind, there was hardly a passenger on board who did not suffer from seasickness. Even seasoned mariners were known to seek the comfort of the ship's rails during the early stages of a voyage; landlubbers might be sick for weeks. Within days of leaving port, the ship stank of vomit and garbage and food scraps and other foul leavings that were discharged or that seeped into the ballast area. The stench was made even worse by the mingled odors of unwashed bodies crowded together like animals. With so much space belowdecks taken up by stores, there was scant room left on the roughly one-hundred-foot ship for mariners and passengers to live and sleep. The crew was berthed in cramped quarters forward, in the forecastle (pronounced "fo'c'sle"), while the officers lived in their own cramped spaced aft. A few of the "gentlemen adventurers"—men like Strachey who were not just gents but also shareholders in the Virginia Company—were almost certainly housed in the mate's cabin (along with Master's Mate Ravens) or perhaps in the gunner's room. The other passengers, all one hundred or so, lived amidship, sleeping on pallets separated by canvas or wood partitions, without enough headroom to stand upright, with little sunlight or air. Whenever possible, for obvious reasons, they took to the deck for a breath of fresh air and a chance to walk or stretch without treading on some neighbor's feet. At night, in fine weather, they slept under the stars or perhaps under the ship's boat, turned turtle on the deck. The most personal acts were performed in public. Passengers in need of toilet facilities were forced to use slop buckets that soon spilled over and added to the general miasma below or to climb into the "beak"—all the way forward beneath the bowsprit—where they would perch precariously on a seat to relieve themselves as the vessel rolled with the waves and then clean themselves using a length of rope that hung from the bowsprit so that it trailed in the ocean below.

Even in these cramped, almost intolerable conditions, there was still the awareness of rank that permeated English society as a whole and that made Gates and Somers unwilling to cede any preference to the other. Gentlemen, even those like Strachey and Henry Paine whose purses were empty, whose shoes were worn, and whose clothing was threadbare, hardly would have mixed with those they thought of as "the lesser sort." At meals, Mr. and Mrs. Rolfe and the Reverend Mr. Bucke and Mistress Horton would have dined with Strachey and other gentry, at a safe remove from the scruffier passengers who had obtained passage only by pledging their lives and labors for the next seven years.

The food the passengers ate—and all ate the same meals unless they managed to bring some personal stock of delights on board—was cooked over an open flame in a "cook room" positioned just aft of the forecastle. Even in the best of times, meals were rough affairs. Once their private stores ran out, not long after the voyage began, Gates and Somers and all the other important men and women on the vessel were forced to eat the same bad food as the lowliest of the deckhands: a hard biscuit and perhaps some cold porridge, washed down by sour beer or foul water.

As the *Sea Venture* sailed west, pushed by steady winds that drove her slowly closer and closer to the Chesapeake, those on board—mariners as well as passengers—fell into a routine. The sailors stood their regular watches, adjusted sails to take full advantage of the wind, repaired canvas and rigging, and performed all the tasks needed to keep the ship, as complex as a clock, sailing well and true. Hours were spent cleaning the vessel in a vain attempt to reduce the smell and keep the vermin at bay. One unlucky sailor, who had been branded a liar by his shipmates, was given the unenviable job of cleaning the slop buckets and swabbing the privy in the ship's beak. Passengers soon discovered that an ocean voyage was largely a tedious affair.

Of course, there were moments of reprieve on the voyage across the Atlantic. The passengers and crew gathered each morning and evening and each Sunday for prayers, led by Mr. Bucke or, if he was indisposed, by Stephen Hopkins, who had a good working knowledge of the Bible along with his Puritan bent. Meals, of course, were a high point of each day, an opportunity for passengers to gather and take part in something that approached a normal shoreside activity, no matter how bad the food. The crews of many sailing vessels in those days included musicians brought along to play for the entertainment of the ship's officers and the passengers. Sir Francis Drake, for example, included trumpeters and violinists in his crew for his famous *Golden Hind* voyage round the world; he had music played when meals were served. Though none of the surviving documents mentions any players on board the

Sea Venture, it is likely there were a few men who could weave a tune to break the monotony of the voyage.

For almost seven weeks, the ships of the fleet sailed their leisurely way across the Atlantic. Since the ships' captains wanted to stay in contact, the fleet could sail no faster than its slowest vessel. That meant even the larger, faster vessels only made about five or six knots under ideal circumstances.[13] During these weeks, Strachey, one of the few passengers who had been to sea before, would have spent as much time on deck as possible, away from the heat and stench belowdecks. An observant man, he no doubt paced the top deck, studying the sea or observing his fellow passengers. Surely he took great comfort when he caught sight of the sails of the other vessels, just knowing the *Sea Venture* was not completely alone in the middle of the immense, seemingly endless ocean.

Navigation at sea in 1609 was, at best, a haphazard affair. Mariners had long had compasses—since the twelfth century, in fact—but a compass gives only a relative bearing, not very useful in the middle of the ocean where there is no real point of reference. To determine their position at sea, then, mariners were forced to measure the position of the sun or a star. Simply put, at the equator, the sun follows a path directly overhead. Depending on a ship's position—either north or south of the equator—the sun follows a path closer to either the northern or southern horizon. If a sailor can figure out precisely how far the sun is from the zenith (the point directly over the equator) or what that point would be if he were sailing right on the equator, and measures the difference between that position and the actual position of the sun (or, for that matter, another celestial body), he can determine his latitude—that is, his position north or south of the equator.

To make this measurement, Master's Mate Ravens, as the ship's navigator, would have used a cross-staff. This was a piece of wood thirty inches long with a sliding crosspiece. By holding the long end against the eye and moving the crosspiece until its bottom edge aligned with the horizon while its top edge lined up with the rim of the sun (no easy task on the deck of a pitching vessel), he could read the angular height of the sun. Then, if Ravens wasn't blinded by looking at the sun, he would have consulted an astronomical table, which gave the sun's declination, or its degree of angle from directly overhead for that date. By subtracting that number from the cross-staff reading, he would be able to determine the ship's latitude.

But that's just the first half of the information needed to figure out just where the ship was in the middle of the ocean. And accurately determining longitude—a ship's east-west position—was a matter of luck since it required an accurate timepiece of a sort that was not invented until well into the eighteenth century. The best that Ravens, or anybody else, for that matter, could do was measure the *Sea Venture*'s speed through the water using a log—a weighted piece of wood tied to a reeled line with knots at equal distances along its length. After throwing the wooden log overboard, a sailor would count the number of knots that were unreeled in a half minute, as measured by a sandglass. That number would give the navigator the ship's speed through the water, in knots, for obvious reasons. The average speed, coupled with the direction taken from compass readings, gave him a rough idea where he was headed and how fast and, hence, a rough idea where he was in terms of longitude. In fact, no sailor really knew where he was at any given moment unless he was anchored within sight of some landmark. All he could do is guess. It's not by accident that this method was known as "dead" reckoning since many a sailor ended up dead when his captain's reckoning was faulty and his ship ran aground on some coast that was supposed to be a day's sail away. But it was the best a mariner in 1609 could hope for. Newport, though, was a practiced sailor. So were Somers and Ravens, so they were certainly not far off course as they headed west, though they could not have said with any certainty where the *Sea Venture* or the other ships were once they were a week or so out of sight of land.

Their exact location was not the only thing those on the ships did not know. They also had no idea what the weather might be even a day or two in advance. And all unknown to the mariners and passengers in the Virginia-bound fleet, as they sailed in calm seas and steady winds, they were sailing into the path of destruction.

<h1 style="text-align:center">3</h1>

<h1 style="text-align:center">"A Dreadful Storm and Hideous"</h1>

In mid-July, as the *Sea Venture* and the rest of the fleet sailed slowly north and west across the Atlantic only slightly faster than a man can walk, a low-pressure area built just off the west coast of Africa. Warm, moist air began rising rapidly from the ocean's surface thousands of feet into the summer sky. As the warm air rose, it cooled and, as it reached a point about a mile above the earth's surface, its water vapor condensed, releasing tiny droplets of water, so tiny that they did not fall to earth as rain but floated in the still-rising air like millions of pieces of ash hanging suspended in the air over a huge, natural chimney.

Still the air rose, updrafts that carried the water droplets higher and higher still until, at more than twenty thousand feet above the earth's surface, the droplets froze, filled the air with billows of white clouds like colossal cotton balls with dark bottoms. Within these clouds, what today's scientists call the "latent heat of condensation" propelled the rising air even higher into the atmosphere, higher than the height of the highest mountain, some fifty thousand feet from the earth's surface. There, the cloud tops flattened to form the huge anvil-shaped thunderheads that any mariner knows are the sign of dangerous weather.

Slowly, this huge system moved west and then veered slightly north. As it crossed the ocean, warm air flowed from the water's surface through the system and into the atmosphere. The spinning of the earth caused the rising air to curve slightly as it entered the system. Soon, the air entering the system was spinning around a center, forming a vortex like a whirlpool. Meanwhile, air pressure near the top of the storm began rising in response to the latent heat being released by the system. This higher air pressure aloft caused air to flow outward around the top of the storm's center, air that dropped toward the earth's surface only to be violently sucked back into the center of the system.

Pushed by steering currents, this storm system made its way west and farther west, on a course that would ultimately bring it directly into the path of the *Sea Venture* and the other vessels that were sailing placidly on their route to Chesapeake Bay. Not for nothing were storms like the one headed for the fleet named "hurricanes" in honor of Huracan, a god of evil and destruction recognized by the Tainos, an ancient Central American tribe.

Most of the ships' passengers—and certainly those who had never been to sea—were lulled into a sense of complacency by the steady good weather. The mariners who had sailed the Atlantic before, including Captain Newport and Sir George Somers, were not lulled at all, for they knew the ocean's unpredictability. Jan de Hartog, the sailor-author, described the mercurial nature of the Atlantic in his book, *The Call of the Sea,* and his words, penned in the twentieth century, would have held true in the seventeenth.

> Ever since antiquity the Atlantic has been the threshold to the edge of the world. All fantastic stories, from sea serpents to the Aldebran and Atlantis, have come from the Atlantic, and no one who has not sailed that incredible sea knows what it means to be a sailor. All other oceans have their schedule: the Indian Ocean has a bad period and a good one; the Pacific gives ample warning of its mood; even the Mediterranean harbors few surprises to the experienced navigator. Only the Atlantic is completely and utterly unpredictable. . . . All the adjectives used to describe the sea since the beginning of man's consciousness can be applied to the Atlantic. The only way to predict her aspect . . . is to write all those adjectives on separate bits of paper, roll them into little balls, put them in a tin, shake them and let the cabin boy draw. It may be "azure" and it may be "fickle"; it may be "terrifying" and it may be "pewter"; the only safe ones are "deep" and "wet."[1]

On Sunday, July 23, as the sun set after another quiet day, the peaceful ocean known to the passengers and crew of the *Sea Venture* since their departure from England was about to be replaced. If Captain Newport had written all the adjectives he could think of to describe the Atlantic on paper, rolled them into little balls, shaken them in a can, and had his boy reach in and pull out a rolled-up ball of paper to predict the ocean's countenance, the words on the paper would have read "tempest" and "terrifying."

The next dawn found the *Sea Venture* and the rest of the fleet moving steadily north and west at a point about one thousand miles west of the Azores at roughly twenty-seven degrees north latitude—or about level with Cape Kennedy, Florida. When the passengers and mariners on the vessels woke and made their way from their crowded and uncomfortable quarters topside, they discovered the sky, which had been blue and clear save for a few high clouds for so many days, was a lowering gray punctuated by high, scudding clouds that seemed to race before gusty, fickle winds. The ocean's blue-green calm was replaced by rolling seas topped by confused, wind-whipped waves. No doubt the leaders of the fleet—Somers and Newport and, of course, Master's Mate Henry Ravens—stood on the *Sea Venture*'s poop as they studied the sky and the sea from horizon to horizon. They would have looked at the scudding clouds and turned their faces into the wind to taste the salt air. They would have seen the sails bellied out and straining and the seas building, and they would have known with the certainty of experience that the *Sea Venture* and the other ships were sailing into a storm. Still, early on July 24, the ship's officers and the mariners would have felt little concern. Storms at sea were unremarkable and all on board, all except for the least traveled, would have expected heavy weather at some point on a transoceanic voyage. For now, all seemed secure. The *Sea Venture* was making good speed with her sails straining. The *Diamond* and the *Blessing* and the other vessels in the fleet were all within sight and sailing true and steady. In fact, they had not lost sight of each other for more than a few hours at any time since they left England. The mariners had reason to feel confident, even if the weather was turning foul.

Of course, the sailors on the *Sea Venture* and the other vessels had nothing but their instincts and lore, passed from one generation to the next, to warn them when they were sailing into trouble. Evangelista Torricelli, the Italian physicist who invented the barometer, the instrument used to forecast storms by registering fluctuations in air pressure, was an infant in mid-1609. The instrument he invented would not be in common use at sea for another hundred years. Without science to guide them, Somers and Newport and the other *Sea Venture* mariners were forced to rely largely on signs and portents to warn of bad weather.

Apparently, if there were any of the traditional portents of heavy weather—a halo around the moon or a distant rainbow or a brick-red sky—they weren't seen or noted by any on board. No one, not the admiral or any of the other mariners or any of the passengers, seems to have had any reason to expect the weather to turn as it did on July 24.

Through that day, the wind grew stronger and stronger still. The ocean swells built higher and began tumbling over each other in the rising wind. The ship's motion, easy for so many weeks, became labored. Sailors were sent aloft to shorten canvas and sent aloft again and again to trim the sails as the wind shifted direction from east to north to south and back again. As intermittent rain lashed the ship, pigs penned on the *Sea Venture*'s deck grunted and squealed. Chickens and geese hurled themselves against the sides of their pens. Below, in the crowded, reeking main deck area, passengers fidgeted uncomfortably or looked nervously around, their eyes wide at the sound of the building wind's mournful cries in the rigging.

Late that same day, mariners and passengers who took to the deck watched tensely as menacing, towering clouds, lit by frequent flashes of lightning, closed in on the *Sea Venture*. As their world turned dark, Admiral Somers must have stood on the ship's poop and looked aft to where the ketch, towed behind the *Sea Venture* since the fleet entered the open ocean, pitched and yawed in the high seas at the end of a thick line that linked the two vessels like an umbilical cord. In the distance, he would have seen the *Diamond* and the *Virginia* and the other ships in the fleet as they labored from wave to wave. The admiral ordered extra lanterns flown from the flagship's high yards in hopes that the other ships would not lose contact with the *Sea Venture* during what he knew would be a long, difficult night.

Indeed, few, if any, on the ship were able to sleep after the sun set on July 24. Frightened passengers prayed or whimpered or laughed too loud and too often, started at each strange noise or simply sat without moving as the wind's moaning grew to a shrill keening and the vessel groaned and creaked its way through steadily building seas. Rain, growing more steady by the hour, forced all but the hardiest to stay below. The mariners were only a little better off. The common seamen, sheltered in the crowded, dank, malodorous forecastle, fought to snatch a few moments' rest. Again and again in the dark hours they were called to hasten above, to secure the livestock and cargo carried on deck, to check the lashings of the heavy cannon, or to cling to the yards in the driving, wind-whipped rain, trimming the sails in the face of the shifting winds. The ship's officers, too, slept little, if at all, knowing the safety of their vessel, of the entire Virginia-bound fleet, lay in their hands. Through the long night they stood braced against the wind and rain and the ship's jerky motion, soaked to the skin, shivering from the cold, with rain pouring from their beards as they peered into the darkness ahead and shouted commands to the steersman who was waging his own battle with the elements on the main deck below, struggling to hold the ship steady, bow to the waves, lest the vessel turn turtle or sink her bowsprit in some towering wave and pitchpole, never to be seen again.

Morning brought little light and less relief for those on the *Sea Venture*. It is safe to say that all on board hoped the new day would bring sunshine and a return to the calm seas and light winds of the past weeks. Instead, the winds grew stronger with every hour that passed and the seas wilder still. At some point, William Strachey, who would later write the most detailed account of the storm, must have made his way from his quarters to the deck so he could see conditions for himself. As he stood in the stinging rain and looked around, he saw the sky thick with towering, threatening clouds. By that time, he said, the winds "were singing and whistling most unusually."[2]

On July 25—it was St. James's Day, according to the Church of England's calendar—the storm grew in intensity throughout the day. The seas swelled until waves were ten feet high, then fifteen, their tops torn free by the gusting, moaning wind. Sailors working the ship, officers on the high poop, and passengers like Strachey who braved the rain-scoured deck for a breath of fresh air would have felt their clothes pulled taut by the wind, tasted salt spray flung from the wave tops by the ever-strengthening gusts, and been forced to squint against the flying spume and stinging rain. By that time, the flagship and other ships of the fleet were laboring in winds that drove the pelting rain sideways, soaked a man in an instant, and seeped through every crack or crevice in the ship's planking to leak into the storage areas and living quarters below. Somers, or maybe it was Captain Newport, shouted orders to further shorten the *Sea Venture*'s canvas against the building wind. Sailors scurried aloft, despite the howling wind and lashing rain, to strike or reef sails that flapped and cracked wildly in the gusts.

To those on the ship, it seemed the storm could not grow any stronger. But with each turning of the glass, the wind strengthened until the *Sea Venture* was in the midst of what Strachey described as "a dreadful storm and hideous." The storm was like a live thing in its ferocity, he said, "swelling and roaring as it were by fits." The passengers—and crewmen, as well—were terrified by the unremitting violence of the waves and by the "terrible cries and murmurs of the winds."[3]

It soon became clear that the ships of the fleet could not maintain contact. Somers ordered the little ketch cut free, knowing that he was almost certainly sentencing all on board to death when he did so, but also knowing it was just too risky to continue towing the smaller ship. At any moment, the ketch could be pooped or broached by a wave, devoured by the ocean, and she would drag the flagship and all her passengers and crew with her to the bottom. A sailor jumped to hack his way through the towrope with an ax. In minutes, the ketch with its twenty crewmen and passengers fell astern, unable to keep pace with the admiral.

With the ketch gone from view, Somers and Newport and Gates and those on deck searched for some glimpse of the *Diamond* and the *Falcon* and the other ships in the fleet. By that time they were out of view, scattered by the raging winds. For all that those on the *Sea Venture* knew, they could already have slipped beneath the waves or have been driven so far off course that they might never be found. All any on the flagship could do was hope the other vessels were safe, pray that the other ships and their crews and passengers would survive the storm.

There are few experiences as frightening as being in a small vessel, at sea, in a violent storm. There is no surcease from the howling of the wind, from the furious and ceaseless pitching and bucking of the vessel itself, from driving rain and spindrift, from nausea, from dread. A sea storm attacks the senses, the mind, the spirit, until the gut is filled with terror that can make a brave man cower belowdecks, curled into a ball like a whimpering child. There is no shelter to be found on a small, storm-battered ship at sea, no place or time to gather one's wits, no rest, even for a moment, no escape. Strachey said that no storm on land, no matter how bad, could be compared to a storm at sea. On land, he said, there is "commonly no such unmerciful tempest" capable of working "upon the whole frame of the body" to "loathsomely affecteth" all its powers while it "gives not the mind any free and quiet time to use her judgement."[4]

During that day, the first full day of the storm, it is likely that only a few of the gentlemen adventurers who were housed in the mate's cabin or the gunner's room, men like Strachey and John Rolfe and Master Bucke, the minister, were able to venture on deck. The rest were forced to stay below. Passengers who thought they were uncomfortable before the onset of the storm found themselves coining new words to describe their misery. There was no hot food or drink. Slop buckets filled and quickly spilled over. Floor planks were slick with waste and vomit. The deck hatch and the gun ports, the only likely sources of fresh air and light for those who were housed in the 'tween deck area, were battened and lashed closed as the rain began. The normally fetid air below grew even more close and disgusting as passengers vomited almost without ceasing, relieved themselves where they could, and sweat out their fear in the crowded, airless space. Anything not tied down tumbled and pitched wildly as the ship rolled and jerked from wave to wave. Unwary passengers who tried to move without a firm handhold were no doubt injured. And through it all, over it all, the sound was terrifying and unceasing: a mix of howling winds, crashing waves, groaning, creaking timbers, and the moans and prayers and screams of passengers, frightened witless.

As the storm continued, all on the vessel—the experienced crewmen struggling to keep even a scrap of canvas aloft so the *Sea Venture* did not broach (turn sideways to the wind and waves); the mariners struggling with the whipstaff that steered the vessel; the shrieking, crying, praying, frantic passengers; even old salts like Somers and Newport—kept telling themselves there was no way the storm could grow worse. But they were all wrong. "For four-and-twenty hours the storm in a restless tumult had blown so exceedingly as we could not apprehend ... any possibility of greater violence," Strachey wrote, "yet did we still find [the storm] not only more terrible but more constant, fury added to fury, and one storm urging a second more outrageous than the former."[5]

Hour after hour, as the wind screeched and waves built so they towered as high as the *Sea Venture's* topmast, the vessel struggled to climb one mountainous swell after another, then teetered drunkenly at the top before sliding into the trough to wallow helplessly for a moment before starting to claw its way to the top of yet another wave. At some point during the second day, Captain Newport ordered all the *Sea Venture's* sails struck. It was impossible, and too dangerous, to carry sail for, as Strachey said, "if at any time we bore but a hullock [a scrap of sail] ... to guide her before the sea, six and sometimes eight men were not enough to hold the whipstaff" as the "sea swelled above the clouds and gave battle unto Heaven." And during all these hours, rain, he said, "did flood in the air."[6]

Strachey was widely traveled, had visited the Barbary Coast of North Africa and sailed on the Adriatic on his journeys between England and Turkey. He had experienced storms in his travels, yet nothing compared with this tempest. "What shall I say?" he wrote. "Winds and seas were as mad as fury and rage could make them." There was not, he added, "a moment in which the sudden splitting or instant oversetting [capsizing] of the ship was not expected."[7]

But that was not all. Like other ships of her time, the *Sea Venture* was built of long, thick planks laid flush, edge to edge and end to end over oak frames. These planks were laid just close enough to one another to allow the ship-builder to pound caulking between the planks. This caulking, called oakum, was typically made using fibers from unraveled rope. Impregnated with tar, these fibers were packed into seams and joints, making the ship watertight. Under ideal, or even usual, circumstances, oakum caulking worked well. Over time, however, as a wooden vessel was worked by pounding waves in a storm, its planks moved and shifted. Eventually, the caulking between the planks would begin to work itself free, opening the vessel like a sieve. And that's exactly what happened to the *Sea Venture*. "The ship," Strachey said, "in every joint almost having spewed out her oakum before we were aware (a casualty more desperate than any other that a voyage by sea draweth with it), was grown five foot . . . deep with water above her ballast."[8]

The news that the ship was taking on water, that the hold was filling, spread through the *Sea Venture* in minutes, shouted or whispered or croaked from sailor to sailor and from passenger to passenger. Belowdeck, exhausted, dirty men and women fell to their knees in prayer, clasped each other in terror or sat stunned and silent, suddenly seeing the ship in which they were trapped as a huge coffin, ready to plunge to the bottom of the wild and raging sea. Strachey thought that the news the ship was taking on water was like "a wound that was given to men that were before (already) dead."[9] Though he did not say so, he must surely have thought he was going to die. Why, he must have asked himself, why on earth did he ever leave London?

Somehow, though, Strachey and others on the vessel found the will to keep struggling, to fight for their lives though it seemed all was lost. Terrified now, the passengers forgot all class pretensions. Sir Thomas Gates and Admiral Somers and Captain Newport joined Ravens and Strachey and Rolfe and other crewmen and passengers in the half-flooded hold, where they began frantically searching the ship's innards to find places where the planks had separated and seawater rushed in. Their chests heaving with exertion, their breathing ragged, their eyes wide with fear, they scrabbled in the dark, flooded belly of the pitching, rolling vessel, holding guttering candles high as they searched the ship's ribs, the planks, every corner of the hold, listening to discover where the water was flowing in. "Many a weeping leak was this way found," Strachey would later report. When a leak was found, Strachey or one of the others tried to stem the flow, using whatever was at hand. Perhaps one of the mariners, or possibly even Strachey himself, had heard how Magellan's crew, almost a hundred years earlier, had used chunks of beef to stop leaks in the hull of their vessel as they sailed around the world. The *Sea Venture*'s crew tried the same remedy, using pieces of the beef taken on board in Plymouth to try to stop or slow the flow of water into the ship's rapidly filling hold. But all, Strachey said, "was to no purpose."[10] The ship kept taking water despite the crew's best efforts.

The *Sea Venture* was, of course, fitted with rudimentary pumps, which were worked madly, but still the water rose and rose. At some point, the pumps became clogged with sodden biscuit—some of the five tons that had been loaded aboard in England—so that Captain Newport or Admiral Somers or Sir Thomas Gates thought perhaps the most serious leak might be found in the ship's bread room. While some men worked in the depths of the vessel, tearing the pumps down and clearing them of soggy, waterlogged biscuit, the ship's carpenter and some other crewmen were sent to rip up all the planks in the bread room so the hull and frame could be investigated. But no leak was discovered—and still the vessel settled lower and lower in the ocean as the storm continued to rage.

Under ordinary circumstances, Sir Thomas Gates—the landsman and soldier who was to take command of the colonists once they reached Jamestown and who was to hold that post until the arrival of Lord De La Warre—would not have given orders about the running of the vessel. But this struggle for survival was anything but ordinary. With the ship ready to sink at any moment, Gates divided the men in the company—about 140—into three groups. He sent one group to work the forward pump, one to work the pump in the stern, and the third group amidships to form a bucket brigade.

"Then men might be seen to labor, I may well say, for life," Strachey said. And it made no difference whether one was highborn or not. "The better sort, even our governor and admiral themselves, not refusing their turn," worked in the hold. Stripped naked as men in galleys, the "common sort" worked alongside the knights and gentlemen and esquires, passengers and crew, all united in the cause of survival. For "three days and foure nights" the struggle continued, Strachey said.[11] Strachey, of course, took his turn, pumping or bailing with hands that blistered, then bled, from the work. His chest ached with the effort, his arms felt as if they were ready to drop off, his mind first raced, then emptied as exhaustion overtook him. He pumped or hoisted buckets for an hour, then fell to find what rest he could until he was shaken awake to return to the grueling labor.

During all this time, the ship—without so much as an inch of sail flying—was being driven nine or ten leagues (roughly thirty miles) in each four-hour watch. And all this time, Strachey said, those on board, even those who had never done a hard day's work in their lives, struggled to keep the sinking ship from slipping beneath the waves.

At some point in the midst of this terror, a huge wave swept over the *Sea Venture* from stem to stern, filling the vessel "brim full from the hatches up to the spardeck." When the wave struck the ship, she stopped in her track, Strachey said, as if the *Sea Venture* had been "caught in a net" or as if a "fabulous remora" (a fish with the ability to attach itself to a ship and, according to myth, stop it in its course) had stuck to her forecastle. Tons of rushing water swept along the deck, knocked the helmsman off his feet, and carried him away from the helm. Freed from the helmsman's grasp, the whipstaff flew violently from side to side so that when the helmsman tried to grab it, he was thrown from one side of the deck to the other. "It was God's mercy," Strachey said, "that it had not split him."[12] Some other mariner, seeing the ship was out of control, ran to grab the helm.

When the helmsman lost his grip, Gates and other men working below were thrown off their feet, hurled against the ship's side and oaken ribs. Women and passengers who were not helping bail or pump tumbled like tenpins. Heads were split, arms fractured, men left too broken to keep pumping. In the darkness and the wet and the roaring, the only thing they could imagine was that the ship had finally lost its battle with the sea. Strachey, who was working below with Gates, thought the ship was "already at the bottom of the sea."[13] Even Gates, who had labored almost without rest to save the ship and who had urged and cajoled his fellow passengers to bail and pump and then pump and bail some more, was ready to concede defeat. He waded out of the flooded hold saying that if he was to die, he did not want to perish in the hold of the ship, but on the deck, under the open sky, in the company of his friends. But the *Sea Venture* was not sinking—not yet, at least. And, proba-bly at screamed orders from Admiral Somers, Strachey and Gates and the other men who were still able—and women, too, no doubt—went back to the pumps, back to the buckets and pails, and back to the exhausting, ceaseless, lifesaving work.

On Thursday night, some sixty hours after the start of the storm, Somers was at his place on the sterncastle, on watch. During all these hours the sky had been so dark that "nor star by night nor sunbeam by day was to be seen."[14] There was no way to know where on the vast ocean they were, no way to know what heading to follow or what course to maintain. There was no reason, in fact, to believe survival was possible.

Suddenly, Somers saw a "little, round light, like a faint star, trembling and streaming along with a sparkling blaze, half the height upon the main mast and shooting sometimes from shroud to shroud, 'tempting to settle." The little star danced and quivered as it hung suspended in the air like some kind of ghostly apparition. The admiral shouted for others to join him on the poop deck to see the magical light. Strachey and a few other exhausted men who were resting between their turns at the pumps climbed to the deck to watch as the bluish silver light danced and wobbled, "running sometimes along the main yard to the very end and then returning."[15]

The starlike light was a corona, or point discharge; they can appear on an object like a ship's mast or a church steeple during an electrical storm, when the air is highly charged with electricity. While Somers and Strachey and the others on the *Sea Venture* had no idea what caused the beautiful, eerie light, they knew that it was not unusual to see such lights during storms. Strachey said, rightly, that Greek sailors knew the lights as Castor and Pollux and that Italians called the phenomenon *Corpus Santos*. Spanish mariners called the lights St. Elmo's Fire, a name derived from that of the patron saint of the early sailors who challenged the Mediterranean Sea in their tiny ships. The ap-pearance of St. Elmo's Fire during a storm was commonly believed to be a sign of good fortune. While sailors viewed St. Elmo's Fire as a favorable omen, the light dancing and bobbing in the rigging of the *Sea Venture* did noth-ing to help the men on the vessel. By Friday morning, when the light finally faded from view, the ship was listing heavily to starboard, in danger of turn-ing turtle. Frantic, knowing they could be lost at any moment, the sailors be-gan to lighten the vessel. Masts were stripped and rigging was hurled overboard along with chests and trunks and anything that wasn't tied down.

Butts of beer and hogsheads of oil, cider, wine, and vinegar were staved in and emptied. All the armament on the starboard side of the vessel was dumped overboard to ease the ship's list. It was proposed that the mainmast be chopped down, a serious move since it would leave the ship helpless, or almost helpless, if she managed to somehow ride out the storm.

By that time, the crew and passengers were in miserable condition. For three full days they had struggled to keep the ship afloat and themselves alive. There was no way to get food or beer or fresh water from the flooded hold. Every man, woman, and child on the vessel—officer, sailor, or passenger—was soaked to the skin. Many were injured; almost all were sick. Even sleep was impossible, Strachey said. "Carefulnesse, grief and our turn at the pump or bucket were sufficient to hold sleep from our eyes."[16]

By that point, those on the vessel were almost beyond caring. Mountainous seas, driving rain, lightning, and screaming winds continued as the ship labored simply to stay afloat. Sylvester Jourdain, Somers's gentleman friend from Lyme, later said all the men on the ship "being utterly spent, tired, and disabled for longer labor, were even resolved, without any hope of their lives, to shut up the hatches and to have committed themselves to the mercy of the sea." While there was no water or beer to drink, a few of the gentlemen and highborn passengers, he said, had kept back some "good and comfortable waters"—wine and spirits. These passengers quit work, fetched their "waters," and started drinking, "taking their last leave one of the other until their more joyful and happy meeting in a more blessed world."[17]

Sir George, meanwhile, remained on the ship's poop, conning the vessel. As the morning hours passed, the storm abated slightly. Suddenly, the admiral jumped to his feet. He wiped the driving rain from his face and stared ahead, hoping his tired eyes were not deceiving him. Suddenly, Somers cried a word that brought amazement, and then joy, to all on the struggling ship. "Land!" he cried. "Land!"

Somers pointed dead ahead from his place on the poop. All on the deck turned to look. He was right. There, ahead on the horizon, was a gray outline that did not move like a wave. It was land! It was salvation, if only they could reach it.

After a moment, Jourdain reported, Somers urged the men on the ship not to give up. He urged them to get back to the pumps and continue bailing. The men, "spent with long fasting and continuance of their labor," were stretched out "in corners and wheresoever they chanced first to sit or lie," Jourdain said, "but hearing news of land, wherewith they grew to be somewhat revived. Every man bustled up and gathered his strength and feeble spirits together to perform as much as their weak force would permit him."[18]

Though the fearsome storm had started to ease by that time, the weather was still foul, with gale-force winds and heavy seas. Sometime earlier, Newport or Somers must have ordered sailors aloft to unfurl enough of the ship's canvas to enable the vessel to maintain steerage through the still-chaotic ocean. With the wind over her stern quarter, the *Sea Venture* moved heavily to the west or slightly south of west, toward the land those on the deck could barely discern ahead. As the exhausted passengers and crew continued their battle for survival, the *Sea Venture* inched closer and closer to the small hump of land that thrust itself from the waters dead ahead. At an order from Somers or Newport, the leadsman moved forward and heaved his weighted line. He let the line—knotted or marked some way every six feet—play through his fingers. When the weight hit bottom, he shouted above the howl of the wind, reporting thirteen fathoms—just under eighty feet of water—under the keel. The vessel edged closer to the land. The leadsman heaved his line again. He reported seven fathoms, or forty-two feet of water. Once more the weighted line was heaved. Four fathoms! Just twenty-four feet. By this time, the ship was within a mile of an island, close enough to see trees—palms and cedars—blowing in the wind.

Somers and Newport, too, knew there was no way to bring the *Sea Venture* to anchor. Her hull was so open, her planks so sprung, that the ship would sink like one of the cannon they'd already jettisoned if they tried to anchor in deep water. Their only hope was to run on until the battered ship took the ground. Closer and closer to land the vessel inched. By this time, Somers and the others could see a beach ahead. Sir George may have wanted to try to run the ship up on the beach. He surely wanted to get as close to terra firma as possible. For a few moments, as the ship wallowed toward land, the old salt may have thought he would be able to drive the ship high and dry on the beach. Suddenly, though, Somers would have seen white water ahead and probably heard the sound of waves breaking on what he would have instantly known was a reef. Even if the old admiral had wanted to, there was no way to turn the vessel—barely time, in fact, to shout a warning to the passengers and crew on the deck. Then the *Sea Venture* struck, driving into a V-shaped opening in the reef that surrounds the Bermudas like a ship-killing necklace. She plunged like a wedge between massive coral heads that tore at the vessel's hull like the claws of a huge beast. The air was filled with a heart-stopping shriek as the thick oak planks of the ship's broad hull deep below the waterline were ripped by knife-sharp coral outcroppings. In an instant, the ship ground to a stop, then staggered like some massive wounded creature as the following waves lifted her for a moment, carried her forward, driving her even harder aground. Miraculously, though, the same coral heads that split the ship's sides held the wounded vessel fast, upright as if she were in the jaws of a vise.[19]

It was, William Strachey later said, the work of a merciful God on Friday, July 28, when the *Sea Venture* came to rest between two coral outcroppings just off the shore of what is today known as St. George's Island in the Bermudas. Perhaps Providence did guide the vessel to her final resting place, or perhaps it was masterful seamanship on the part of Sir George Somers. What is certain is that if the vessel's track had carried her just a few yards to either port or starboard, the *Sea Venture* would have been battered to pieces by the coral reef and all on board almost certainly would have perished.

It is not difficult to imagine what it was like on the *Sea Venture* in the moments immediately following her grounding. In seconds following the impact, as the vessel's forward momentum was suddenly halted, the heavy cannon— the sakers and demi-culverins and minions that were still lashed on the port side of the upper deck—tore free from their lashings and careered forward along the heaving deck to crash against the aft of the forecastle. The ship's masts trembled and cracked, leaning drunkenly forward as a hail of broken rigging and spars and furled sails tumbled to the deck. Passengers and crew on deck were hurled off their feet or sent cursing and reeling against the ship's bulwarks and rails. Belowdecks, all was bedlam as those who were still working the pumps and those who had not made their way topside were spilled off their feet or toppled from their berths, tumbled to the deck along with sea chests, lamps, crockery, cookware, books, bottles, anything that wasn't securely lashed in place.

As the *Sea Venture* came to rest, held unmoving in the grip of the reef, the terrible noise of the grounding died and the air was filled with the prayers and cries of frightened and injured passengers. Mariners cursed as they struggled to their feet and looked around the stricken vessel that had carried them so far. Belowdecks, seawater poured into the ship through holes torn in the hull by coral outcroppings. All those below thought only of escaping from the dark, wet terror that surrounded them. Crewmen abandoned their pumps, threw buckets aside, and scrambled for ladders leading to the decks. Seasick and suffering passengers snatched what valuables they could find and groped their way through the blackness to battle the sailors in a mad dash to the ship's deck and light and air and survival.

On deck, passengers and sailors alike clambered to climb the ship's rails and up the rigging, straining to see the island that lay to the west. They saw a shallow white beach, surmounted by green hills, topped by wind-whipped palms and cedar trees. From where they were stranded, they may well have been able to smell the fecund scent of the island. Overhead, seabirds wheeled and spun, screaming and cawing wildly. William Strachey—for he was surely on the deck, perhaps standing on the rail or clinging to the rigging or on the poop with the ship's officers—would have stared with wonder and anticipation at the land that represented salvation. To him and the others on the vessel, the cawing and crying of the seabirds may well have sounded like mocking laughter. As terrible as it had been to fear death when they were in midocean, their situation seemingly hopeless, it was cruel and terrifying now to face death with land—sweet land with swaying trees and green hills and a sandy beach—in sight. In fact, though the beach lay only about a half mile or so from where the ship was held in the grip of the reef, it might as well have been over the horizon. Almost no one on the *Sea Venture* would have known how to swim, not even the mariners who spent their lives at sea. That meant the only hope any on the vessel had for reaching the salvation of the wind-swept beach were the ship's boat and a smaller craft, described by one survivor as a skiff. As the realization of their continued peril became clear, crewmen and passengers—men and women and older children—clawed and battled for position along the ship's rails, terrified that the horribly wounded ship would be torn to pieces or slip beneath the waves before the boats were launched.

Somehow, Gates and Somers and Captain Newport managed to impose order on the ship's terror-stricken passengers and the equally frightened crewmen. Fortunately for those on board, by the time the *Sea Venture* took ground, the storm had abated enough to allow the crew to lower the ship's boats—a longboat and the skiff—into the relatively calm water that lay in the lee of the stricken ship. Sailors who could man the oars for the long pull through the surf to the beach clambered into the boats, followed by Sir Thomas and Sir George and quite possibly Captain Newport.[20] They may have been joined by other people of rank, including Strachey, Sylvester Jourdain, and Mistress Horton and her maid. John Rolfe, the gentleman-farmer, and his pregnant wife may have been among the first to abandon ship. Although it can't be known for certain, Rolfe may have carried a few valuable tobacco seeds from the West Indies in his pocket when he clambered into the ship's boat. Soon, other men of rank and some women were lowered or clambered over the ship's side and into the boats until there was no more room. Dozens of passengers and crewmen lined the ship's rails, watching anxiously as the boats made their way to land. A story—it may be apocryphal—has it that as the boats carried their first loads toward the breakers that rolled steadily to the beach, Gates elbowed his way forward to stand in the bow of the lead boat. Even before the boat was fully beached, he jumped into the shallow water. "Gates, his bay!" he supposedly shouted as he slogged ashore. Whether or not the tale is true, the bay on the eastern shore of St. George's Island still bears Gates's name.

Over the next several hours, the *Sea Venture*'s two boats made hurried trips between the beach and the grounded vessel. Remarkably, all 150 men, women, and children on the ship were eventually brought safely to shore. Even the ship's dog was saved. As the dog, probably a mastiff, ran up and down the beach, barking excitedly, the men and women from the ship looked around with wonder at the miracle of their salvation.

4

The Isle of Devils

By the time all of the *Sea Venture*'s passengers and crew made their way to the beach, the sun was beginning its descent to the western horizon. William Strachey and the others who had battled for four days to survive the hurricane threw themselves to the sand above the high-water mark to rest and to dry their sodden clothing. Meanwhile, Sir Thomas Gates and Admiral Somers and Captain Newport looked back to sea, to where the *Sea Venture* sat perched in the grip of the reef. Though the ship seemed secure, the steady wearing of the waves or a sudden squall could easily send her sliding off the reef or batter her to pieces, scattering the valuable supplies still in her hold, supplies that would be sorely needed if they were to survive.

During the course of the afternoon of July 28, the ship's crew made several more trips between the beach and the vessel. They salvaged whatever provisions they could find that had not been spoiled by salt water. They carried a few squealing hogs that had weathered the storm to the waiting boats. They gathered loose rigging and rope and spare canvas and clothing and any crates or trunks that remained and hauled them ashore. By the end of that first day, these items and any salvageable pieces of the *Sea Venture* scattered the shore. The hogs were placed in a hastily constructed enclosure above the high-water line.

As the sun set that evening, the Reverend Richard Bucke, the Anglican clergyman on the *Sea Venture*, held a thanksgiving service. For four days, since the onset of the tempest, those on the vessel had been too busy to gather for the morning or evening prayers that would have been routine during the voyage. Now, having survived the tempest and the *Sea Venture*'s grounding, having made their way to the safety of the shore, the sailors and passengers had a great deal to be thankful for. The evening service of the Anglican Church for July 28 in that year, according to the Book of Common Prayer, started with the Lord's Prayer and proceeded through the Third Collect of Evensong. No doubt the shipwreck survivors, thankful for their salvation, but terrified still as they considered their situation, prayed the words of that collect with particular fervor that evening as they stood together on the beach. "Lighten our darkness, we beseche thee, O Lorde, and by the greate mercye, defend us from al perilles and daungers of thys nighte."[1]

No doubt those who huddled together on the beach with the sound of the ocean surf loud in their ears found special relevance in the scripture reading for that day, a reading from the prophet Jeremiah, including the verse, "Will ye not tremble at my presence, which have placed the sand for the bound of the sea by a perpetual decree, that it cannot pass it: and though the waves thereof toss themselves, yet can they not prevail; though they roar, yet can they not pass over it?"[2] And it can be assumed that as the survivors prayed and sang psalms together more than one turned to gaze seaward at the grounded vessel that had carried them from home to the forlorn beach, the vessel that looked like nothing more than a dying creature, parts of its skeleton already exposed, in the waning day.

At some point, probably during this first evening ashore, Gates and Somers—who, with Captain Newport, the well-read Strachey, and some of the more experienced mariners were certainly the only ones on the island who had any idea where they were—surely called all in the company together and announced that they had landed in the Bermudas. To those on the beach who had any knowledge of the island chain at all, the announcement would have been terrible news. The Bermudas were known, as passenger Sylvester Jourdain noted, as "the most dangerous, infortunate, and most forlorn place in the world." Small wonder, then, that they had never been inhabited, as he wrote, "by any Christian or heathen people."[3]

The Bermuda Islands were born in violence one hundred million years ago, coughed from the molten belly of the earth as a volcanic seamount rising more than a mile from the Atlantic's floor to just below the water's surface. Eventually, the fiery birth of the seamount ended and for aeons the undersea volcano lay undisturbed except by the cooling waters of the ocean as they swirled and roared around and above the mount.

Roughly 1.6 million years ago, at about the time that early hominids were learning how to exploit fire in East Africa, the earth's temperature dropped. As temperatures declined, much of the Northern Hemisphere was covered by a massive ice cap. The Atlantic Ocean's level slowly dropped until the seamount's head and shoulders broke the ocean's surface for the first time. Tumbling waves crashed against this newly exposed land in the ocean's midst, hewing and shaping the seamount's top until, after the passage of thousands of years, the ice began to melt in the northern ice cap and the water returned, submerging all but the seamount's top.

Again and again, over ensuing millennia, this cycle repeated itself. Temperatures decreased and increased, the northern ice cap expanded and contracted, and the ocean's waters fell and rose. Over time, the exposed top of the seamount was visited by shelled sea creatures that lived and died, their shells crushed by waves and turned to sand that was, in turn, blown into dunes and hardened by rain. And, with the final receding of the waters some two hundred centuries ago, turtles crawled out of the ocean to burrow in the sand and lay generations of eggs while seeds carried to the land by the Gulf Stream's northflowing current or deposited by birds sprouted and turned the craggy, exposed top of the seamount green in a profusion of grass, shrubs, graceful palms, towering cedars, and gnarled mangroves that protected the shoreline. And over time, more birds came, countless birds that nested and turned the air into a cacophony of screeches and caws and chirps.

For thousands of years, then, the islands were left to flourish, known only to birds and insects and creatures of the sea. In faraway lands, in those millennia, humankind took root, spread, and eventually flourished. Turning from the land, man began investigating the waters that make up most of the earth's surface, sailing from ports in Europe and England and Ireland west and north and south into the trackless and unknown oceans.

Even after westward-looking explorers began sailing the Atlantic in search of new lands to conquer or settle, the Bermudas were, as Sylvester Jourdain noted, forlorn indeed, in the sense of being left alone. There's no surprise here. The roughly 150 islands in the tiny archipelago—commonly lumped together under the name *Bermuda*—are little more than specks in the middle of the vast, tumbling ocean. They sit roughly 900 miles north and east of the

Bahamas; roughly 600 miles east of Virginia; and about 3,500 miles south and west of London.

Most of the islands in the group are far too small to be inhabitable. The total land mass of the archipelago is only about twenty-one square miles, spread in a rough fishhook shape (with the hook's eye at the eastern end) across twenty-five miles of ocean surface. The largest of the Bermudas is only about fourteen miles long and about a mile wide at its widest point. The highest point of land in Bermuda, now known as Town Hill, has an elevation of just 250 feet. It is much easier to miss a Bermuda-sized target in the middle of the ocean than it is to hit it.

Yet Strachey and Jourdain and the others from the _Sea Venture_ were not the first to set foot on this island chain. Legend—and it is almost certainly no more than wishful thinking on the part of Irishmen and -women—has it that the first visitors to Bermuda were a band of Irish monks led by St. Brendan the Navigator in the sixth century of the current era. A narration written in the tenth century tells of a fantastic seven-year voyage made by this Irish saint and a band of his followers late in the saint's life. Brendan is a real figure, born in 484 c.e. at a place now called Church Hill on the north shore of Tralee Bay in County Kerry. According to the _Navigatio Sancti Brendani Abbatis_ (Voyage of Saint Brendan the Abbott), the monks set out in a skin boat very much like the curraghs still made in the west of Ireland today. Their voyage took the holy men from Dingle on Ireland's west coast, to the Faroe Islands to the north, and then across the ocean to a place Brendan called the Promised Land, believed to be the coast of North America.

The _Navigatio_ is filled with oddities, not the least of which is an accommodating whale that surfaced each Easter Sunday so the monks could celebrate mass on its back. These curiosities make the story seem much more a fairy tale than history. Also included is the description of an island that was filled with flowers and fruit and birds that began singing as if with one voice as the sun set in the west. According to the legend makers, the description of this island's birds makes it clear that Brendan and his monks were the first cruise passengers to visit Bermuda. Though now endangered, Bermuda's native cahows—properly known as Bermuda petrels (_Pterodroma cahow_)—have a habit of gathering each evening and filling the air with incessant chattering and cacophonous cries that Brendan and his band, it is surmised, heard as angelic singing.

It is impossible, at this point, to either prove or disprove Brendan the Navigator's voyage. The whole story may well be no more than a myth woven out of earlier myths by a seafaring, storytelling people. It is known, though, that a map drawn by the German navigator and cartographer Martin Behaim in 1492 depicted a spot of land he called "St. Brendan's Isle" west of the Canary Islands. Behaim noted that St. Brendan came to this island in the mid-sixth century, saw many wonders, stayed for seven years, then returned home. In medieval times and even later, the story was widely believed. John Smith was one who accepted the story of St. Brendan. In his *Generall Historie of Virginia, New England and the Summer Isles,* Smith says "Brandon" visited North America "a thousand yeares agoe."[4]

More believable recorded history dates the discovery of the Bermudas to 1503. In that year, the islands were visited by a Spanish sailor, Juan de Bermúdez, on board his vessel, *La Gar Ha* or *Garza.* The Bermudas were, by that time, ripe for discovery. They lay just south of the sea route that was regularly followed by Spanish ships making their way between their home ports and Mexico and the West Indies. When Bermúdez saw the islands—often called La Bermudez or Garza by early mapmakers—he was on his way to Spain following such a voyage to Hispaniola. He imagined the Bermudas as a potential haven for passing Spanish vessels, a place where they might find water and food. In 1515 Bermúdez returned to the islands with Gonzalo Fernández de Oviedo y Valdés, a Spanish explorer, hoping to land hogs on the islands so passing ships could stop and replenish their stores. While contrary winds kept Bermúdez and Oviedo from landing themselves, they did manage to send a few hogs ashore. Oviedo, who later became the official Spanish historian of the West Indies, left a record of his impression of the islands along with a description of a "strife and combat" he observed between flying fish and fish he called "giltheads"—probably dolphins.[5]

Even after its discovery, Bermuda remained a no-man's-land. The maze of reefs and coral heads that nearly surround the islands make approaching the Bermudas a scary business. Samuel Eliot Morison, the sailor-historian, said it was amazing that anyone ever managed to find his way to a safe anchorage at Bermuda without the help of navigation aids. Small wonder, then, that the islands are more closely fringed with a necklace of shipwrecks than any part of the New World other than the famously deadly Outer Banks of the Carolinas.

As challenging as the islands were to mariners, a few Spanish and Portuguese and, later, English sailors did make their way to stand on one of Bermuda's beaches or to climb its rocks or investigate its many caves. None of these early visitors came to stay, though. Bermuda was just too difficult to reach, too dangerous to approach.

By 1527, Spanish treasure fleets were regularly making their way from Havana, steering north and then northeast off the east coast of Florida, aided by the Gulf Stream's north-setting current until they reached the ship-friendly westerlies north of Bermuda. There, these waddling galleons would put their whipstaffs over and steer north of Bermuda, bound for the Azores Islands and the safety of home. At that time, Spanish interest in the idea first floated by Bermúdez—to use Bermuda as a supply depot for Spanish fleets—increased. The king, it was reported, desired that the Bahamas "should be inhabited so that there could be found a roadstead and also assistance for so long a voyage."[6]

As a consequence of the king's interest, the Spanish offered an adventurer named Fernando Camelo a grant to settle the islands. Camelo, more of a thinker than a doer, created an elaborate plan that included landing cattle and planting the island with trees and shrubs. Nothing came of Camelo's offer, though, and the islands remained uninhabited and unpeopled, visited only by sailors under duress.

According to Oviedo's history, a Portuguese ship bound for home port from San Domingo was driven onto the Bermudan reefs in 1542 or early 1543. Fortunately for the thirty seamen on the vessel, the ship—like the *Sea Venture* almost seven decades later—was held in the grip of the coral, kept afloat long enough for the crew to salvage provisions, tools, spars, sails, and shrouds. Over the next four months, they constructed a new vessel they used to sail to San Domingo.

It may have been one of the sailors from this Portuguese vessel who climbed to a cliff seventy feet above the sea on Bermuda's south shore where he carved a cross, the date—"1543"—and what appear to be the letters TF or RP. No one knows for sure just what this carving represents. If the letters are TF, they might be some marooned or shipwrecked mariner's initials, carved as a memorial to himself as he stared out to sea, searching for the sight of a friendly sail. If RP, they may stand for *Rex Portugaline*, representing an early Portuguese claim to the islands.

Over the next fifty years or so, the island chain was, for the most part, left alone by Spanish mariners, the most likely to come close to the islands. Still, there were a few reported visits. On December 17, 1593, a French ship under the command of a Capitaine de la Barbotière struck the Bermudan reefs. Sailing in the vicinity of the island chain, the captain was assured by his pilots that they were safely past the islands and their coral necklace. Supposedly having steered the ship past all danger, these pilots demanded, and received, their "wine of height"—a ration of wine or spirits traditionally given to pilots when they had safely discharged their duty. Then, wrote Henry May, an English passenger on the ship, "after they had had their wine, carelesse of their charge . . . being as it were drunken, through their negligence a number of good men were cast away."[7] In fact, most of the men on the ship drowned. Twenty-six, including May, made their way to land in the ship's boat and a jury-rigged raft. For the next four months, May and his shipmates used tools salvaged from the wreck to cut cedar trees found on the island, hew planks, and build a small bark, using trunnels ("tree nails" or wooden dowels) in place of nails. They rigged the vessel with sails and tackle salvaged from the wreck. On May 11, 1594, the survivors set sail with a store of water and thirteen live tortoises for food. After a voyage of nine days, May and the others spied land at Cape Breton, Nova Scotia.

Another mariner, Captain Diego Ramirez, found himself an unwilling visitor to the islands in early 1604 when his ship, one of a fleet of five treasure galleons under the command of Don Luis De Cordova, was struck by a winter storm. Four of the five ships, including Don Luis's flagship, were never seen again. Ramirez and his shipmates had better luck. Their vessel came safely to rest in a pocket of sand near what is, to this day, called Spanish Point. While his men worked to repair and refloat his ship, Captain Ramirez explored the islands. He drew a map which then lay, along with an account of the voyage and wreck, in the Spanish archives in Seville for 350 years before being found and translated.

By the time Ramirez and his shipmates found themselves cast ashore in Bermuda, the island chain had achieved such a terrible reputation, thanks to its reefs and to the unearthly screams of the island's millions of cahows, that mariners were calling Bermuda the Isle of Devils. Ramirez, like other visitors before and after, was pleasantly surprised by what he found in this place supposedly inhabited by evil spirits.

"It is not high having good black soil, is thinly wooded and is good level country," he wrote. "All the islands and keys are covered with cedar forests, tufted palmetto trees"—these would have been Bermuda sabal palms—"and underbrush of various kinds. There is good timber for vessels. . . . There are great droves of hogs, very well grown."[8]

He described very large herons and sparrow hawks "so stupid" the Span-ish were able to club them and crows that came and perched on the sailors' heads. "The headlands," he wrote, "are ... the haunts of certain nocturnal birds which during the day remain in their caves but at night come out to feed.... At nightfall these birds come out from their caves with such an out-cry and varying clamor that one cannot help being afraid until one realizes the reason."[9]

These birds were, of course, the Bermuda cahows. They were seen up close by a sailor named Venturilla, believed to be the first black person to have left his footprint on Bermuda's soil. According to Ramirez, Venturilla was sent ashore with a lantern and an ax to cut a piece of cedar. "When he landed and entered the bush," Ramirez wrote, "he began to yell so that I shouted, 'The devil is carrying off the Negro. All ashore!' The men jumped into the boat. The Negro's outcries, the signals he made with the light and his hands and the clamor of the birds was augmented now by that of the men. It was these nightbirds!"

Finally, the men were able to rescue the badly frightened Venturilla. In the process, they killed five hundred birds. "We cooked them with hot water," Ramirez said, "and they were so good and fat that every night the men went hunting and we dried and salted more than a thousand for the voyage besides what the men ate." The birds were so plentiful, the captain went on, "that four thousand could be killed at the same spot in a single night."[10]

Ramirez also noted the great number of fish—grouper, parrot fish, and red snapper—that were so unafraid that men could catch them in their bare hands or with pointed sticks. He and his men also spied the mast of a wrecked ship on the shore and a stand of tobacco that seemed, he said, as though it had been planted by man.

If, as is likely, at least a few of the *Sea Venture* survivors had heard of the Bermudas, it is unlikely that any—even Gates and Somers and Strachey and the other well-educated men on the island—knew that earlier visitors to the islands had found them pleasant, stocked with fish and fowl and even hogs, and thick with cedar trees that could be used for shipbuilding. What they knew, in all likelihood, was only that Bermuda had a fearsome reputation and that it was unlikely any English vessel would come looking for them so far off the beaten track.

While survivors had been able to salvage some limited supplies from the stricken vessel, it might be months before a rescue vessel appeared or they were able to construct a ship to escape. After their first night on what is now known as St. Catherine's Beach, some of the shipwreck survivors were sent by Gates or Somers to search for sources of food and water. According to Sylvester Jourdain, "Every man disposed and applied himself to search for and seek out such relief and sustenation as the country afforded."[11] In fact, it is unlikely that all the men on the island went in search of food and water. While some went foraging, others would have set about building rough shelters, thatched with palm fronds, above the high-water mark. At the same time, sailors, probably under the watchful eye of Sir George Somers, made repeated trips to the grounded vessel, salvaging anything that might be of service. Planks above the waterline were torn from the ship's oaken frames and hauled ashore along with hatches and any undamaged spars that could be removed and metal fittings and canvas and cordage and tools and even books and the important charts from Newport's cabin and, of course, the instructions and a copy of the new Virginia charter given to Gates by the officers of the Virginia Company in London. Somehow the heavy ship's bell was hauled ashore, as were several heavy cooking kettles and at least one of the smallest cannon.

Within days, though, the salvage operation came to an end as the *Sea Venture* slipped beneath the waves, to rest where her bones still lie, between the two coral outcroppings that trapped her. Even though the survivors must have known the ship was lost once it struck the reef, they must have felt truly forlorn as the vessel, their only link to England, disappeared from view.

Meanwhile, like other mariners who found themselves cast ashore in the Bermudas, the *Sea Venture* survivors were amazed by what they discovered as they moved from the beach on what is now St. George's Island, climbing rolling, wooded hills as they moved to the island's interior. The country afforded more of what Jourdain described as "all fit necessaries for the sustentation and preservation of man's life" than any could have imagined.[12]

In William Strachey's record of the shipwreck and what followed—given the unmanageable title *A True Reportory of the Wreck and Redemption of Sir Thomas Gates, Knight, upon and from the Islands of the Bermudas: His Coming to Virginia and the Estate of that Colony Then and After, under the Government of the Lord La Warre, July 15, 1610, Written by William Strachey, Esquire*—the former poet and onetime lawyer told how the shipwreck survivors found an abundance of riches from the sea. Not long after coming ashore, he reported, Gates set a large net, designed for use trapping deer in the forests of the New World, across the mouth of what would become known as Frobisher's Building Bay, just south of Gates Bay on

St. George's Island. With the net, Strachey said, "we have taken five thousand of small and great fish," including pilchards, bream, mullets, "and other kinds for which we have no name." Fat crayfish and crabs and oysters and edible conch were so plentiful, he added, that "I think no island in the world may have greater store or better fish."[13]

Jourdain agreed, saying that fish were so abundant "that if a man step into the water they will come round about him; so that men were fain to get out for fear of biting." There were rockfish, "very fate and sweet," and such an abundance of mullet that one thousand could be taken with a net at a time; and lobster and pilchard and other fish Jourdain could not identify. Soon after landing, Jourdain reported, Somers set the ship's carpenters to building a small, shallow-draft rowboat he could use to supply the survivors with fish. Apparently, both the skiff and the ship's boat that had been used to ferry survivors from the *Sea Venture* to the beach drew too much water to go safely over the reefs that almost surrounded the island. On his first fishing trip, Somers found it easy to hook enough fish to feed the whole company of survivors for a day.[14]

But there was more sustenance than "just" seafood. Explorers found edible berries in profusion. The few women among the survivors were soon put to work weaving baskets from palmetto fronds and filling the baskets with sweet, ripe berries. But the greatest find was the wild hogs, the descendants of those left on the islands by passing Spanish and Portuguese vessels. The survivors first discovered the wild hogs when a few of the swine brought ashore from the *Sea Venture* wandered into the woods near the beach and attracted the attention of a "huge wild boar" that followed the hogs back to the hut. That night, one of the sailors hid in the hog enclosure, enduring the filth and the stench until the wild boar came "and groveled by the sows." The sailor was able to slip a rope around the animal's back legs to hold him fast. Eventually, the survivors found they could easily capture "sometimes fifty boars, sows and pigs in a week alive," using the ship's dog, who would "fasten on them and hold whilst the huntsmen made in." These hogs were kept in sties near the beachfront quarters, where they were fed with berries that dropped from the cedars and palms. "And," Strachey reported, "when there was any fret of weather . . . that we could not fish nor take tortoises, then we killed our hogs."[15]

In addition to the wild hogs and abundant seafood, there were also plenty of fowl and eggs to fill the shipwreck survivors' bellies. Like earlier visitors to the island, the *Sea Venture*'s survivors were amazed by the ease with which they were able to kill or capture hundreds of birds. According to Strachey, he and the others found "sparrows ... robins of divers colors ... heronshaws, bitterns, teal, snipes, crows, and hawks ... oxbirds, cormorants, bald coots, moor hens, owls, and bats in great store." Then there were the cahows, the same plump, almost tame birds that had so terrified Ramirez's crewman, Venturilla, and whose eerie cries had led some mariners to believe the islands were populated by demons. The English found they could easily capture these birds for the cookpot by "lowbelling"—a method of trapping birds, usually at night, using bells, lights, or sticks to confuse and frighten them. In the Bermudan version of this sport, described by Strachey as a "pretty way to take them," men would stand on the rocks or beach, "hollooing, laughing, and making the strangest outcry that possibly they could." The noise would attract the birds that "would come flocking to that place and settle upon the very arms and head of him that so cried." So trusting—or perhaps stupid—were the birds that the survivors would "take twenty dozen in two hours of the chiefest of them," Strachey said, adding that the cahows were "a good and well-relished fowl, fat and full as a partridge."[16]

There were other sources of food, as well. There were sweet-tasting tortoises so large that one, said Jourdain, would "suffice fifty men a meal, at the least," and these were so plentiful that forty could be taken in a day by men in two boats.[17] Strachey also waxed rhapsodic when writing about the Bermuda tortoises. Each of the fat, tasty creatures was large enough, he said, to feed "a dozen messes, appointing six to each mess." The meat, he added, tasted neither like fish nor flesh, not surprising since, as he said, it keeps "most in the water and feeding upon sea grass like a heifer in the bottom of the coves and bays."[18] There were tortoise eggs, too, "sweeter than any hen egg"; and there were prickly pears and mulberries and cedar trees that produced what Jourdain called "a very sweet berry and wholesome to eat."[19] These same berries produced a pleasant drink when they were boiled and strained, then allowed to stand for three or four days.

Then there were the palmettos, the only palms native to the Bermudas. These palms, unlike any tree ever seen England, provided both shelter and food. "With the leaves we thatched our cabins and roasted the soft tops which tastes like fried melons, and, when sod (stewed), they eat like cabbages, but not so offensively thankful (gassy) to the stomach."[20] Though there's no mention of it in the survival narratives, the *Sea Venture* mariners and those Strachey referred to as "the common sort" were probably the first Bermudans to make an intoxicating drink, known as bibbi, from the fermented juice of crushed palmetto leaves.

By early August of 1609, the survivors had established their tiny settlement on the beach overlooking Gates Bay. The quarters were described as "cabins" thatched with palmetto fronds. Nearby stood the small enclosure they had built to hold the hogs ferried ashore from the *Sea Venture* wreck. Men had dug a well not far from the beach, near the site where Fort St. Catherine would be built in 1616. Because there was no salt on the island and none had been salvaged from the ships, Somers ordered a hut built near the shore where fires were kept burning beneath three or four of the ship's kettles filled with seawater to produce salt.

By the first week of August—within a week or so of the wreck—Sir George "squared out a garden" where he planted muskmelons, peas, onions, radish, lettuce, and other herbs and good English plants.[21] In ten days the seeds, carried as cargo on the *Sea Venture,* had sprouted and pushed their way above ground. The island's birds made quick work of the sprouts, though, and none of the plants matured. Somers had no better luck with several sugarcane sprouts he planted in the garden area near the little gathering of thatched huts; they were almost immediately rooted up and eaten by the island's wild hogs. Despite these early disappointments, Somers and the other survivors thought that the Bermudas would prove to be a likely place for English settlers to grow the lemons, oranges, sugarcane, and even grape vines that thrived in some of the Spanish islands of the Caribbean. In fact, as fertile as the Bermudas appeared to the survivors, the island chain's soil and subtropical climate were ill suited to producing most crops. Still, the survivors found plenty of food and lush surroundings and mostly pleasant weather and ready shelter.

Of course, Sir George and Sir Thomas and Captain Newport had worries other than just food and water and shelter. They were bound, by duty and by desire, to fulfill their obligations to the Virginia Company. The men and women in Jamestown were waiting for their arrival and the supplies they carried, while others in Virginia and in England and in Bermuda, too, had invested heavily in the Virginia venture. Somehow, the *Sea Venture* survivors had to escape the islands and make their way to the Chesapeake.

Within a week or two weeks of their grounding, Gates and the others knew that the other ships in the fleet had either been lost in the storm or had sailed on to Jamestown. If any of the other sea captains had decided after the storm to search for the *Sea Venture* and those who sailed in her, they had abandoned those efforts as futile within just a few days. Those in Bermuda knew that they had to try to let the Virginia colonists know of the shipwreck and, if possible, to arrange for their own rescue.

Sometime around mid-August, the ship's carpenter, Richard Frobisher—described by Strachey as "a painful and well-experienced shipwright and skillful workman"—set about making the ship's boat ready for a sea voyage.[22] Using hatches salvaged from the wreck, he built a deck and made the longboat "so close that no water could go in her."[23] He fitted the little vessel with sails and checked its caulking and made the boat—probably about twenty-four feet in length and unballasted—as ready as he could for a voyage across almost six hundred miles of dangerous, open ocean.

Henry Ravens, the *Sea Venture*'s master's mate and hence a top-notch navigator, was tapped to sail the "bark of aviso" (advice boat) to the Chesapeake to bring back help. Raven's crew was made up of six sailors. Thomas Whittingham, a settler, was chosen to carry the news of the wreck. Sir Thomas Gates and others in Bermuda sent letters with Whittingham, including instructions from Gates to the Virginia colonists: he appointed Peter Winne, who had sailed on one of the other ships in the fleet, acting governor until he, Gates, arrived and he declared that six advisors should be chosen to serve as Winne's assistants. Gates also wrote to "gentlemen" of quality in the colony, asking them to assist Winne in any way they could and to set a good example to keep others in Jamestown from trying to usurp the government.

On Monday, August 28, Ravens and his crew of six set sail. It is easy to imagine Strachey and the other survivors as they gathered on St. Catherine's Beach and watched with a mix of anxiety and hope as Ravens and his boatmates sailed away from Bermuda. It is just as easy to imagine their dismay when the longboat-turned-pinnace sailed back to the beach just two days later, having circled the island without finding a safe way through the reefs.

Two days later, on Friday, September 1, Ravens and his crew departed again. This time, Ravens followed the track the *Sea Venture* had sailed when approaching the island. By following that course, Ravens and the others were able to find water deep enough to handle the longboat's twenty-inch draft. Before his departure, Ravens promised Gates and Somers and Strachey and the other survivors that if he lived and arrived safe in Virginia, he would return by the time of the next new moon, or by late September. Ravens, in turn, was told that the survivors would light a signal fire to guide him back.

As the weeks passed, the survivors began searching the sea, hoping to catch sight of a ship, any ship, bearing help from Virginia. At night, Strachey made his way by boat to what is now St. David Island—a smaller island lying slightly south and east of St. George's—where he clambered to a hilltop on the easternmost point of land and lit a signal fire that could guide Ravens to the survivors. Night after night, Strachey would sit by the fire, waiting and watching and hoping.[24] Perhaps it was at this time that he began his long report on the shipwreck or perhaps he simply gazed seaward and thought of what the uncertain future might hold. September turned to October and October to November, however, with no sight of Ravens or of any rescue vessel from Jamestown. His fate and the fate of his mates was never determined. Almost certainly, they were lost in a sudden storm—after all, it was still hurricane season—that sent their tiny vessel to the bottom.[25]

Even before those in Bermuda knew that Ravens's mission was unsuccessful, Sir Thomas Gates ordered the construction of a pinnace that could carry survivors on to Jamestown. He may have figured there were no ships in Virginia large enough to rescue all the survivors—more than 140 following the departure of Ravens and his shipmates—or he may simply have been pragmatic about the likelihood that the longboat might never make it to the Chesapeake. In any event, the same day that Ravens left, the keel of the pinnace was laid on Buildings Bay, just south of the beach on which Gates and the other survivors first came ashore. There, a group of men set about building a large pinnace under the direction of Frobisher, the able ship's carpenter. But even as they laid the keel and began fashioning the ribs of the vessel they hoped would carry them to safety, trouble was brewing, trouble that would ultimately threaten tragedy for all the *Sea Venture* survivors.

5

"That Disorderlie Company"

In early August of 1609, while Sir George Somers was busy squaring out his garden just above St. Catherine's Beach on St. George's Island and planting the muskmelon and onion and other seeds so carefully carried from England, he must often have thought of the other ships that had sailed in company with the *Sea Venture*. As the admiral of the Virginia-bound fleet, charged with the safety of all the settlers in the fleet, he must have wondered what had happened to those other ships and the hundreds of men and women who had left their homes with such high hopes, only to sail into the teeth of the hurricane. Sir Thomas Gates and William Strachey and John Rolfe—indeed, all of whom were safe in Bermuda—must also have wondered as they hunted for wild hogs or fished in the blue-green waters that lay just off St. Catherine's Beach or stared out to sea if the other Virginia-bound settlers had survived the storm, and—if they were still alive—what conditions they had found in Jamestown. More than one of the Bermuda survivors, remembering the terror of the tempest, must have breathed a prayer for those on the other vessels even as they gave thanks for their own salvation. Many would have been certain, not without some cause, that the other ships must have been lost with all hands in the same storm that had hurled the *Sea Venture* on the Bermudan reef.

In fact, the balance of the fleet—other than the little ketch that was lost after separating from *Sea Venture* in the early hours of the storm—had survived the tempest, if barely. On August 10, four of those ships passed between Cape Henry and Cape Charles, named for the sons of King James I, and sailed slowly up the Chesapeake Bay on the rising tide. The ships—the *Blessing*, the *Falcon*, the *Lion*, and the *Unity*—were battered, their masts broken or missing, sails in tatters, decks scoured by roaring seas. Over the next two days, the ships moved north and east to the mouth of the James River and then crept up the James River, described by George Percy, one of the original Jamestown settlers, as "one of the famousest Rivers that ever was found by any Christian . . . where ships of great burthen may harbor in safety."[1]

As the ships threaded their slow way up the James, the sea-weary passengers and sailors who had never been to the Chesapeake—and that was the vast majority—would have been awed by the landscape, different from anything they had ever seen in England. Both sides of the river were fringed by broad meadows and what Percy described as "goodly tall trees, with such fresh waters runing through the woods as I was almost ravished at the first sight thereof."[2] Those on the vessels would have been amazed, too, by the lack of people in the landscape they viewed. For mile after mile they moved through the verdant country, breathing in the sweet smell of land and trees and flowers, looking in wonder at the woodlands filled with deer and other game and at the river teeming with fish and waterfowl, almost certainly without seeing so much as a hair of the native people who occupied the Tidewater region. Of course, their passage was undoubtedly observed by the Indians, who immediately sent runners through the woods to spread the news that more of those the native people called the "coat-wearing people" had come to the banks of the river.

Sometime on August 11, the ships rounded into the wind off Jamestown Island and came to rest, wallowing in the river's easy swells. By the time the vessels' anchors were loosed, settlers had streamed out of the palisaded town's main gate to stand on the riverbank and stare at the storm-battered vessels and chatter and wave excitedly at the newcomers. Sailors threw heavy hawsers from the vessels to men on shore so the ships could be tied off to trees just above the high-water mark.

After more than two months at sea, having suffered through the tempest and through the seemingly endless days of tedium and constant motion, most of those on the ships rushed ashore to enjoy the feel of solid land beneath their feet. Others, too sick to walk or injured during the storm, were lowered into waiting boats and carried to the beach and into the settlement. In addition to their crews, the vessels carried about four hundred men and women along with some provisions for the always struggling settlement.[3] The mares and horses loaded on the *Blessing* in Plymouth Harbour somehow weathered the hurricane and they, too, were hauled ashore, no doubt somewhat the worse for wear. Over the next several days, three more ships of the fleet sailed up to moor in the deep water that lay just off the settlement. These were the *Diamond*, the *Swallow*, and a third vessel, not named but presumed to be the ketch *Virginia*.

Sadly, none of those who were on the *Blessing* or any of the smaller ships in the fleet left anything like William Strachey's description of the storm to tell us what conditions were like on those ships during the tempest. William Box, an "honest Gentleman" who sailed as a passenger on one of the vessels, did write a brief report in which he said, "In the tayle of a Hericano wee were separated from the Admirall.... Some lost their Masts, some their Sayles blowne from their Yards; the Seas so over-raking our Ships, much of our provision was spoyled, our Fleet separated, and our men sicke, and many dyed."[4] And Gabriel Archer, one of Jamestown's original colonists who had departed from the settlement in 1608 and was returning in 1609 for a second stint in Virginia, said, in a letter sent to the Virginia Company soon after the *Blessing* landed him in Jamestown, that the "tempest . . . was so violent that men could scarce stand upon the Deckes, neither could any man heare another speake."[5]

Even with the lack of detail in these reports, it is not difficult to imagine what those on the smaller vessels in the fleet endured after leaving the company of the *Sea Venture*. The first thing that happened—and this was reported by every witness—was that the ships scattered. Contact was soon lost and it was every vessel for herself. In reality, even if the ships' captains had wanted to stay in contact, it would have been impossible. The only way for ships to communicate was by flag or other visual signals, by lights at night, or by horns or cannon. At the height of a storm, such communication was obviously out of the question. As the wind increased and waves grew, every ship's master would have had his hands full saving his own ship and passengers and crew.

It seems that the *Blessing*, the ship carrying Gabriel Archer, was only in the high winds and seas for about forty-four hours, or about half as long as the *Sea Venture*. But even if the *Blessing* and the rest of the smaller vessels were able to avoid the hurricane's strongest winds, they would have spent days that seemed interminable—there's no way of knowing for sure how long—battered by mountainous seas and ferocious winds like those that tortured Strachey and the others on board the *Sea Venture*. During those long hours, the mariners on those vessels as well as all those passengers who had never experienced anything even remotely like an Atlantic hurricane would have been every bit as terrified as those on the *Sea Venture*.

Finally, though, the storm moved on its course, leaving the battered vessels and exhausted survivors in its wake. Some six days after the winds and waves calmed and the skies cleared, the *Lion*, relatively unscathed, somehow established contact with the equally fortunate *Blessing* and the fleet's rear admiral, the *Falcon*, which had also survived the storm without major damage. Not long after that, they were joined by the badly damaged and seriously undermanned *Unity*, with all but ten of the seventy settlers on board sick or injured. Of her crew, only the ship's master, his cabin boy, and one sailor were healthy enough to perform their duties.

The three other vessels that had sailed away from the *Sea Venture* when the fleet met the leading edge of the storm on July 25 were also terribly battered by the tempest. Both the *Diamond* and the *Swallow* had either lost their mainmasts or cut them free at the height of the storm. Many on the two ships were sick, so sick that Archer reported that "the Viceamirall (*Diamond*) was said to have the plague in her."[6] Though what Archer called the plague may well have been smallpox or even heatstroke, the death toll on the *Diamond* and the *Swallow* was terrible. Between the two vessels, thirty-two passengers and crew—well over 10 percent of their total complement—had died at sea, their bodies thrown overboard. Somehow, during the crossing, perhaps at the height of the storm, two of the women passengers gave birth to babies. Not surprisingly given the circumstances, the two children, both boys, died in mid-Atlantic.

According to Archer, all the captains had been instructed before leaving port to sail directly for Virginia, to avoid the West Indies unless the ships in the fleet were separated, in which case, he wrote, they were to "repaire to the *Bermuda* (Archer's italics), there to stay seven dayes in expectation of the Admirall." It seems very likely that Archer meant to write "Barbuda" and not "Bermuda" since—until that time—no English vessel had ever voluntarily made landfall at Bermuda, the Isle of Devils. Equally important, unlike Barbuda, Bermuda was not then or ever considered part of the West Indies.[7] In any event, it is unlikely that any of the ships' captains seriously considered steering their damaged and undermanned vessels to either Barbuda or the

Bermudas in search of the *Sea Venture*. Instead, the storm would have convinced all the captains to steer for Virginia and what they hoped and prayed would be safety.

The arrival of the seven ships in Jamestown did not come as a surprise to the English settlers, who had been forewarned by Samuel Argall—the mariner who arrived in Virginia in mid-July after plotting a new course across the Atlantic—that a large fleet under the command of Sir George Somers and Sir Thomas Gates was being dispatched from England. However, the settlers in the little fort on the banks of the James must have been dismayed when they discovered that the "admiral" bearing Sir Thomas and Sir George was missing in action along with the lion's share of provisions meant to help the colony survive the winter, when food was scarce at best. Of course, the seven ships that survived the hurricane did carry at least some food and other supplies, but nowhere near enough to satisfy the growling bellies inside the fort. Then, too, there was the fact that the ships carried all those new settlers whose presence could only add to the colony's seemingly endless food shortages.

Obviously, while those in the settlement hoped against hope that the flagship had survived the storm, no one knew when or if the *Sea Venture* with its supplies—and the new leadership promised by Samuel Argall—might appear in the James River. Of course, the colony was not leaderless. Captain John Smith, who had taken the colony's reins in September 1608, was fully able to continue leading and he was entitled, under the terms of the original charter, to hold the office for a full year, or until September 10, 1609. However, several settlers, men who saw themselves assuming the leadership of the settlement, had other ideas. This group was almost certainly led by two of the colony's original settlers who had left the colony only to return in the fleet of 1609. One of the two was Gabriel Archer, the *Blessing* passenger who wrote about conditions on the vessel in the hurricane. His right-hand man was John Sicklemore, a settler who, for reasons no one has ever been able to determine, used the alias John Ratcliffe. These two men soundly despised Smith—a feeling he returned in kind. Now, they saw an opportunity to supplant Smith as the colony's leader or, at the very least, to force him to step down in accordance with the terms of the new charter.

The bad blood that pitted Archer and Ratcliffe against Smith had its beginnings in 1607, in Jamestown's earliest days, when the three men served together on the colony's ruling council. In the months when colonists were dying of hunger and illness, Smith discovered that the duo, along with a few others, were planning to steal supplies and a small boat they could use to flee Virginia for the safety of England. While Smith would almost certainly have been happy to see the last of the two men he thought of as cowards and traitors, he knew the colony could not survive without the boat and that the supplies the men were about to steal were sorely needed by the hungry colonists. Smith, in typical John Smith fashion, soon spiked those plans when he ordered several of the settlement's cannon turned on the boat and ordered those on board to come ashore or be shot out of the water.

Neither Archer nor Ratcliffe was the type of man to take such effrontery lying down, especially from a man they would have considered their social inferior. A few weeks later, the two saw an opportunity to even the score. At that time (it was after Smith's rescue by Pocahontas, when he returned to Jamestown), Archer and Ratcliffe used the Bible as a legal text and charged Smith with murder under Levitical law. Ludicrous as it seems, the two argued that the "eye for an eye" verse made Smith responsible for the deaths of two of his men who had been killed when Smith was captured by the Powhatan people. It is a measure of Smith's unpopularity with the "better sort" of colonists (not only Ratcliffe and Archer) that he was—within hours of his return to Jamestown—charged, tried, found guilty, and sentenced to die, with the execution scheduled for the next morning. That night (it was in early 1608), Smith was saved from death when Captain Christopher Newport, the man who later served as the _Sea Venture_'s captain, unexpectedly sailed up to Jamestown with a handful of new colonists and a shipload of food and other supplies. Newport, who recognized Smith's value to the colony even if some of the other leaders did not and who, no doubt, saw the idiocy of making Smith responsible for the death of the men who had been killed by the Indians, immediately ordered him freed and all charges against him dropped.

Now Archer and Ratcliffe and, to a lesser degree, John Martin, another of the original settlers whose laziness had angered Smith in the colony's early days, and who had departed in 1608 only to return on the _Falcon,_ all saw their chance to repay Smith for his cheek by stripping him of his office. Of course, Smith was not about to give up without a fight. He said, with justification, that since the colony's new leaders and the new charter authorizing the change in leadership were somewhere out on the Atlantic (or at its bottom), there was neither need nor authority for him to give up his post. And he certainly did not want to turn the leadership of the colony over to men he knew were ill suited to guarantee its safety or survival.

For his part, if Smith had known what lay in store in the next few weeks, he might well have simply thrown up his hands and ceded control to the men he found so distasteful. As it was, at one point, he said he would give up his commission to Martin, a man he apparently found slightly less offensive than Ratcliffe and Archer. Martin accepted, but kept the job for only three hours before deciding the responsibility was more than he wanted to shoulder and turning the task back to Smith.

As much as Smith disliked Ratcliffe, Archer, and Martin, he felt no better when he surveyed the new settlers dispatched by the Virginia Company. They were, in Smith's view, a pretty sorry lot. According to Smith's fellow colonists Richard Potts and William Phettiplace, the newcomers were nothing more than a "lewd company, wherein were many unruly gallants packed thither by their friends to escape il destinies. . . . Happie had we bin if they had never arrived." The newcomers, Potts and Phettiplace said, would either "rule all, or ruine all," adding that their arrival led to nothing but "confusion, or misery."[8]

Still, John Smith knew he had to have backing if he was to lead the colony successfully even for a few weeks. He would have deeply felt his responsibility to both the four hundred or so newcomers who had survived the hurricane as well as the approximately two hundred already living in Jamestown when the remnants of the 1609 fleet arrived. The roughly six hundred settlers living within the triangular palisade on the shores of the James—more than had inhabited the settlement at any time since its founding—had to be fed and housed and somehow kept alive. In an effort to make friends and gain support for his leadership, Smith appealed to the mariners, rough-and-ready men whom Archer and Ratcliffe and the others would have sneered at as unworthy of respect. George Percy, the journal keeper who would later prove to be a terribly inept governor in his own right, said that Smith, "fearing . . . thatt the seamen and thatt factyoin mighte growe too stronge and be a meanes to depose him of his governmentt," bribed the mariners "by the way of feasteings Expense of mutche powder and other unnecessary Tryumphes That mutche was Spente to noe other purpose butt to Insinewate wᵗh his Reconcyled enemyes and for his owne vayne glory for the wᶜh we all after suffered."[9] In reality, Smith, the man of action who had won respect as a soldier in Europe, would not have had to expend much in the way of bribes or feasting to earn the mariners' support. They certainly knew they had a better chance of surviving long enough to reboard their ships for the return voyage to England by following John Smith's lead than by throwing their lot in with Archer, Ratcliffe, or John Martin. Whether by bribery or, more likely, simply by dint of his personality, Smith quickly garnered enough support to convince his opposition to leave him in control of the colony. With as much good grace as his enemies could muster, which was not much, they allowed Smith to remain in office as their soon-to-be-replaced leader.

By this time, Wahunsonacock (Powhatan) and his people all along the Chesapeake were fully aware of the arrival of the hundreds of settlers on board the ships that rode at anchor off Jamestown. The paramount chief, while not privy to the plans that had been made in London, was savvy enough to know in his bones that the occupation of his lands and the threat to his rule—his very survival and that of his people—had been ratcheted to a new level. Thanks to his spies close to the colony and to several colonists who abandoned the settlement to take shelter with the natives, he also knew that the settlement was once again short of food and, even more important, that John Smith's rule was under attack from within. Since his first meeting with Smith, the old chief had known Smith was the colonist most worthy of respect and fear. Now less fearful of the short, red-bearded captain than at any time since that first meeting, Wahunsonacock determined to abandon his policy of more or less peaceful coexistence and to do what was needed to force the coat-wearing people from his lands once and for all or to force them to submit to his rule.

At the same time, Smith decided that the best way, indeed the only way, to guarantee Jamestown's future was to disperse settlers. In making this decision, he was taking a page out of the Indians' playbook since the Powhatan people routinely broke into small groups when food was scarce so that they could better forage and live off the land. Smith opted to send about sixty colonists downriver under the leadership of John Martin and George Percy (two of the men he counted as enemies). At the same time, he dispatched roughly 130 colonists up the James to a spot near the village of Powhatan, ruled by Wahunsonacock's son, Parahunt. This group he placed under the leadership of Francis West, whose only claim to leadership was that he was the twenty-three-year-old younger brother of Thomas West, Lord De La Warre, the man who had been named "governor for life" of the Virginia colony, and who was expected to arrive in Jamestown at almost any time. These groups, Smith believed, would be able to trade for supplies and live off the land, enabling those who remained in Jamestown to survive the fast approaching winter. Smith, as well as the men who left the protection of the settlement to live off the land,

were unaware that Wahunsonacock was no longer willing even to feign friendship for the *Tassantassas* (strangers)—except, of course, when it served his own
purposes.

It took no time at all for trouble to break out between the colonists sent
north with West and the natives living near the falls on the James River, near
the site of present-day Richmond. More interested in searching for gold—
that nonexistent Virginia gold yet again!—than in planting crops or in peaceful trade, the colonists built a fort of sorts on some low land close to the river
and then simply demanded that the natives supply them with food. When the
natives resisted, the English took what they wanted. "That disorderlie company so tormented those poore naked soules [the Indians], by stealing their
corne, robbing their gardens, beating them, breaking their houses, and keeping some prisoners," wrote one of Smith's supporters, that the natives "daillie
complained" that the settlers were worse than their worst Indian enemies.[10]
Not surprisingly, the Indians retaliated, attacking any man who dared set foot
outside the fort.

When Smith heard of the troubles at the falls, he headed up the river with
a group of men. What he found there filled him with a mix of dread and
anger. The little satellite settlement was in disarray, with no discipline, no rule
other than every man for himself. West himself, the putative leader of the settlement, was gone, searching for gold. The situation was so bad that Smith
was unable to smooth relations between the colonists and the Indians, despite
the fact that he had always been on good terms with Parahunt and his people.
Disheartened, Smith headed back downriver to Jamestown, apparently planning to recruit some men loyal to himself and ferry them back to the falls
where they might instill some discipline in West's disorderly group.

Smith and his men did not go far before their vessel ran aground. While
he was stranded, a handful of natives attacked some men working outside the
fort at the falls, killing several and driving the rest inside. They then made
their way inside what must have been a flimsy palisade and freed a few Indians that were being held captive. Smith, hearing of the new troubles at the
fort, went back to try to calm relations between the English and the natives.[11]

While Smith was at the fort, it seems that Francis West returned and immediately got into a heated argument with Smith, who berated him for building his fort on low land where it could be easily attacked. Smith then used his
persuasive skills to cobble together an agreement with Parahunt, allowing the
English to take possession of an already fortified Indian village of about two

hundred acres, a site with arable land, a place Smith described as one of the most "pleasant and delightfull in Virginia."[12] In exchange for the parcel of land, Smith promised copper and "gave" Parahunt a teenaged English boy named Henry Spelman to serve as a translator. With the deal closed, Smith ordered West to move into the Indian village with his men and then made his way back to the ship for his journey downriver to Jamestown.

Unknown to Smith, almost as soon as he departed, West and his men abandoned the Indian village and moved back to the underprotected location next to the river. Smith, meanwhile, did not make it back to Jamestown unscathed. No one knows for sure what happened on the seventy-four-mile return voyage down the James except that at some point Smith fell asleep in his canoe and somehow, accidentally or on purpose, a bag of gunpowder he carried on his belt ignited. The burning gunpowder "tore the flesh from his body and thighes, nine or ten inches square in a most pittifull manner. . . . To quench the tormenting fire, frying him in his cloaths he leaped over-board into the deep river, where ere they could recover him he was neere drowned." By the time he reached Jamestown, he was near death.[13]

Even as Smith lay in bed in his cottage in the settlement, writhing in agony, his enemies were not satisfied. According to Smith, an assassin crept into his tent and stood over him, pointing a pistol. The plan went awry, he said, when the would-be killer's "heart did faile" before he was able to "fire that mercilesse Pilstoll."[14] Finally, John Smith had had enough of Jamestown. He knew he had no choice but to return to England and to leave the settlement to stew in its own juices.

By October 4, 1609, several of the ships that had survived the storm that wrecked the *Sea Venture* were ready for their return voyage to England. Smith made arrangements to sail as a passenger, departing just a day or so later. By that time, Smith, the only man who had been able to bring anything like order to the struggling colony and the only colonial leader with a proven ability to deal with the native people both firmly and fairly, was not only physically torn, he was also emotionally exhausted and confused. Aged about thirty by that time, Smith was old, or certainly middle-aged for his times. As the ship that would carry the wounded old soldier back to London fell down the James toward the Chesapeake Bay, someone on board helped him to stand erect on the deck where he was able to look back at the settlement whose survival he had helped to ensure. By this time, according to Smith, the town itself

was strongly palisaded and contained some fifty or sixty houses. Its population numbered about 490 persons, including the newcomers. Livestock included six mares and two horses, carried to Jamestown on the *Blessing*, along
with more than five hundred pigs, kept on Hog Island, a few miles down the
James from the settlement. There were also hens and chickens, goats, and
sheep. The colonists were well armed with muskets and other small arms as
well as twenty-four cannon of various sizes. There were three ships, including
the pinnace *Virginia*, and seven boats, including a canoe or two. There was
food too, enough to last ten weeks. The colony seemed to be on more solid
footing than ever before. Smith had reason to feel proud and he would have,
for he was sage enough to know that if it had not been for his leadership, the
colony almost certainly would not have survived. He was also saddened and
fearful of what the future might hold.

Jamestown colonist Richard Potts, an admitted Smith backer, saw Smith's
departure as what it proved to be: a tragedy in the making. "What shall I say,"
he wrote, "but thus we (lost) him, that in all his proceedings, made Justice his
first guide, and experience his second, even hating basenesse, sloath, pride,
and indiginitie, more then any dangers; that never allowed more for himselfe,
then his souldiers with him, that upon no danger would send them where he
would not lead them himselfe; that would never see us want, what he either
had, or could by any meanes get us; that would rather want then borrow, or
starve then not pay; that loved action more than words, and hated falshood
and covetousnesse worse then death; whose adventures were our lives, and
whose losse our deaths."[15]

However, many, if not most, in the colony were happy to see Smith sail
away. He had his supporters, to be sure, but many of the better-born settlers, and many of the more common sort who had been forced to work
rather than trade for food, found him overbearing and insufferable. It
would not be until later that the colonists realized how much they missed
his leadership.

At that time, though, no one in Jamestown knew what suffering and death
lay ahead. Nor did any in the colony have any idea what had happened to the
Sea Venture and her passengers, including the men who had been sent to take
the reins of leadership from John Smith. By the time Smith departed, all in
Jamestown certainly must have believed the vessel, her crew, and the one hundred or so men and women who had been sent to Virginia were lost in the

storm that had savaged the *Lion*, the *Blessing*, and the other ships in the Jamestown-bound fleet. Along with Smith, the ships returning to England carried with them news that the admiral as well as the unnamed ketch had been lost in the storm, news that would set wives and mothers and fathers and children and other loved ones mourning across all of England.

6

Mutinies

By early October, as John Smith, wounded and disheartened, sailed away from Jamestown, a small ship was taking shape on stocks set on the Buildings Bay beach in Bermuda, just a long stone's throw from where the *Sea Venture* survivors had struggled ashore in July 1609. Each day, the sounds of saws and hammers and shouting, cursing men sent seabirds cawing and skittering into the air over the beach as Richard Frobisher, the shipwright from Limehouse, oversaw a group of untrained men—"an ill-qualified parcel of people," according to William Strachey[1]—as they slowly crafted a seaworthy vessel from the keel up. Her ribs and knees were made of oak timbers salvaged from the *Sea Venture* wreck and hewn to shape. Her hull was shaped using planks torn from the wreck and hauled ashore before she slipped beneath the waves or painstakingly cut from the cedar trees that grew so profusely on the island. Sir Thomas Gates, the governor designate of Virginia, worked alongside Frobisher and other laborers, hewing and toting and sawing in the summer heat, providing an example to men, Strachey said, who were otherwise unwilling to work.

By this time, Strachey, the onetime lawyer and poet, certainly had his eye on Sir Thomas as a patron who might help him get a leg up in Virginia. Given Strachey's hunger for position and financial security, it would have been perfectly natural for him to make himself useful to a man whose patronage could help him in Jamestown or, for that matter, with the leaders of the Virginia Company of London. For his part, Gates probably welcomed Strachey's attentions. After all, the failed lawyer was a gentleman, like Gates, as well as an educated and well-read man, undoubtedly able, as his writing showed, to tell a good story. Strachey would have been ready to pass on an exciting tidbit of gossip about Shakespeare or Ben Jonson or the actors who lived near him in Blackfriars. In fact, Strachey seemed willing to be a bit of a toady in his relationship with the man who would be governor of Virginia. In writing about those days in Bermuda, Strachey later gushed how "happy" it was for the survivors that Gates was with them, able by his "example . . . and authority" to both shame and command the survivors to work at building a ship that would carry them all to safety.[2]

As Sir Thomas and his workmen—farmers and shopkeepers and other landsmen, for the most part—toiled away at the building of a vessel, the mariners seem to have been content to wait for Henry Ravens's return with a rescue ship from Jamestown. These were men, after all, who staked their lives and fortunes on the sea. Perhaps they thought, even as September turned to October and October turned to November, that a ship would appear to carry them to safety. Perhaps—and this was hinted at by John Smith, in his history of Bermuda—there was some open hostility between, on the one hand, Admiral Somers and his men and, on the other, Sir Thomas Gates and his followers. This was certainly a possibility given the lack of regard mariners had for those who never went to sea, and vice versa.[3] In any event, as Gates and his men worked to build a vessel, Somers and the mariners filled their hours keeping the survivors well fed, fishing for grouper and mullet and other fish that teemed in the waters near shore, and hunting for wild hogs and tortoises and cahows and other tasty birds. During this period, too, Sir George had a small boat built, probably by Frobisher, and spent hours alone or perhaps rowed by an oarsman as he coasted the islands and drew the first detailed map of the Bermudas.

While the sailors hunted and fished and the landsmen sawed and hammered and hauled planks under Sir Thomas's watchful eye at Buildings Bay, the women were busy at their own chores.[4] There were berries to be gathered, firewood to be hauled into the camp, fires to be tended, hogs to be fed, huts to be thatched with palm fronds, and oysters to be plucked from the shallows. Someone had to watch over the kettles filled with boiling seawater so the salt wouldn't be spoiled, and someone had to wash clothes and bake bread with the scant flour saved from the dead ship's hold and cook the cahows and tortoise and fish and other delicacies. Those were chores that almost certainly would have been done by the women.

Soon enough, the days in the little settlement that rose above the high-water line on St. Catherine's Beach became ordered, as routine as the days had been on board the *Sea Venture*. The Reverend Richard Bucke preached two sermons each Sunday and feast day—usually, Strachey said, about "thankfulness and unity"—and there were prayers each morning and evening when the ship's bell was rung and all the survivors were expected to gather for prayers. Not many missed the services since names were called and those who did not answer were, according to Strachey, "duly punished."[5] In England, so-called recusants who chose not to attend required services were typically fined. Given the lack of ready cash in Bermuda, it is likely that the punishments were both physical and harsh.

Secular life in the little settlement also achieved a rhythm. Guards were posted and changed on schedule. The same tasks were performed, day after day, in the same order, from sunrise to sunset. But there was time enough, too, for socializing. Some spirits had almost certainly been salvaged before the *Sea Venture* slipped beneath the waves—perhaps they were rescued even before the flour and other victuals. The better born in the company—Sir George, Sir Thomas, Captain Newport, John Rolfe, Strachey, Henry Paine, and Mistress Horton, the lady who took ship with her maid—almost certainly sat together of an evening, drinking and talking of life in London and of what might lie ahead in Virginia. The sailors and the farmers and craftsmen and other common people may have been able to save some beer or sack and, if not, they almost certainly had bibbi, the home brew made from palmetto leaves. There was even time enough and sufficient privacy—in the woods, if nowhere else—for a romantic dalliance or two and for proper courtship: in late November, Mistress Horton's maid, Elizabeth Persons, wed Sir George Somers's cook, Thomas Powell, in a religious ceremony performed by the Reverend Bucke.

By the time Miss Persons and Thomas Powell exchanged vows, it was apparent to Sir George Somers that Ravens must have been lost at sea and that there could be no more realistic expectation of help from Virginia. By that time, as well, it would have been obvious to Somers that the ship being built by Gates and Frobisher and the other landsmen—it was to be called the *Deliverance* and would be about forty feet on the keel with a beam of less than twenty feet, displacing eighty tons—would be too small to carry all the ship-wreck survivors across the Atlantic to Virginia. Sir George met with Gates and asked for the use of two carpenters and other men along with enough supplies to build a second pinnace.

It surely seems from the governor's response that Sir Thomas and Sir George were not on the most amicable terms. Gates was willing enough to lend Somers two of the four carpenters he had working on the *Deliverance* and to assign twenty men to help the admiral, but when it came to supplies, Gates was stingy indeed. While the governor and his men were constructing their pinnace using metal fasteners and other materials salvaged from the *Sea Venture*, he told Somers that he could spare no materials at all other than a single iron bolt and the tools that his own men were not using.

Somers must have been enraged at what he would have taken as discourtesy. At sea, of course, as admiral of the Virginia-bound fleet, he would have been the undisputed leader of the entire expedition, and Gates's superior. With the *Sea Venture* now lying on the bottom, Gates could make the case—and no doubt did—that Sir George's command had come to an end. As the governor-designate of Virginia, Gates would have felt justified in throwing his weight around. It's easy to imagine these two knights of the realm—one accustomed to command at sea, a man who had sailed, after all, with Sir Francis Drake, and the other a brave soldier, a commander in the Netherlands, used to giving orders and having them followed without delay—as they growled and circled each other like a pair of wary dogs, each searching for an opening that would allow him to show dominance over the other. Ultimately, though, Gates had his way, and Somers took his band of twenty workmen (almost certainly mariners) to what Strachey described as "the main island"—presumably Bermuda Island, the largest of the group—and set about building from scratch a thirty-ton vessel—large enough to haul about sixty passengers and supplies for an open-ocean voyage from Bermuda to the Chesapeake.[6]

The labor was tedious and backbreaking. Every beam and joint and plank had to be fashioned by hand from cedar trees that grew across the islands.[7] A keel was laid, probably hewn from a single, tall, straight tree trunk. Other trees were felled and sawn into planks to serve as beams and overheads. Boughs found in the forest were muscled into shape to serve as elbows. Slowly, the hull took shape as one hand-hewn plank after another was fastened in place. The single iron bolt given to Somers by Gates was used to attach the keel to the keelson (the first plank laid on top of the keel). All the other joinery was accomplished using trunnels whittled out of cedar wood and hammered into holes bored in planks and beams.

Meanwhile, in those weeks while the ships took shape and life in the camp took on something of the appearance of normalcy and routine, trouble was brewing among the band of shipwreck survivors. To be sure, they were surrounded by plenty, by fish and fowl and eggs that kept their bellies full. There was water from the well on St. Catherine's Beach. The weather was fine, for the most part, though squalls frequently struck without warning, turning the sky pewter gray and lashing the palms and cedars—not to mention the survivors in their rough shelters—with high winds and driving rains. Still, there were problems in paradise.

According to Strachey, by early September, barely five weeks after the *Sea Venture* wedged herself between two coral heads off the coast of St. George's, a group of discontented mariners began muttering that there was no need, no real reason, why they should be forced to sail on to Virginia. The mariners, of course, led miserable lives, filled with hard work, little comfort, terrible food, and constant exposure to danger: conditions vastly different from those they found in Bermuda. Soon, the unhappy grumbling began to influence others, both among those William Strachey described as the "common sort" and those he called "the better sort." The discontented—mariners and landsmen both—had obviously heard of the trials faced by the early Jamestown settlers. In Virginia, they muttered, "nothing but wretchedness and labor must be expected." In Bermuda, though, "ease and pleasure might be enjoyed." And, they said, since "in both the one and the other place they were (for the time) to lose the fruition both of their friends and country, as good and better were it for them to repose and seat them where they should have the least outward wants the while."[8] A powerful argument, almost undeniable in its common sense. Why, indeed, go to Virginia where men starved or lost their lives in Indian attacks? Why not stay in Bermuda? But it was a dangerous argument as well, for, as Strachey later said, such discontentment "had like to have been the parents of bloody issues and mischiefs."[9]

Eventually, a group of six men, all mariners, decided simply not to do any work that would further the building of the pinnace being constructed by Gates and his helpers. These six—their names were John Want, Christopher Carter, Francis Pearepoint, William Brian, William Martin, and Richard Knowles—soon convinced a carpenter named William Bennett and a blacksmith whose name is not known to join in their plotting. Their plan was simple. They would steal a boat and make their way to a nearby island, one where they could stay without toil or worry, living lives of leisure while the others sailed on to the Chesapeake.

The conspirators were obviously a talkative group, since before they were able to put their plan into action, they were found out by Sir Thomas Gates and hauled before the old soldier for punishment. Probably since no real harm had been done, the governor decided to treat the would-be mutineers gently. Since they wanted to stay in Bermuda, wanted to live alone on an island, he determined to grant their wishes. The six men (minus the carpenter and blacksmith, whose services were too important to the rest of the survivors and to those in Jamestown) were exiled to a distant, rocky island and supplied with just enough in the way of rough provisions to keep them alive.

Soon, the six found their lives on the island much harsher, and lonelier, than they had imagined. Their bellies missed the good food to be enjoyed in the little settlement on St. Catherine's Beach. They missed their companions and wondered why their co-conspirators had not been banished. John Want, the ringleader of the mutineers, a man described by Strachey as a "sectary in points of religion," apparently was a preachy fellow whose company would have quickly grown tiresome. Somehow the conspirators managed to get several letters, "humble petitions," in the words of Strachey, to Gates, admitting their wrongdoing, begging forgiveness, and promising to mend their ways. They also told Gates they could, and would, provide services that would help the company as a whole.

Gates could be (as his rule in Virginia would later show) a harsh man when circumstances warranted severity. He was, Strachey said, "not easy to admit any accusation and hard to remit an offense." However, he was, Strachey added, "at all times sorry in the punishment of him in whom may appear either shame or contrition"—a soft touch, in other words, when it came to dealing with any miscreant who exhibited the proper degree of remorse.[10] Gates forgave the conspirators and allowed them to return to the main camp. While Gates's show of mercy might have been laudatory, it proved to be a mistake, at least in the long run.

Over the next few months, as the season changed and the winds grew colder, flocks of migratory birds appeared in the rocky hills overlooking the little settlement and on the beach. Turtles crawled out of the water to nest and lay their eggs. As many as forty in a day were taken by the men who roasted their succulent meat over open fires or salted it away for use on the coming voyage to Jamestown. On Christmas Eve, Reverend Bucke preached a sermon and celebrated communion along with Sir Thomas and most of the company of survivors. On New Year's Day, Gates and one of the gentlemen among the passengers, Master James Swift, went hunting and killed a pair of large, tasty swans. But, once again, all was not well on the island that must have seemed like a paradise to many of the shipwreck survivors.

Sometime around Christmas, Stephen Hopkins, the pious and preachy nonconformist who served as a "clarke" to Reverend Bucke, assigned "to read the psalms and chapters upon Sundays," began fomenting mutiny much like the earlier group of malcontents. Like the earlier mutineers, Hopkins spoke glowingly of life in Bermuda, of the abundance of good food and the lack of toil and trouble. According to Strachey, the pious Hopkins proposed "substantial arguments both civil and divine," misquoting the scriptures and putting his own spin on the law, to convince others (and perhaps himself) that they had every right to disobey Gates's orders, if that was their desire, and to remain in Bermuda if they saw fit. Gates's authority ceased with the shipwreck, he argued; hence, "it was no breach of honesty, conscience, nor religion" for him or any like-minded survivor to refuse to acknowledge Gates's leadership—in other words, to commit mutiny.[11]

By January, the weather was miserable. The little settlement of survivors was lashed by biting, sharp north winds, scattered rains and hail, thunderstorms that turned the sky so dark that it seemed the sun might never shine again. In that month, Hopkins plotted. He tried to attract converts. On January 24, according to Strachey, the would-be mutineer disclosed his plans to Samuel Sharpe and Humphrey Reede, hoping to enlist their support. Instead, Sharpe and Reede hurried to warn Sir Thomas Gates that mutiny was afoot.

Gates would have been shocked by the disclosure. Hopkins was a trusted and respected man, a cut above the ordinary sort. He stood at prayer services and read the scriptures to all the survivors. He was not the type of man one would expect to stage a mutiny, even a nonviolent one. If Hopkins could be a mutineer, everyone was suspect. Gates knew he had to take action, quickly and firmly. Hopkins must be punished if for no other reason than to serve as an example to other survivors who might have similar mutinous ideas or leanings.

Gates ordered Hopkins arrested and placed in manacles. "By a tolling of the bell"—the same ship's bell that was hauled ashore and used to call the survivors together for prayer—the entire company was assembled. Hopkins, charged with mutiny, was dragged before the company, under guard. The two witnesses, Reede and Sharpe, told their tales and Hopkins was given an opportunity to respond. At first, Hopkins denied the charges, weeping abjectly. Soon, though, he saw his denials were falling on deaf ears. He admitted his guilt, pleading, Strachey said, "simplicity." Through his own sobs, he heard himself sentenced to death for mutiny and sedition. Hopkins then changed his tack and began begging piteously for mercy, if not for his sake, then for the sake of his wife and young children. His pleas for mercy worked. "So penitent was he and made so much moan, alleging the ruin of his wife and children," Strachey reported, that all the "better sort of the Company"— including Strachey himself and Captain Christopher Newport—went to Gates's quarters later that day and begged the governor to pardon Hopkins until, in response to their pleas, Gates relented and issued a pardon to a mutineer once again.[12]

The next trouble that arose was in Admiral Somers's camp on the main island, where the mariners were building the *Patience*. One evening, just after twilight, two of the sailors, Edward Waters and Edward Samuell, got into an argument that quickly escalated into a full-blown fight. Men who lived at sea were not known for finesse when it came to fighting. It's easy to imagine the two hard men, weathered by the sun and wind, using fists and knees and elbows and the few teeth they had left as they battled by the campfire, surrounded by a circle of yelling, cursing shipmates. At some point in the fight, the tide turned against Waters who, in a moment of desperation, picked up a shovel and struck Samuell on the side of the head with the tool's knife-sharp edge. Samuell was probably dead before he hit the sand.

While the watching mariners probably enjoyed the fight, some in the crowd grabbed Waters and took him before Gates for punishment. In this instance, Gates immediately sentenced Waters to hang for the murder. Since the sun had set, however, he decreed that Waters should be tied to a tree, alongside his victim, "with many ropes and a guard of five or six to attend him." In the night, though, the guards fell asleep and Waters escaped with the help of shipmates who, Strachey said, "not taking into consideration the unmanlinesse of the murder nor the horror of the sinne," cut the ropes that bound Waters and his victim together and then led Waters to a hiding place in the woods where they were able to bring him food each night.[13]

Though search parties hunted for the fugitive, he managed somehow to remain free, hiding in the forest or in one of the caves that dotted the islands, almost certainly with the collusion of some of the other mariners. Perhaps, and this may have been the case given the way the other sailors reacted, or didn't react, to the murder, Samuell was one of those men who had many more enemies than friends. There certainly did not seem to be many men in the *Sea Venture*'s crew who mourned his loss.

In fact, Waters or his friends eventually convinced Sir George Somers that the murderer deserved mercy. Somers, in turn, petitioned Gates and, no doubt, appealed to that gentle streak in the governor that had caused him to be merciful to the mutineers and to Stephen Hopkins. Waters was allowed to rejoin his shipmates in the mariners' camp.

At about the same time, the little camp on St. George's Island was being battered by fierce winter gales, with winds that pushed seas high up the beach where the pinnace *Deliverance* sat vulnerable on stocks. According to Strachey, wave after rushing wave "endangered her overthrow and ruin" by threatening to tumble the half-built pinnace in pieces from the stocks that held her upright. Had that happened, of course, the hours of backbreaking work erecting stocks and hewing joints and elbows and cutting timbers would have been for nothing. Worse, all the timbers and gear so carefully salvaged from the *Sea Venture* might well have been swept to sea and lost for good. Sir Thomas hurriedly ordered laborers into the hills, where they dug a hundred loads of stones that were carried to the beach to construct a sort of jetty between the stocks and the sea. The jetty, Strachey said, "brake the violence of the flow and billow" and saved the ship.[14]

The *Sea Venture* survivors must have been miserable as the winter deepened and one furious gale after another swept across the islands, with cold winds that howled around the little cabins on St. George's Island and in the mariners' camp. The damp and cold seemed to penetrate to the bone, set the survivors shivering as they huddled in their drafty quarters or worked—as they had to work—to gather food or firewood or to build the ships that were to carry them on to Jamestown. What flour was left turned moldy, as did clothing and books and bedding. Tools and weapons seemed to rust overnight.

Meanwhile, not all in the Bermudas was intrigue and mutiny and the misery of endless toil and dampness. In February, as the first hints of warm weather made themselves known, a baby girl was born to John Rolfe and his wife. Reverend Mr. Bucke christened the infant with the name Bermuda, with William Strachey, Captain Newport, and Mistress Horton standing as witnesses. It would have been natural for Rolfe and his wife to feel a joy at the birth of their daughter, but that joy soon turned to sorrow as the first-ever child born in Bermuda died soon after her birth. The infant was buried somewhere on St. George's Island. Another child, a boy named Bermudas, was born just a few days later. This baby, too, died in infancy.

As the weather turned fair, as work progressed on the two small ships that represented salvation to most of those in Bermuda, a number of the shipwreck survivors—some in the settlement on St. George's and some in Somers's camp on the main island—once again began plotting a mutiny. This time the plan was more sweeping and bolder than earlier attempts to overthrow the "government" of Sir George Somers and Sir Thomas Gates; it was so brazen that Strachey called it both "deadly and bloody."[15] And it was. The mutineers—the band included Henry Paine, the "gentleman," as well as second offenders Christopher Carter and Robert Waters (the pardoned murderer)—planned to kill Gates and men loyal to him, seize all the supplies and food, and take full control of the little settlement. Though Strachey does not make clear what the mutineers might have done if they had been successful, it is likely that they planned simply to stay in Bermuda or perhaps flee in the *Deliverance* to the West Indies, where they might turn piratical and find Spanish ships to loot. Of course, failure was always a possibility. But, the ringleaders certainly figured, if their plot was discovered, Gates lacked the spine to execute any of their number, no matter how treacherous their behavior.

According to Strachey, the mutineers had little difficulty attracting converts. Apparently, though, they proselytized too much, told too many other men of their plans. "Some of the association who, not strong enough fortified in their own conceits, brake from the plot itself and . . . discovered the whole order and every agent and actor therof."[16] Several of the would-be mutineers skulked into Sir Thomas's cabin—no doubt terrified at the thought of his reaction—and laid out the plan, chapter and verse, naming all the names.

Gates knew this third mutiny was a serious affair. Not only was it widespread but, for the first time, mutineers were planning the murder of the little settlement's leaders, including, of course, Gates himself. The old soldier, who had been knighted for valor at Cadiz by Queen Elizabeth's favorite, Essex, knew his duty and, despite what the mutineers thought, was not afraid to perform it. He also knew that if he acted too soon, some of the conspirators might escape. Most, including the leader, were in the secondary camp with Sir

George Somers, not in the main camp above St. Catherine's Beach. And, as far as Gates knew, all the mariners, including Sir George himself, might be tainted. Gates called the men closest to him—including, no doubt, William Strachey and John Rolfe and, of course, Captain Newport—and told them of the plot. While there were probably some in Gates's camp who wanted to rush to vengeance, Sir Thomas advised patience. The trusted men were advised to go nowhere without their weapons and to be constantly on guard since, in Strachey's words, every man's life was "not . . . in safety whilst his next neighbor was not to be trusted."[17] At the same time, Gates ordered the watches doubled. Armed men patrolled the paths and passageways leading to Gates's camp, hands on their swords, muskets primed. For the time being, though, while all were on guard, suspicious and watchful, no arrests were made.

On the night of March 13, matters came to a head when Henry Paine, described by Strachey as a man who was "full of mischief, every hour scheming something or other," openly rebelled when he was called for guard duty.[18] Instead of taking his place with the rest of the watch, he shouted insults at his "captain"—perhaps one of the many men who had served with Gates in the Netherlands—and then struck the officer. Other men who saw the attack grabbed Paine before he could make matters worse. If things had gone no further, Paine might have gotten away with what could have been viewed as a momentary aberration. Paine, though, refused to stand guard and walked away laughing at the idea that a double watch was necessary.

Paine's friends were quick to warn him that if Gates heard of his actions and his refusal to stand watch, he would almost certainly would pay with his life. Strachey, who later wrote about the incident, hesitated to repeat Paine's response except to say that the angry gentleman used such language "as would offend the modest ear too much to express it in his own phrase." The substance of Paine's comments, spat out with what Strachey described as "bitter violence," was that Gates had no authority to judge any man in the colony, certainly not a gentleman like himself, and that the governor should "kisse etc."[19]

By the next day, the story of the fracas between Paine and his captain, and Paine's remarks—including the words so tastefully omitted by Strachey— were known by every man and woman in the two camps. Gates immediately called the entire company together, Somers and the mariners from their camp on the main island along with the other survivors from the gathering of huts on St. George's Island. Paine, now in shackles, was hauled before the governor where charges—of treason, no doubt—were read aloud. The evidence was clear. The captain of the guard told how Paine had refused to obey orders and attacked him violently. The men of the watch corroborated the captain's testimony, told how Paine walked away from guard duty. They repeated Paine's comments. Paine never stood a chance and must have known it as soon as the "court" was convened. Gates immediately pronounced him guilty and ordered him hanged without delay. He wasn't about to take a chance that Paine might escape, as Waters had, following *his* death sentence, nor did he want to risk an uprising by Paine's friends. A ladder was hauled out and a noose quickly prepared. When Paine saw the makeshift gallows, he became instantly remorseful, confessed his guilt, and—though Strachey doesn't say so—undoubtedly pleaded for his life. Gates, though, knew he was being carefully watched by all the survivors, especially by other discontented men who might themselves be plotting mutiny. He ordered the execution to proceed, though he did grant Paine's last wish that as a gentlemen he be shot rather than suffer a traitor's death by hanging. "Toward the evening," Strachey said, Paine "had his desire, the sun and his life setting together."[20]

The news of Paine's execution sent shock waves through the mariners' camp. Those in the camp who were involved in the conspiracy—and that seems to have been most of the men assigned to work with Somers—had no idea if Paine had fully confessed before his death. For all they knew, their compatriot had named names in an effort to save his own skin. In the hours following the execution, men in the little camp near the spot where the *Patience* sat almost ready for launching must have looked nervously at each other, fingered their knives or swords as they wondered when or if they would be arrested, wondered, too, what chance, if any, they had of avoiding punishment. Finally, those who had been involved—and there is no indication just how many of the men that was—panicked and fled into the woods.

Strachey—and perhaps Somers, too—seems to have been baffled by the mutineers' actions. Strachey said he thought the men who fled might have been motivated by a "greediness after some little pearl" (for a time it was hoped that oysters that abounded in the Bermudas might be pearl-bearing, a hope that was as fruitless as the hope that gold would be found in Virginia) or simply by a desire "forever to inhabit here."[21] In reality, having learned of Paine's end, they probably hoped only to stay hidden and safe from execution until they saw Gates and Somers and the others sail away for Virginia.

In any case, while the mutineers—now fugitives—seemed bent on staying in Bermuda, they soon discovered that they missed some of the comforts of civilization. Soon after fleeing into the hinterland, they sent "an audacious and formal petition" to Sir Thomas Gates, signed by all the company, begging not only to be allowed to remain in Bermuda but also for two suits of clothes for each man along with enough meal—flour or oats salvaged from the ship's stores—to last them for a year.[22]

From Strachey's narrative, it seems the petition was sent to Somers, who then forwarded it to Gates, the man ultimately responsible for the survivors. Once Gates received the petition, of course, he knew that Somers was in contact with the mutineers. Knowing, too, that Somers had taken no steps to bring them to justice, Sir Thomas had reason to believe, or at least suspect, that the admiral supported the mutineers, if not in their plot then at least in their desire to stay in Bermuda. In his response to the mariners' petition, written to the admiral, Gates pleaded with Somers "by the worthiness of his (heretofore) well mayntayed reputation, by the powers of his own judgement, by the virtue of that ancient love and friendship which had these many years been settled between them" to do his best to convince the mutineers to give themselves up.[23]

At the same time that Gates implied that Somers was aiding the mutineers, it seemed he went out of his way, in his answer to the petition, to convince the admiral of his goodwill toward him, and indeed all the mariners, stressing that his plan had never been to abandon the sailors in Bermuda without adequate supplies or without plans to return as soon as practical. Perhaps the conflict that John Smith had talked about in his history of Bermuda had, by that time, developed into a festering sore. Perhaps Gates felt that the split between the two groups had contributed to the mutiny and he wanted to smooth relations. Whatever the reason, Gates made it plain he felt no ill will toward Somers and the mariners.

It was true, Gates said, that when the *Sea Venture* survivors were first stranded in Bermuda, it appeared that they would not be able to fashion a vessel that could carry all of them on to Jamestown. It was also true, he said, that it seemed for a time that what he called "the tyranny of necessity" might have forced him to leave some of the men behind while the rest sailed away. Though Gates never came out and said so, the men who would have been abandoned—for the most part, at least—would have been the common sailors, members of the *Sea Venture*'s crew who would not have been needed to sail a much smaller vessel the six hundred miles or so from Bermuda to the

Chesapeake. But, Sir Thomas said, he never intended to abandon or forsake the men he left behind "like savages." No, he would have left them "all things fitting to defend them from want and wretchedness . . . for one whole year or more," or plenty of time for him to arrange their rescue. Gates urged Sir George to tell his men, "if by any means he could learn where they were," that he would have spent his own money, used all his authority in Virginia, or called on his friends in England, if necessary, to send ships to rescue them before a year passed, if it had been humanly possible.

After going out of his way to convince Somers and the men who were hiding in the woods that he had always had their salvation as his goal, Gates went on to say that any fears the mariners had of being left behind were senseless since *Deliverance,* the ship he and his workers had built, proved to be larger than originally thought, spacious enough to carry all the survivors on to Virginia. Then there was *Patience,* the ship the mutineers themselves had constructed. Between the vessels there was ample room for all and then some.

Having made his case that he wanted only the best for the *Sea Venture* survivors, Gates went on to say he was obliged, by duty to King James I and to the Virginia Company, to see to it that they all continued on to Jamestown. Besides, he added in English that was convoluted even for a Jacobean gentlemen, if he allowed them to flout his authority it would be "an imputation and infamy . . . to their proper (personal) reputations and honors" since it was right and duty "to compel the adversant and irregular multitude at any time to what should be obedient and honest." In other words, it was up to the honest men in the company of mutineers to convince—or force, if need be—the recalcitrant to come back to the fold.[24]

If all that wasn't enough, Gates then promised the mutineers that if they surrendered and expressed remorse and promised to mend their ways, he was ready to forgive and forget. If anything, he said, he pitied them, though he did not say why. But, in any case, he promised that "whatsoever they had sinisterly committed or practiced hitherto against the laws of duty and honesty should not in any sort be imputed against them."[25]

According to Strachey, the letter so moved Sir George Somers that the admiral turned on all his charm to bring the mariners to heel. "He did so nobly work and heartily labour," Strachey said, "that he brought most of them in."[26] Of course, Somers was able to hold out Gates's promise of lenient treatment as bait to the mutineers. Perhaps that was enough to convince most that they should return to work. Others would have been convinced, no doubt, when Gates reminded them, as he must have, that if they did manage to stay hidden, if they were able to remain in Bermuda when the others sailed away, they could not hope, not in their wildest dreams, that they would simply be left to eat fish and birds and turtles in the islands forever. Eventually, a fleet of ships from England or from Virginia would sail into view, anchor off the little settlement while armed men rowed ashore to take the mutineers into custody and haul them to Jamestown or London for imprisonment or, more likely, execution.

As persuasive as Sir George's arguments were, two of the men— Christopher Carter and Robert Waters—still refused to give themselves up. Carter, of course, was a twotime offender, a man involved in the first mutiny who had been pardoned by Gates. Waters was the man who murdered his shipmate, was sentenced to death and freed by his friends, only to be, like Carter, pardoned by the governor. No doubt the two were fearful that, despite Gates's promises of pardon, they would be executed as habitual offenders. That makes sense. There may, however, have been more to the story. Nathaniel Butler, who later served as Bermuda's governor and who knew Carter personally, said that there was so much animosity between Gates and Somers that the two mariners, Carter and Waters—staunch Somers supporters who were guilty of "cleaving notoriously" to the admiral—were singled out to "receive sharp rewards" by Gates and his faction. Somers, unable to prevent what he viewed as the unjust treatment of the two sailors, convinced the two that they should stay in hiding or even run deeper into the woods to avoid capture. According to Butler, Somers made them a "faithful promise that he would speedily return to their relief."[27]

By the time the mutineers, save for the two fugitives, returned to camp, where they were indeed forgiven by Gates, it was the end of February. The *Deliverance* was far enough along that her planks were ready to be caulked using oakum made from old cables salvaged from the *Sea Venture* along with salvaged tar and pitch that was used to seal her bilge. When the tar and pitch and oakum ran out, Frobisher saw to it that the vessel was "breamed ... with lime made of whelk shells and an hard white stone which we burned in a kiln, slaked with fresh water and tempered with tortoises' oil."[28]

By late March, the ship was ready for launching. She was, Strachey said, roughly forty feet long on the keel and about sixty feet overall, taking into account her rake forward and aft. With a beam of almost twenty feet, she had a burden of eighty tons. A small cannon, salvaged from the wreck, was mounted on her slightly raised forecastle so that the deck might be scoured with small shot "if at any time we should be boarded by the enemy"—the Spanish were never far from the minds of seafaring Englishmen in 1610—and far aft she had a "great cabin" and a steerage room complete with four windows.[29]

When the tide rose on March 30, the *Deliverance* was manhandled from the beach on Buildings Bay down to the water. Buoyed by four empty casks and left unrigged, she was towed, probably by Sir George's little rowboat, to the back side of St. George's Island, where she was tied up to a small round island protected from the ocean waves but close to a channel that led to open waters. Sir Thomas and Frobisher the shipwright and Strachey, who by this time had established himself as one of Gates's most loyal followers, would have stood on the beach with all the men who had spent so many difficult hours building the ship watching, beaming with a sense of pride and accomplishment as the little vessel bobbed on the blue-green waters just off the beach. Over the next few weeks, though, there was more work to do, loading tons of stones into the vessel's hold to serve as ballast and stepping her masts and fixing spars and hundreds of feet of standing and running rigging and making last-minute adjustments and repairs that were never ending on board any sailing vessel.

During those weeks, Somers and his crew of mariners also finished work on the *Patience*. The smaller vessel—just twenty-nine feet long on the keel—was launched near the end of April. Matthew Somers, Sir George's nephew, served as her captain and stood at her tiller as she made her way to a mooring close to the *Deliverance*, near the channel by which the two ships would make their way to sea. Soon, the shipwreck survivors were busily loading the two vessels with supplies, including turtle and fowl meat and fish and water for the voyage. Thinking that they would find ample food in Jamestown, they laded no more than they projected they would need for a voyage to the Chesapeake, taking into account the reality that they might be blown far off course.

While the ships were being prepared, Sir Thomas Gates visited the garden that had been prepared by Sir George near the little settlement on St. Catherine's Beach. He found a tall cedar tree and lopped off its upper branches to make sure it wasn't blown down in a storm. Using two pieces of timber rescued from the *Sea Venture*'s carcass, he fashioned a cross and, using trunnels, attached it to the tree. He nailed to the cross a picture of King James I—a silver twelvepence—along with a piece of copper on which he had engraved a memorial in Latin and English:

> In memory of our great deliverance, both from a mighty storm and leak: wee
> have set up this to the honor of God. It is the spoil of an English ship (of
> three hundred ton) called the *Sea Venture*, bound with seven ships more (from
> which the storm divided us) to Virginia or Nova Britannia in America. In it
> were two Knights, Sir Thomas Gates, Knight governor of the English forces
> and colony there: and Sir George Somers Knight, admiral of the seas. Her
> captain was Christopher Newport; passengers and mariners she had beside
> (which all came safe to land) one hundred and fifty. We were forced to run
> her ashore (by reason of her leak) under a point that bore southeast from the
> northern point of the island which wee discovered first the eight and twenti-
> eth of July, 1609.[30]

With the *Patience* and the *Deliverance* ready for sea, all that was needed was a favorable wind to carry the vessels through the channel and out to sea. For several days in early May, the wind blew from the east and southeast, making departure impossible. During this period, Sir George Somers and Captain Christopher Newport took a boat—probably Sir George's fishing boat—out to the reef, where they took soundings and placed "canoes" (buoys) to mark the sides of the channel so the two deep-draft ships could find their way to deep water. Finally, when the survivors woke on May 10, the winds were friendly and favorable. The survivors—settlers bound for Virginia and the mariners who had been recruited as part of the fleet—hurried to board the waiting ships. At 10 A.M., the ships' sails were unfurled and the lines that held them fast to land were cast off. The wind died soon after that but Somers ordered the longboat out with oarsmen to tow the two ships through the channel. The *Deliverance* went first, with the *Patience* following close behind. Though the channel had been marked and the mariners were careful, the *Deliverance* ran aground once. Luckily, the coral heads were soft. They shattered under the weight of the ship's hull or, as Strachey said, "we might have been like enough to have returned anew and dwelt there, after ten months of carefulness and great labor, a longer time."[31] Instead, the two ships, with more than 140 survivors, made their way out of the channel and into open water where soundings showed more than three fathoms (eighteen feet) depth. As the ships cleared the channel, the winds picked up, the sails bellied out, and the vessels heeled slightly as they headed away from the Bermudas. William Strachey and John Rolfe and Gates and Somers and Mistress Horton and all the other survivors must surely have stood on deck, watching, as the stretch of water between the islands and the ships' sterns grew slowly wider and wider.

On land, somewhere on a hilltop or perhaps on the beach, two men—Christopher Carter and Edward Waters, the two mutineers who had gone into hiding in February—also stood watching as the two ships made their slow way toward the heaving and distant horizon.

7

Famine Ghastly and Pale

As the *Sea Venture* survivors sailed away from St. George's Island, most would have been understandably apprehensive, if not downright terrified. It was not likely that any of the passengers or crewmen on the *Deliverance* and the *Patience* would have forgotten their experience in the hurricane that drove the *Sea Venture* to her doom on the Bermudan reef. Memories of that terrible storm must have been fresh in every mind as the two pinnaces moved into open waters and William Strachey and John Rolfe and the other shipwreck survivors watched the green islands that had been their refuge and salvation slowly slip below the horizon. Soon, though, all but the most nervous passengers would have been lulled into a sense of complacency by the fine weather, friendly breezes, and relatively calm waters. All on board were comforted, too, by the knowledge that, if all went well, they would see land within a week or ten days.

For hour after hour, then, the two small ships built by the survivors in Bermuda sailed on, heeled slightly to port, their sails taut as the vessels plowed steadily through gentle ocean swells in the direction of the Chesapeake. Strachey, who wrote the only known narrative of the journey, said the trip was uneventful, except for a few times when the wind turned "scarce and contrary."[1] At those times, Strachey, who was on board the *Deliverance* with his new friend Sir Thomas Gates, lost sight of the smaller *Patience*, bearing Sir

George Somers, his nephew Matthew, and most of the mariners. Soon enough, though, as the wind steadied and Newport, on the *Deliverance,* ordered sail shortened, the smaller pinnace hove back into view and the two vessels joined company again.

On May 17, 1610, just one week after the ships left Bermuda, Strachey noted what he described as a "change of water"—a sudden difference in the ocean's color as the Atlantic shallowed over the continental shelf off the coast of North America. At about the same time, those on the ships saw "rubbish"—leaves and twigs and perhaps a dead bird or two swept from some Virginia beach—floating in the water, a sure sign that "we were not far from land."[2]

At about midnight the following day, May 18, some mariner, probably coxswain Robert Walsingham, went forward with a sounding lead line, measured the water's depth, and found the bottom at 37 fathoms, or about 225 feet. By the morning of May 19, the lead found bottom at just under 20 fathoms, or about 120 feet, and showed the bottom was stony and sandy, a sure sign that some wave-swept shore was just over the horizon.[3] Late the next day, Strachey and the others on the two ships caught a whiff of a "marvelous sweet smell" on the breeze, the smell of trees and flowers, the smell of land itself. The aroma reminded Strachey, who had traveled in the Mediterranean, of the smell of land when he neared the coast of Spain in the Straits of Gibraltar. It made it all on the ships "not a little glad," he later said.[4]

As soon as the light allowed the next morning, a sailor scurried to the top of the larger vessel's mainmast, where he spied a low mass of land lying to the south and west. His cry—"Land ho!"—brought all the survivors on both vessels running to look where he pointed until a low, dark smudge edged its way over the horizon. Later that same day, the ships anchored just off the broad mouth of the Chesapeake, forced to wait for the ebbing tide to change. At about 11 P.M., with the flood starting, Somers ordered the ships' anchors weighed. Sails were trimmed and the vessels moved into the bay.

Strachey does not describe what happened on the ships as they entered the Chesapeake, but it is safe to assume that Master Bucke led a prayer of thanks and joy for their safe passage, a prayer that was happily seconded by all the shipwreck survivors. Sir George Somers certainly had reason to give thanks, as did Christopher Newport. They, after all, had been charged with the safety of the colonists and now their duty was discharged. For his part, Sir Thomas Gates must have looked around with wonder and at least a little apprehension. Finally, he had reached the place where he was to serve as the king's representative in a position that could add immeasurably to his reputation—or spell his ruin. All the settlers bound for Jamestown would have wondered what waited in this strange new world and all would have been anxious to land. Strachey, having almost certainly ingratiated himself firmly with Gates by the time they arrived in Virginia, would have been eager to start his new life, to discover what opportunities he would find and how he would fare. All must have been anxious to move up the Chesapeake to the James River and from there to the settlement that would be their home.

In fact, if Strachey and the others on the vessels had known what awaited them on the banks of the James, they might well have turned their little ships to head back to Bermuda or steered north to try to find the English fishing fleets that regularly worked the cod-rich banks off the coast of Newfoundland. Instead, they waited impatiently as the *Patience* and the *Deliverance* made their slow way into the vast mouth of the Chesapeake.

A little over six months earlier, when the wounded, disheartened John Smith sailed away from Jamestown, he left George Percy in charge of the colony and responsible for the safety and survival of the roughly five hundred men, women, and children living along the James. Percy, one of the original Jamestown settlers, was twenty-nine years of age when the leadership of the colony fell into his lap in 1609. The eighth son of Henry Percy, the eighth earl of Northumberland, and the brother of another Henry Percy, who became the ninth earl of Northumberland, he was one of the highest-born colonists. His high birth did not count for much, however, since, as an eighth son, he was—in a society that practiced primogeniture—too far down the list of heirs to expect anything meaningful in the way of an inheritance. In fact, George Percy would have been fully aware that his prospects were dim in his native land. Like many another young man with no hope of inheriting position or fortune, Percy decided at an early age to make the military his career, and joined the army to serve in the long wars in the Netherlands. Though he served with some distinction, Percy's prospects grew even dimmer in 1605, when his older brother Henry was rather loosely implicated in the Gunpowder Plot, an almost laughable plan cobbled together by a group of Roman Catholics to blow up Parliament and kill King James I and his family. While Henry Percy avoided the headsman's ax, he was thrown into the Tower of London, where he remained in relatively cozy confinement until 1621. For his part, George knew that, with his brother in the tower and his entire family under a cloud of suspicion, it was a good idea to put as much mileage between himself and King James I as possible. He jumped at the opportunity to invest in the Jamestown venture and to sign on as a colonist in the 1606 expedition. It is telling that as highborn as he was—and the Percy family was one of the most powerful and famous in England, dating back to the Norman conquest—George Percy was not named to the ruling council in Jamestown in 1606. Still, he was one of the colony's old-timers and, in 1609, he was, it seems, the only man willing to take the colony's reins after Smith's departure.

Winter was setting in when Smith's ship dropped down the James and Percy took command at Jamestown. The thick cedar and oak and elm trees that blanketed the rolling country along the bay were turning color, losing their leaves. The breeze was more often out of the north and northeast now and it was cool when it wasn't downright cold. There were fewer mosquitoes and gnats, and that was a blessing, but the biting wind and the increasingly dark skies and gray waters of the river gave warning that the weather was about to turn bitter. Those who bothered to think ahead as they wrapped their cloaks tighter around themselves or held their cold hands closer to the snapping fires inside the fort knew it was going to be a rough few months before new crops could be planted and harvested.

Sometime that fall, as the weather turned cool, it seems that Pocahontas—John Smith's friend and the one person who could have served as a peacemaker between the Powhatan people and the colonists—visited the settlement only to learn that the short, red-bearded captain was gone. She must have asked more than one of the Englishmen where Smith was, what had happened to him, when he would be back. For some reason, the English decided to lie to her. "They did tell us always you were dead," she said to Smith much later, when they met in an England she could not in 1609 even begin to imagine.[5]

By that time, Wahunsonacock (Powhatan), heartily sick of dealing with the *Tassentassas,* had made the decision to avoid all contact with the foreigners who had invaded his lands. The paramount chief had moved his headquarters from Werowocomoco, the village on the banks of the York River where he had his fateful meeting with John Smith, to Orapaks, a remote town high up the Chickahominy River, virtually out of reach of the interloping Englishmen.

As soon as Pocahontas heard the lies about Smith, she no doubt sent messengers racing to Wahunsonacock's new capital, bearing the news that the man she considered a friend, or more than a friend, was dead. Wahunsonacock, we can be sure, heard the news of Smith's demise—there was no reason at all for him to have doubted the story—as a welcome opportunity to rid his lands of the coat-wearing people. The chief knew from his dealings with Smith and Edward Maria Wingfield, the first president of the council in Jamestown, as well as from Captain Newport, John Ratcliffe, and other Englishmen that Smith was head and shoulders above the other men who arrived on the big ships from across the sea. He recognized that Smith was a man much like himself—wily, tough, not to be fooled or fooled with. He knew that while Smith treated the Powhatan people with respect, going so far as to learn the Powhatan tongue, he would fight like a warrior—or like a cornered animal—if he ever felt threatened. With Smith out of the picture, Wahunsonacock realized he faced what might well be his last chance to convince the foreign invaders that their only hope of remaining in the land he called Tsenacommacah was to become his subjects. At the same time, he knew that there was no way his warriors could defeat the English in open warfare, especially with the arrival of the several hundred new English who landed on the *Blessing* and other ships of the 1609 fleet. So Wahunsonacock told his people to fight a guerrilla war, to attack only when their chance of victory was assured, to use guile as a weapon sharper than any stone knife. He also told his people to refuse to share their own sparse food, not to trade. Knowing that the English were short of victuals, he was perfectly willing to sit back and watch nature do to the English what his warriors could not.

Percy, of course, had no way of knowing what was going on in Wahunsonacock's head. That wasn't his problem. His problem was that in his own head he would have thought himself much more than Smith's equal. His blood, he would have thought, the blood that linked him to all those earls of Northumberland, made him better than Smith, more able to lead, more deserving of success.

A portrait of Percy shows he was a foppish young man, a dandy's dandy dressed in a loose-fitting, flowing shirt adorned with a massive lace collar that spreads from shoulder to shoulder beneath a face that appears unattractive at best and, at worst, weak-willed and spoiled. His weak chin fairly cries out for a beard and, even in a painting that, it must be assumed, was meant to be laudatory, his lips seem pursed in a kind of dismissive, condescending sneer. Despite the fact that Master George Percy's portrait shows him missing the middle finger of his left hand—a finger he lost in honorable battle—the por-

trait displays none of the soldier-of-fortune, devil-take-the-hindmost assertiveness seen in John Smith's portrait. Sadly for the colonists in Jamestown,
what the settlement needed in the winter of 1609 was more of John Smith's
strength and assertiveness and less of George Percy's condescension.

To Percy's credit, he seems to have learned from Smith who, in turn, had
learned from the Indians, the value of dispersing small groups of settlers
when food was scarce. Not long after taking over as leader, he sent John Sicklemore (alias Ratcliffe) to Point Comfort on the north side of the entrance to
the James River to build a fort and establish a satellite settlement. According
to Percy, he did this "for towe Respectts The one for the plenty of the place
for fisheinge The other for the comodious discovery of any shippeinge w^ch
sholde come uppon the Coaste."[6] This fort was across the James from the
spot where John Martin had earlier established a satellite colony on what is
now Dumpling Island.[7] Not surprisingly, given Percy's temperament, he instructed Captain Ratcliffe to name the new colony Fort Algernon, in the apparent hopes of gaining favor with his eldest brother, the earl, who controlled
the family's purse strings and whose eldest son bore the name Algernon. The
plan to establish a fort at the mouth of the James, along with the earlier outpost settlements at the falls below the site of modern-day Richmond (under
the command of Francis West) and on Dumpling Island, made sense. The
problem was that all these satellites were placed under the command of men
who were ill equipped by temperament or experience to deal with the native
people or with their own followers. Indeed, it took no time at all for the settlers in the outposts to run into trouble.

Martin and his men on Dumpling Island had appropriated Indian land to
build their fort, ransacking Indian holy sites in the process and aggravating
the Nansemond people who, with Smith gone, had been given free rein by
Wahunsonacock to retaliate. One of the settlers, a man named George For-
rest, wandered away from the little camp only to be shot by seventeen arrows,
one of which passed right through his body. After clinging to life for a week,
he died, "for want of Chirurgery."[8] Even if a surgeon had been available on
Dumpling Island, Martin was not about to go out of his way to stake a claim
as a brave man. He quickly decided that his safety was much more important
than his reputation. Leaving his men under the command of Lieutenant
Michael Sicklemore, he fled as fast as he could back to the relative protection
of Jamestown. According to Percy, Martin came to Jamestown "pretending

some occasions of business" but, in truth, he was, Percy said, motivated by "his owne safety . . . feareinge to be surprysed by the Indyans."[9]

The Lieutenant Sicklemore left in charge at Dumpling Island is not to be confused with John Sicklemore, who used the name Ratcliffe as an alias. Michael Sicklemore was one of the colony's early settlers, arriving with John Smith in 1607. He had accompanied Smith on most of his explorations and trading voyages and had proved his courage and worth on more than one occasion. In Smith's history of the colony, Sicklemore is described as "a very honest, valiant, and painefull [dedicated] soldier."[10] He was not, though, able to deal with the unruly company on Dumpling Island. Not long after Martin fled for the safety of Jamestown's palisade, seventeen of his men mutinied, stole a boat, and headed across the James to trade for food in the Indian village of Kecoughtan. A few days later, when the mutineers did not return, Sicklemore and a party of men went in search of them. The seventeen mutineers were never seen again and, it is safe to say, were killed by the natives. Sicklemore and his men were no luckier. They were found dead, in the words of George Percy, with "their mowths stopped full of bread." As Percy noted, the message was clear, "being donn as it seamethe in Contempte and skorne thatt others mighte expecte the Lyke when they shold come to seeke for breade and reliefe." The well-read Percy even saw a parallel between the way Sicklemore and his men were killed and the execution of a Spanish general in Chile who was forced to drink molten gold by the Indians. While Percy does not say how he was privy to his information, he claimed to know that the Chilean natives had told the general, a man named Baldivia, "Now glutt thy selfe wth gowlde, Baldivia!" as they poured the molten metal into his open mouth.

With Martin fled, seventeen men lost and presumably killed, and Sicklemore and what Percy described as "dyvers others" executed by Indians, the rest of the men at the Nansemond outpost decided that it made perfect sense to abandon their fort and run for cover. "The reste of Sickelmors company wch weare liveinge Retourned to us to James towne to feede upon the poore store we had lefte us," Percy reported. [11] That left Fort Algernon at Point Comfort as the only colonial outpost downriver from the main settlement.

Meanwhile, life was not much better upriver at the falls, where Francis West was proving to be an inept leader in his own right. Having thoroughly antagonized the natives with their never-ending demands for food, the settlers found themselves under almost constant attack by Indians who wanted nothing more than to drive the hated English from their lands. After natives killed eleven more of his men and stole one of the outpost's boats, West gave up and ordered all his people—roughly one hundred—to abandon the camp and return to Jamestown.

By this time, the settlement must have been getting truly crowded. Even with the desertions and killings, roughly 450 people were jammed inside the palisaded town, many more than at any other time since the English stepped ashore. But overcrowding was the least of the colonists' problems. The return of West and his people and the men from the falls meant that the already limited food supply at Jamestown would be further strained. Percy instructed Captain Daniel Tucker, one of two men in charge of the colony's stores and trade, to calculate just how much food remained. When Tucker made his way to the storehouse inside the fort and looked around, he must have wanted to flee. By his calculations, if each colonist was restricted to a half can of corn a day (probably about a cup), the colony might survive for three months. Percy and Tucker and anybody else who bothered to think ahead would have known there was no way a new supply would arrive from England before food ran out. And it would have been equally apparent to any who bothered to think about it that the colony's supplies would run out in late winter, just when the Indian storehouses would be empty. That meant the natives would be unable to supply corn, even if they were willing.

By that time, Percy must have wondered why on earth he had ever left the safety and security of London and why he had ever aspired to leadership in Virginia. Even the Tower of London might have appeared preferable to what he faced in Jamestown. He had aspired to leadership, though, and he must have been desperate as he tried to figure some way to fill the settlers' bellies, to stave off starvation and disaster in the settlement, to save his own skin. Finally, Percy made a fateful decision to send Ratcliffe north to Orapaks, Wahunsonacock's new capital, to "(pro)cure victewalls and corne by the way of comerce and trade"[12]—that is, to obtain food the beleaguered settlement needed badly if it was to survive. As it turned out, he could not have chosen a less able man to lead the expedition into danger.

The accounts of what happened—one by Percy himself and another, in broken and puzzling English, by Henry Spelman, the young man "given" by John Smith to Parahunt to serve as a translator in exchange for the Indian village at the falls—are contradictory and confusing at best.

According to Percy, Ratcliffe went up the York River in a pinnace, probably the *Virginia*, one of the ships that survived the hurricane that scuttled the
Sea Venture in Bermuda. He was accompanied, Percy said, by fifty men (Spelman said twenty-four or twenty-five). Somewhere along the way, Ratcliffe
came across "Powhatans sonne and dowghter" and invited them to board his
pinnace. Percy doesn't say who these royal offspring were and, given the size
and extent of the old chief's family, it is impossible to know. It is safe to assume, however, that the daughter invited aboard his pinnace by Ratcliffe was
not Pocahontas since she was well known to Percy and most of the other settlers and he would not have hesitated to use her name. In any event, what
Percy called Ratcliffe's "creduletie"—or his prideful willingness to believe in
his own invincibility—led him to let the chief's children go when he arrived at
Orapaks instead of holding them hostage to guarantee his safety and that of
his men. John Smith certainly would not have made the same mistake.[13]

Worse than that, once the party arrived at Orapaks, Ratcliffe did not
mount an armed guard and did not keep his men close. Instead, he allowed
"his men by towe and three and small Numbers in A Company to straggle
into the Salvages howses" to trade on their own or to try to win the favors of
Indian women who may well, at this point, have been compliant.[14] Still,
things seemed to go well at first, but only because the man Percy described as
"the subtell owlde foxe" made a show of being friendly, although "his intente
was otherwayes onely wayteinge A fitteinge tyme for their destruction."[15]

During the first day ashore, Ratcliffe and his men were treated well, Spelman said. Wahunsonacock received them, appointed a house for them to stay
in not far from his own dwelling—but about half a mile from where the
barge and pinnace were moored. He welcomed them with open arms and exchanged bread and venison for "copper and beades and such like."[16]

The next day, according to Spelman, the English were led to the village
storehouse where the real trading was to take place. Again, all seemed well as
the Indians handed over grain for copper and beads. At some point in the
bartering, though, the English discovered that the Indians were cheating by
pushing up the bottoms of the soft woven baskets that were used to measure
out the grain so that the English would get short rations in exchange for their
goods. When the English protested, Wahunsonacock left the storehouse, taking with him his wives, Spelman himself, and several other colonists who had
gone to live and work with the Indians.

With the trading over and tempers inflamed, Ratcliffe and his men gathered the corn they had obtained and set out on the half-mile trek back to their barge. This seems to have been the opportunity Wahunsonacock had been waiting for. As the English struggled along a trail through the forest, Indian warriors attacked. Only two of the men on shore escaped, running into the woods and eventually making their way back to Jamestown overland. The others—and there's no way of knowing exactly how many—were killed. Ratcliffe himself was captured and turned over to Indian women, whose job it was to torture enemy warriors captured in battle. He was tied naked to a tree. A fire was lit at his feet. The women then used mussel shells, sharp as razors, to scrape the flesh from his bones and, while he lived and watched through terrified eyes, to throw his flesh into the fire before finally putting him out of his misery, perhaps by setting him afire. Percy wasted little compassion on his brutally killed companion, saying only that "for want of circumspection [Ratcliffe] miserably (per)ished."[17]

Still, the Powhatan warriors were not through. After dealing with the Englishmen on shore, they attacked the pinnace where it was moored on the river. Smith friend and loyalist William Phettiplace, in command of the men left on the vessel, heard the screams of those who were dying on land. Seeing Indians pouring from the woods toward the river, firing arrows as they came, he raised anchor and tried to flee back downriver. He and his men were almost overwhelmed as they frantically rowed or poled the pinnace out of danger. As it was, several more Englishmen were killed in the attack on the pinnace. All told, of the fifty men (if we are to believe Percy) who went to Orapaks to trade with Wahunsonacock, only sixteen returned to Jamestown. And the returning men brought back no food for the desperate colonists, none at all.

Not long after that, Percy sent Captain James Davies—the man who had captained the pinnace *Virginia* through the hurricane that wrecked the *Sea Venture*—to take charge of Fort Algernon. Davies had earlier been involved in an attempt to colonize Maine and so was an experienced man who might justifiably be expected to perform well as the leader of the small garrison at the fort at the mouth of the James.[18] At about the same time, Percy sent Francis West, who had already proved his inability to lead at the falls, to try to trade with the Patawomeke Indians. This group, while part of Wahunsonacock's confederacy, lived on the outer edge of Tsenacommacah, on the Potomac River above what is now Fredericksburg, Virginia. Since the Patawomeke lived far from Jamestown and had only limited contact with the English, Percy figured that they might be more friendly—and more willing to trade—than the native people closer to the settlement.

As it turned out, Percy was right, to a degree. The Indians were less belligerent. At least they did not attack the English on sight. West, however, was the wrong man for the job. When the natives exhibited a reluctance to trade, West convinced them to barter by terrorizing them and ultimately beheading two warriors in front of horrified family members and other members of the tribe. After filling his pinnace with corn and sailing down the York to Point Comfort with his badly needed supplies, West met Davies, who told him that the situation at Jamestown was growing desperate. West and his men decided the corn would make little difference to those at the fort, but that it was more than enough to feed them on a voyage back to England. Hoisting sails, West, the brother of Lord De La Warre, the man who was slated to become governor for life and captain general of Virginia, turned his back on Jamestown and its hungry settlers and headed east, across the Atlantic, taking with him his boatload of grain.

Now, in Percy's words, all at Jamestown started to feel "that sharpe pricke of hunger, w^{c}h noe man [can] trewly descrybe butt he w^{c}h hath Tasted the bitternesse therof."[19] Indeed, the settlers were stymied at every turn, either by Indian unwillingness to trade, by their own inept leadership, or by their own unwillingness or inability to hunt or fish. Winter, the season the natives called *popanow*, was settling on the Chesapeake. This was a season when the Powhatan people lived on food gathered and stored during the fall harvest, supplemented by waterfowl taken by the hunters. Food was scarce even in the richest of Indian villages, so even if the natives had been willing to trade—which they weren't, on Wahunsonacock's orders—the English had little hope of obtaining food, no matter what they offered in barter. The settlers might have found a way to keep famine at bay if their only difficulty had been their inability to trade for grain. But there were other difficulties. The Indians fell on the colony's pigs on Hog Island and slaughtered them gleefully, not to eat, but simply to guarantee the settlers were made more desperate. And anytime the English stuck their noses outside the fort to forage for food in the woods, they ran the risk of being turned into human pincushions by Powhatan archers.

With the settlement's hogs slaughtered, the colonists ate their way through their supply of chickens, sheep, and goats, even the horses, including those carried from England on board the *Blessing* a few months earlier. Bones were gnawed, sucked dry. The animals' skins were boiled for soup, their hooves boiled, too. They ate their cats, the descendants of ships' cats carried from England, and their dogs, mastiffs used for hunting mostly, and when their domestic animals were gone, they ate rats and mice. "All was fishe thatt came to Nett to satisfye Crewell hunger," said Percy, a better writer than leader.[20] Some of the higher born—men who routinely wore wide starched ruffs around their necks—discovered that the starch used to stiffen the collars was edible, and so that, too, was boiled into a kind of sticky mush. Other settlers were soon forced by hunger to boil their shoes and boots and belts and any other scraps of leather they could find. As winter deepened and grew more cruel—and 1609, like 1608, was one of the coldest winters in Virginia history—more than one set of bloody footprints would have painted the snow that covered the ground inside the palisade on the banks of the James.

With their food supplies shrunk away to nothing, the English suffered what Percy called "a world of miseries."[21] As the days grew shorter and the weather colder, as snow fell and the ground hardened, men and the few women and children in the fort grew gaunt. Their skin turned ashen. Fires burned but there was no meat to cook, no fish or fowl, only a handful of weevily meal per settler per day, and only enough of that to last weeks or a few months at most. And there was no relief in sight.

As the store of firewood within the fort was used, settlers, too terrified of the Indians to roam the forest for a new supply, tore the doors and shutters off their cabins, tore the clapboard sides off the dwellings, burned whatever they could burn for warmth. A few desperate men, only a few, left the safety of the fort to search the woods "and to feede upon Serpents and snakes and to digge the earthe for wylde and unkowne Rootes."[22] They moved like scavenging dogs, skulking, looking over their shoulders for any sign of the Indians, jumping at any strange sound, a twig crack or the sudden cry of a bird. Frantic, they used knives or half-frozen fingers to dig the icy ground, tugged dirty roots free, scrabbled for fallen nuts, dislodged hibernating snakes, or pounced on other vermin and ate greedily. As careful as they were, many of the men were slain by the natives.

One day, Henry Pryse (Price?), a settler described as a "Leane, spare man," was so maddened by hunger that he ran into the marketplace, the little square within the fort, crying that there was no God, that if there was a God, "he wolde nott suffer his creatures, whom he had made and framed to indure those miseries and to (per)ish for wante of foods and sustenance." That same day, Pryse went into the forest with a butcher—described as "a corpulentt fatt man"—in search of food. Both were slain by Indians, found in a state that, to Percy at least, signified the Almighty's displeasure with the blasphemer: Pryse's skinny corpse was torn to pieces by scavenging animals while the body of the "fatt Butcher," lying just a few feet away, was untouched, except, of course, for the arrows that still stuck in his body.[23]

As days passed, settlers died, one at a time, then two, then in bunches, their bodies jumbled together and thrown in shallow graves inside the palisade or perhaps dragged out to be hurriedly buried by weak and trembling men, men so hungry they could barely walk and so terrified of Indian attack that they would not have bothered to do more than throw a few handfuls of dirt over the bodies and perhaps mutter a quick prayer for their dead fellow colonists before scurrying back to the safety of the palisade.

Still, the dying continued. In Percy's words, "And now famin [was] begineinge to Looke gastely and pale in every face [so] thatt notheinge was spared to maintaine Lyfe." Hunger and horror can make men mad and that is what happened in the little settlement. Having eaten rats and cats and vermin and shoes and roots, the men and few women left alive in the fort dug up the bodies of the dead to feed on the meat and gnaw the bones of their fellows. Percy adds the comment that some "Licked upp the bloode wch hathe fallen from their weake fellowes." The native dead were no safer. After an Indian was killed in an attack on the fort and buried, a group of settlers exhumed his body and ate his corpse.[24] A number of men, no one knows for sure how many, were executed by Percy, hanged in the marketplace as an example to the rest, for stealing from the general store.

According to Percy, the "moste Lamentable" act committed in this lamentable time was the murder of a pregnant woman by "one of our Colline" driven mad by starvation. At some point in that terrible winter, the colonist, whoever he was, cast a hungry eye at his pregnant wife and found her too tempting to resist. According to Percy, the settler murdered the woman, tore the child from her womb, hurled the unborn baby into the James River, and then chopped his wife into pieces and "salted her for his food." The crime, Percy added, was not discovered "before he had eaten a part therof."[25]

In Captain John Smith's history of Virginia, the same basic story was told—with a touch of macabre humor that must have brought a smile to the old soldier's lips: Smith did not know "whether shee was better roasted, boyled, or carbonado'd [grilled], but of such a dish as powdered [salted] wife I never heard of." The joke must have helped dull the edge of the horror of what came to be known as the Starving Time, a time when, Smith said, "it were to vile to say, and scarce to be believed" what the settlers endured.[26]

Justice had a tendency to be swift in Jamestown. Soon after the "vile" murderer was apprehended, Percy had him tortured, hanging him up by his thumbs "w'h weightes att his feete" until he confessed his crime.[27] The torture, it is safe to say, was brutal, since the guilty man only weathered it for about fifteen minutes before admitting his crime. Within just a few minutes of his confession, Percy had him tied to a stake where he was burned alive.

The whole affair was just too terrible to report in England, without some censoring and the Virginia Company later went to great pains to put its own spin on the tale. According to the company's propaganda, published in a pamphlet hurried into print as a "confutation of such scandalous reports as have tended to the disgrace" of the "worthy" enterprise of Jamestown, Collins "mortally hated his wife" and was driven to murder by that hatred. It was only when his house was searched, the pamphlet explained, and parts of her body discovered, that he fell back on his excuse that he killed her because of hunger. "Upon this his house was again searched, where they found a good quantity of meal, oatmeal, beans, and peas."[28] Obviously, the propagandists implied, there were vile men in Virginia, men who hated their wives enough to murder them, but there was no hunger.

The London Company's propaganda aside, the starvation and suffering in Jamestown was real and it was terrible. The dying continued through the winter and into the spring. Had the settlers been able or willing to fish, they might have alleviated some of their suffering. When Smith left the settlement, the colony boasted at least six and maybe seven small boats, including a canoe. By the spring, when the river's waters should have been teeming with fish, only a canoe and one boat were available for the colonists' use. West, of course, had sailed away in one pinnace. The rest of the watercraft, it seems, had simply fallen into disrepair—along with fishing nets—or perhaps all had been destroyed by natives. Even the boat and canoe left at Jamestown appear not to have been suitable for fishing, for Percy reported that at some point, one of the colonists, Captain Daniel Tucker, managed to build what Percy described as a large boat that the colonists were able to use as a fishing vessel, a move which, Percy said, provided "some helpe and A little Reliefe unto us." It seems at least likely that some of the colonists considered outright murder and cannibalism as the starving continued since Percy said Tucker's fishing vessel kept the colonists "from killinge one of Another."[29]

As the weather began to warm, Percy fell sick. By early May, he was, he said, "Reasonable well recovered," well enough to travel to Fort Algernon at Point Comfort. His motives for finally leaving Jamestown were, he said, to determine how the men under the command of Captain James Davies were faring and to revenge the earlier murder of the settlers by the Indians at Kecoughtan. When he arrived at Point Comfort, Percy was enraged to discover that Davies and his men were so flush with food that they were feeding crabs—crabs that "wold have bene a greate relefe unto us and saved many of our Lyves"—to their hogs. In his narrative, Percy goes so far as to accuse Davies of plotting to take his men and flee to England, leaving the Jamestown settlers to starve. There's no real reason to assume that Davies was going to abandon the settlement and, in fact, Davies had every right to wonder why the colony's leader had not bothered to visit the outpost for six months or more. In any event, Percy made it plain to Davies that he planned to bring "halfe our men from James Town to be there [at Point Comfort] Releved And after to Retourne them back againe and bringe the reste to be susteyned there Also." If that didn't return the men to health, the fort on Jamestown Island was to be abandoned and all the settlers relocated to Fort Algernon.[30]

The two men, Davies and Percy, were in the midst of making plans to move Jamestown settlers to Point Comfort when someone on shore, probably a sentry, cried out that two small vessels were on the horizon, approaching the mouth of the Chesapeake. At the word that ships were approaching, all the English at Point Comfort sprang into action.

The English in Jamestown were—with reason—always fearful of a surprise Spanish attack. That evening, as the two vessels came closer, Percy and Davies and the forty armed colonists in Fort Algernon stood guard. When the sun rose, they saw two strange pinnaces laying just off shore. Percy ordered a warning shot fired from one of the fort's cannon, a signal that the two ships should heave to and not try to pass. In moments, as those on the beach watched nervously, a longboat put out from the larger of the two ships and headed for shore.

As the longboat neared the beach, someone would have shouted for those in the boat to identify themselves. Of course, no one on shore—not Percy or Davies or any of the other nervous armed men—would have had any reason to expect that the two pinnaces were the *Patience* and the *Deliverance* bearing roughly 140 men and women who had left England almost a year earlier on board the *Sea Venture*.

Strachey does not say who was in the longboat, but it almost certainly contained Sir Thomas Gates, who was excited at the prospect of finally reaching the colony he was to command, at least temporarily. And if Gates was in the boat, Strachey almost certainly was as well. One or both would have shouted that they were English, that they were from the *Sea Venture*, come at long last to resupply the colony. At that, someone on the beach called back that they were English, too. Questions flew from both sides. What happened? Where have you been? Are all well? And what of the other ships in the fleet? Were they lost? How go things in Jamestown?

Gates and Strachey and the others in the longboat were overjoyed to discover that the fleet—all save the little ketch—had arrived safely, battered, to be sure, but still safe. Those from the settlement would have been just as happy to hear that all but a few who sailed on the admiral were safe and sound on board the two small ships that lay at anchor not far from the beach.

The joy of the new arrivals was short-lived, however. Soon enough, Strachey said, they learned that the boat that had been dispatched from the Bermudas under the command of Master's Mate Henry Ravens had never arrived in Jamestown. All knew, then, what they must have suspected, namely that Ravens and his six companions were dead. What was worse, though, was what Strachey described as the "new, unexpected, uncomfortable, and heavy news of a worse condition of our people . . . at Jamestown."[31]

8

"Misery and Misgovernment"

The news that Jamestown was tottering on the brink of extinction thanks to disease and hunger and Indian attack must have spread like wildfire through the *Patience* and the *Deliverance* as soon as Sir Thomas Gates and the others who had gone ashore returned to the ships that lay anchored just off Point Comfort. The settlers—men like William Strachey and John Rolfe and women like Mistress Horton, who had all set sail for Virginia convinced that the New World offered their best hope for the future—must have felt as if they'd been kicked in the belly when they heard the news of the death and devastation at the English settlement. They could have been forgiven if they'd thought that the same Providence that delivered them from the storm and provided them a safe haven on St. George's Island had turned into a cruel jester. It is certainly likely that some urged the expedition's leaders to turn the ships' bows back toward England or at least toward Bermuda, where there was plenty of food, a secure little settlement above St. Catherine's Beach, and freedom from fear of attack by natives they would have considered no better than savages.

Gates and Somers and Captain Christopher Newport, of course, were not about to turn their backs on their duty to King James I and the Virginia Company, no matter how tempting the idea of returning to Bermuda or England might have been. Back on board the pinnaces, they ordered the mariners to make ready for the voyage up the James River to the Jamestown settlement.

That day, as the ships still lay at anchor off the Indian town of Kecoughtan—modern-day Hampton, Virginia, and the same place where Michael Sicklemore's men were headed when they disappeared—they were buffeted by what Strachey described as "a mighty storm of thunder, lightning, and rain" that provided them all with a "shrewd [sharp] and fearful welcome."[1] It must have seemed to those on the little ships as if God himself was warning them not to proceed with their plans.

Still, Gates and Somers were determined to press on. As soon as the storm passed, anchors were weighed and stowed and all sails were unfurled. Even now, though, the elements seemed to conspire against the English. The wind, howling just a few minutes earlier, died away to nothing and the ships were forced to spend two full days riding the flood tides up the James, anchoring to hold themselves steady when the tides ebbed.

As the ships made their painfully slow way to the settlement, all on board who were able and not busy working the vessels would have crowded the rails to stare at the strange and wonderful vista of marshes and thickly wooded hills as it slowly unfolded on either side of the river. The weather was warm by that time, at least after the early-morning river fog burned off; trees were dressed in new greenery and the marshes and forests were loud with birdsong and the faint hum of insects. The river, as they entered it, would have sparkled under the high sun and the air would have been thick with the smells of growing things. Perhaps, as the shipwreck survivors moved north and west through the lush landscape—a landscape unlike anything most on the ships could even imagine—they were able to put out of their minds, at least for a few moments, the sad news they had heard of conditions in Jamestown.

The *Patience* and the *Deliverance* came to anchor just off the fort on May 23, 1610, almost a full year from the time the *Sea Venture* and the other ships of the Virginia-bound fleet sailed out of Plymouth Harbour and into the open Atlantic. As the ships neared the settlement, all would have been on deck, straining to catch sight of the palisaded town. At first, it must have appeared to those on the two pinnaces as if the settlement was abandoned. No one, it seems, came through the town's main gate, facing the James, to welcome them or to watch the ships come to anchor. The palisade that surrounded the settlement was unguarded and looked as battered as if it had suffered an attack or perhaps taken a terrible pounding during a storm. Its gates—the one that

faced the river and those in the round bulwarks that stood at each of the triangular fort's corners—were hanging off their hinges. Ports over the gun slits
in the palisade were missing. But what was most troublesome was the silence.
Though those on the ships shouted to raise some welcome from those in the
settlement, there was no reply, no welcoming peal of bells or cannon shot. All
was still except for the sounds of insects and birds, the wind in the trees, and
the gentle lapping of the river's waters against the two vessels' hulls.

The narrative written by Strachey does not say who went ashore first. It is
likely that Gates and Somers were the first to step on land at Jamestown, accompanied by a few chosen men—Strachey himself and Captain Newport
would certainly have been included in this group. While they had been advised what to expect in the settlement, it is not likely that George Percy, a man
who had a tendency to be self-serving, would had given them anything like
details about the death and destruction that had occurred in the little English
outpost while it was under his command. In any event, there is no way those
on the *Deliverance* and the *Patience* could have prepared themselves for what they
discovered as they pushed their way through the main portal and into the
town itself. Houses were empty and in ruins, torn to pieces for use as firewood by settlers who were too weak and sick to go into the nearby forest for
wood or who were wisely unwilling to leave the relative safety of the fort
where, at least, the Indians could not attack at will. Many of the homes that
were still standing looked ready to tumble down. The marketplace, a square at
the center of the "town," was uninhabited. There was not a settler to be seen,
not a cat or a dog stirring, no chickens or hogs or any other livestock.

Reporting to Sir Thomas Smythe and the other officers of the Virginia
Company in London, one of the settlers in Virginia—almost certainly
William Strachey—penned a letter a few weeks after Gates and Somers and
the others arrived in Jamestown. In this report, the author said the town "appeared rather as the ruins of some ancient [for]tification than that any people
living might now inhabit it."[2]

Sir Thomas, who was in sole and unquestioned command now as the
deputy governor of the colony, ordered the settlement's church bell rung to
alert any English in the town that he and the others on the *Deliverance* and the
Patience had arrived from England. As the bell pealed—it must have been a
mournful sound to the Jamestown newcomers as they looked around the dev-
astated settlement—a few men tottered slowly through the doors of the
wrecked houses that surrounded the marketplace. They were emaciated, bare-

foot, wrapped in rags, barely able to put one foot in front of the other. They were, George Percy said, "so maugre and Leane thatt itt was Lamentable to behowlde them for many throwe extreme hunger have Runne outt of the naked bedds being so Leane thatt that Looked Lyke Anatomies [skeletons used for study by medical students]." As they approached the newcomers, Percy added, the skeletonlike figures cried mournfully, "We are starved, we are starved."[3]

Soon enough, perhaps too soon for most on the *Patience* and the *Deliverance*, all the *Sea Venture* survivors made their way into what remained of the fort. It is not difficult to imagine the fear and uncertainty—if not downright horror—they felt as they entered the palisade gates and looked at the ruin that surrounded them. Those who had survived the shipwreck, the months in Bermuda, and the voyage on to Jamestown would have looked at the skeletal faces of the few settlers who struggled into the town square, hoping to catch sight of some friend or acquaintance or maybe even a family member who had sailed on one of the other ships in the fleet that departed from England in company with the *Sea Venture*. What they saw was a tale of deprivation and pain and suffering etched in the faces of the survivors. Someone, probably Percy, gave Gates and the others the news that, of roughly five hundred settlers who were alive in Jamestown just six months earlier, when John Smith left what he thought was a prosperous settlement, only sixty—including these half-dead stick figures that now begged for a scrap of bread, a handful of grain, anything to put in their shriveled bellies—remained alive.

The Jamestown newcomers must have wanted to hurry back to the boats anchored just off shore, to flee from the little settlement even if it meant facing a long, storm-tossed voyage across the Atlantic to England or the safety of the Bermudas. They'd been promised an Edenic existence in Virginia, a life of ease with food aplenty in something like heaven on earth, surrounded by friendly natives who were just waiting to serve them hand and foot. Instead, they had been transported to a hellhole where famine and illness and a savage death awaited. Even the air stank, not just with the usual redolence of unwashed English bodies but also of refuse that had built up inside the fort during the long months when settlers were afraid to leave the palisaded town, of raw sewage, of illness, of death itself, probably even of an unburied body or two or more.

Gates, perhaps more than any other of the new arrivals, must have been heartbroken as he surveyed the little settlement that was to have been his domain. He'd given up a command in the Netherlands for this opportunity that now appeared more like a death sentence than a chance for advancement or enrichment. Having been a soldier for most of his life, he knew that failure in Virginia—and failure was looking more and more like the only possible end of this settlement with each passing moment—would likely spell the end of his professional career. At the same time, he, like any feeling man, would have wanted nothing more than to help the survivors in Jamestown, to prepare a feast to fill their bellies, to restore them to health. He knew, just looking at them as they tottered around the square begging for food and crying piteously, that they were just days from death. He had expected to find a well-supplied settlement, with grain and game and fish for all, not this abattoir reeking of suffering and death. He had not planned at all on having to feed starving settlers with the few stores carried on board the *Patience* and the *Deliverance*. There was some food on board the pinnaces, but Gates knew it was only sufficient to feed the *Sea Venture* survivors and the settlers in Jamestown for about fourteen days, and then only if it were carefully rationed.

Gates also knew that someone had to take effective command of the settlement quickly if they were to survive. He almost certainly would have looked askance at George Percy, no matter what his pedigree, as would the old sea dogs Newport and Somers as they wondered what on earth he had done, or not done, to turn what they believed had been a thriving settlement into a boneyard. Within moments of entering the palisade, Gates called together the newcomers and the Jamestown settlers who were still able to walk. By this time, Strachey was—it seems—serving as Jamestown's unofficial secretary since he was asked by Gates to read the commission appointing him as the colony's deputy governor. With Gates's commission read, Percy, who had served as governor since John Smith's departure, then relinquished his commission, the old patent, and the governing council's seal. Then Richard Bucke, the minister who had served the shipwreck survivors in Bermuda, led all the colonists in "a zealous and sorrowful prayer"—zealous in its requests for sustenance in what all knew were difficult times and sorrowful, as Strachey said, because the newcomers had found "all things so contrary to our expectations, so full of misery and misgovernment."[4] Sometime very soon after this, Gates officially appointed Strachey to the post of colonial secretary, to replace the eponymously named Matthew Scrivener, the former secretary who had drowned in a boating accident not long after John Smith's departure. At that moment, as terrible as conditions were in Jamestown, Strachey must have felt a whole world of possibility opening before him. As secretary, he would be on the colony's governing council, close to the seat of power in Jamestown, in a position that would make his name known to the Virginia Company in London—even to King James himself. Suddenly, anything was possible for the formerly bankrupt lawyer. Of course, the first thing he would have to do was survive his time in Virginia.

Soon, Gates and Somers and Newport and the other men who found themselves responsible for the survival of the settlement gathered with Percy and Captain Davies and a few of the other Starving Time survivors to try to determine what course of action to follow. Gates learned that the Indians were unable to trade—even if they had been willing—since it was the planting time and the natives themselves had no extra food. He was also told that there had been, in all the months when settlers were dying of hunger, no way to take fish from the river since the colonists' nets and, presumably, any fishing lines they had when Smith left the colony for England were either ruined or lost. In any case, probably because of the seven-year drought that started in 1607 (it was the worst dry period in almost seven hundred years, modern scientists have learned through a study of tree rings) sturgeon, the fish that sustained the Indians when food was scarce, had not yet made their way up the James.

Hunting was also out of the question. The native people were all too willing to kill any Englishman who left the safety of the town. In fact, a few days before the newcomers arrived in Virginia, two settlers who strayed outside the fort in search of food were slain, as were another two very shortly after Gates and the others stepped ashore. As a consequence, the settlers, both old and new, were understandably wary about crashing through the forest in search of game. In any event, the deer and bear that were the favorite prey of the Indians were as hard to find in the woods as sturgeon were in the James. According to Strachey, Wahunsonacock went so far as to order his men to drive game north, far out of reach of the *Tassantassas* at Jamestown. Even if game had been plentiful and the Indians had been willing to let the settlers hunt in peace, the majority of the English settlers were neither adept at stalking the woods nor able to shoot their inaccurate muskets well enough to bring down game sufficient to keep their bellies full. As early as 1608, John Smith had bemoaned the fact that the settlers could not feed themselves even in the midst of plenty. "Though there be fish in the Sea, foules in the ayre, and

Beasts in the woods, their bounds are so large, they so wilde, and we so weake and ignorant, we cannot much trouble them," he said.[5]

As soon as Gates realized just how dire the situation was in Jamestown, he announced to the company that he had brought provisions from Bermuda that would alleviate at least some of their hunger pangs. That news would surely have made those who had survived the terrible famine happy, but what pleased them even more was Gates's next announcement: he promised that if he found it impossible to supply them through trade or fishing or hunting, he would carry them all back to England the best way he could. At this announcement, all within the sound of Gates's voice cheered, even the settlers who had just arrived from Bermuda since, Strachey said, "even our own men began to be disheartened and faint when they saw this misery amongs the others and no less threatened unto themselves."[6]

But Gates was not about to give up without a struggle. Having made the colonists his promise to abandon Jamestown if necessary, Gates then wrote—or had Strachey write—a series of orders and nailed them to a post in the church for all to see. While Strachey doesn't say exactly what these orders were, they almost certainly outlined punishments for theft from the common store and proscribed the death penalty for anyone—settler or mariner—who traded illegally with the natives.

While Gates, like every governor before or after his time, tried to curtail illegal trade, he was willing at least to try to bargain with the few natives who came to the town. These natives were, however, much more interested in spying than in helping the English interlopers survive. They wanted information which was, to be sure, quickly sent to Wahunsonacock. Matters were made even more difficult, according to Strachey, by mariners who regularly crept out of the fort at night and sailed their longboats to nearby Indian villages where they traded for "otter skins, beavers, racoon furs, bears' skins, etc., so large a quantity and measure of copper as, when the truckermaster [cape merchant, a kind of purser, in charge of trade] for the colony . . . offered trade, the Indians would laugh and scorn the same." With the copper debased in value by the greedy sailors—men who, in Strachey's view "made prey of our people in want"—any small opportunities there were to trade the valuable copper for victuals disappeared.[7]

With trade and hunting impossible, Gates turned to the Chesapeake in hopes of finding sustenance. Apparently, the store of oysters and other food at Point Comfort, the supplies that had sustained Davies and his men during the Starving Time, was either overlooked as a source of food or, more likely, simply was not sufficient to sustain all the men, women, and children then living in Jamestown. However, Gates knew, or hoped, that enough fish could be taken from the great bay to keep the settlers alive until crops could be planted and harvested. Somers, after all, had supplied the Bermuda survivors by fishing the waters off St. George's Island. Somewhere—perhaps in the supplies brought from Bermuda—the settlers had found a usable net and now Gates sent one of the colony's boats on a fishing expedition down the James to Point Comfort and then on to Cape Henry and Cape Charles and across the Chesapeake. Though they "labored and hauled our net twenty times, day and night," they snared only enough fish, Strachey said, to "content half the fishermen"—certainly nowhere near enough to satisfy the roughly two hundred hungry colonists in Jamestown.[8]

Of course, the settlers might have simply attacked nearby Indian villages and stolen food. This idea would have been particularly attractive following the arrival of the *Sea Venture* survivors in Virginia since the company contained a number of hale and healthy men, including sailors and others who had served as soldiers in the Netherlands. If that idea was ever floated, however, it gained no support even though it had been done in the past, with some success. In explaining why Gates did not order such attacks, Strachey—who may be forgiven for his naïveté since he was new to Jamestown and perhaps unacquainted with earlier instances—staked out the moral high ground in a way that had nothing to do with the realities of life in Virginia: "And to take anything from the Indian by force we never used, nor willingly ever will." Then he went on to be more honest, saying that while the Indians "well deserved" harsh treatment at the hands of the English, given their own belligerence, the settlers did not attack and steal the natives' corn supplies because they (the natives) had just "set their corn, and at their best had but from hand to mouth."[9]

While the English were staring famine in the face, unable to hunt or trade or fish, quickly depleting their scant supplies of food, living in a ghettolike fort in terror of Indian attack, Wahunsonacock, the paramount chief, simply sat back in his headquarters at Orapaks and watched the settlers' troubles through his spies' eyes. He knew that though the number of *Tassantassas* living in the wooden fort had increased, the newcomers had brought little in the way of food, and that these new arrivals were no better at feeding themselves than

the earlier coat-wearing interlopers had been. All he had to do was be as patient as a hunter in the forest, to wait. The hated English would starve soon
enough and either die like dogs—like the many who had died in the months
following John Smith's departure from the colony—or flee back across the
ocean. And this would happen, he would have felt sure, without any further
action on his part.

Within a fortnight, Gates knew that the situation at Jamestown was truly
desperate. The supply of food brought from Bermuda was vanishing and no
one had any idea when—or if—help could be expected from the Virginia
Company in London. Of course, Thomas West, Lord De La Warre, was supposed to be Virginia-bound with more settlers and with supplies that might
keep the colony alive until trade with the natives was possible, but Gates knew
that he and all the others in Jamestown might well be dead long before another English ship sailed into the Chesapeake. As he pondered what to do,
how to proceed in the face of what looked like unconquerable problems,
Gates must have thought more than once of the Lost Colony of Roanoke and
of the more than one hundred English settlers who seemed to vanish into
thin air while they waited—just like those in Jamestown—for supplies to arrive from England.

By the first week of June 1610, Sir Thomas was forced to accept the sad reality that there was no way to avoid abandoning the colony. He called together
Percy and Somers and Newport and Strachey and the other leaders of the settlement and announced his decision. "It soon . . . appeared most fit . . . ,"
Strachey reported, "that to preserve and save all from starving there could be
no readier course thought on than to abandon the country."[10] As Strachey
noted, there were four small vessels now moored just off Jamestown—the
Discovery, the smallest of the ships that carried the first English settlers to Virginia in 1607; the *Virginia*, one of the ships that accompanied *Sea Venture* from
England; and the *Patience* and the *Deliverance*, the two ships constructed by the
Sea Venture survivors in Bermuda. The English would be crowded, to be sure—
there were, after all, the roughly 140 from Bermuda, the 60 Jamestown survivors, along with 30 or 40 men still occupying the fort at Point Comfort.
However, the four tiny vessels would carry the settlers north to the fishing
grounds of Newfoundland where, Strachey noted, "they might meet with
many English ships into which happily they might disperse most of the company."[11] The alternative to the uncomfortable sea voyage to the north was,
everybody knew, almost certain death in Virginia.

No matter how dangerous the voyage, no matter how uncomfortable the passage, the settlers in Jamestown—the old hands as well as the newcomers—wanted nothing more than to turn their backs on the settlement. At the news that they were to take ship, they must have cheered, yelled, sang songs, danced—those that were able—in the dirty, fetid streets of the settlement.

Gates, though, was all business. Having decided to act, he wasted no time. He put men to work inventorying the supplies that could be taken on board for the journey north and made a list of goods that might be taken to England for sale. There wasn't much—perhaps a few feet of clapboard, some soap ash, or a few pelts were the only "riches" that had been found in what was supposed to have been a land where gold and pearls were plentiful—but Gates, a good company man as well as a good soldier, was determined to provide some return for the Virginia Company's investors, no matter how paltry the profits might be compared to the huge investment. While the inventory was being taken and lists of passengers were drawn up, he ordered some men to make pitch and tar to caulk the four ships for the voyage, others to check sails and rigging and to make repairs as necessary. Still others were set to grinding what little grain that was left and baking bread that would sustain them all on their journey up the coast.

By June 6, the Jamestown settlers were loading supplies and weapons on board, along with a few belongings. As the ships were being laded, Gates ordered men to bury the fort's heavy armament, thought to be twenty-four cannon of different sizes, somewhere outside the palisade. It must have hurt the old soldier to mistreat weapons that way, but better to see them buried than to have them fall into the wrong hands—either Indian or Spanish.

On the morning of June 7, Gates oversaw the loading of the four ships, almost certainly with Strachey by his side checking passenger lists and making sure all boarded their assigned vessels. Most of the settlers—at least those who were healthy enough to make it onto the ships under their own power—would have laughed and chattered excitedly at the thought of leaving the inhospitable wilderness behind, the wilderness that killed English like some kind of rapacious beast. A few—men like Strachey, who must have seen his newfound status slipping away even before he became fully used to it, and Gates, who must have come to Virginia filled with hopes and plans, and those who had no future in the old world of England save indebtedness or prison—would have been downcast at the idea of leaving. A few of the colonists, bitter about their experiences in the New World, were all for setting fire to the settlement, gleeful at the prospect of watching the place that had been the scene of so much misery go up in smoke as they sailed away, to the north and eventually back to England where—no matter what their station in life—they could at least live without fear of Indian attack. Gates, though, refused to go along with that idea and stopped the firebugs, saying that the fort should be saved because, in what quickly proved to be prescient words, "we knowe nott butt thatt as honneste men as our selves may come and inhabitt here."[12] The threat of arson was real enough that Gates assigned a company of men to guard the fort until the last of the colonists had walked through the gate. As the settlers departed, a drummer slowly beat the doleful sound of the abandonment of England's only North American settlement.

Sir Thomas and Sir George, along with Percy and James Davies, the man who had met the Bermuda survivors at Point Comfort, were in command of the four ships—Davies on the *Virginia*, Percy on the *Discovery*, Somers on the *Patience*, and Gates on the *Deliverance*. Sometime around noon on June 7, the ships hoisted anchor, cast off the lines that held them moored to the trees on shore, and started downriver toward the Chesapeake. As the vessels carrying the English settlers left Jamestown astern, a "peal of small shot"—a volley of pistol or musket fire—rang out in a ceremonial farewell.[13] Those on board most certainly would have stood on the decks of the four small ships, watching as they moved slowly away from the settlement. Unfortunately, William Strachey did not say how or what he felt as he left the place he had hoped would be the scene of his re-creation, nor did Gates, Percy, or any of the other Englishmen who had been forced to abandon the colony. It is not difficult to imagine, though, the feelings of those on the vessels—a mix of joy and sadness, relief and disappointment. Most of all, though, there would have been a desire to leave the inhospitable wilderness and return to the civility and relative safety of England.

As the ships moved away from the now deserted town, Powhatan warriors and spies watching from the forests would have danced and shouted with joy. Finally, the hated *Tassantassas* were leaving. Messengers sped with the news to the paramount chief in Orapaks and to the chief's brother, Opechancanough, and the other *weroances* (chieftains) up and down the James and York and as far away as the Potomac. The Indians would have breathed a sigh of relief, at least temporarily, though the wisest among them would have known, with certainty, that they had not seen the last of the bearded, coat-wearing people and their big canoes from across the sea. Pocahontas, the chief's daughter who had saved Captain John Smith's life, may well have felt a pang of sadness at the news that the foreigners were leaving the Tidewater, for she of all the native people was one who had seen the coming of the English as an opportunity instead of a threat.

The wind must have been light that day, hardly strong enough to ruffle the river's surface or belly out the ships' sails, for by sunset they made it only as far as Hog Island, about six miles downriver from the settlement. Of course, there were no more hogs on the island (that had been seen to by the Indians during the Starving Time), but the island afforded a safe place to moor for the night. The next day, they sailed on. When they were near a place they called Mulberry Island, not far from the mouth of what is now the Warwick River and still only a short distance from Jamestown, they dropped anchor to wait for the rising tide to turn. As the ships swung at anchor, someone spied a longboat approaching from the direction of Point Comfort. Strachey and the others on the four vessels watched anxiously, wondering who on earth could be approaching. It took about an hour for the longboat to make its way to the four anchored ships. At a shouted challenge from someone on one of the vessels, a voice answered that the longboat had been dispatched by Thomas West, Lord De La Warre, the designated governor for life of Virginia, who had arrived off Point Comfort two days earlier with three ships, about 150 new colonists, and supplies. In moments, Captain Edward Brewster—the son of a colonist who had died in Jamestown during the brutal summer of 1607, when more than half the first settlers had succumbed to illness or starvation—climbed to the deck of the *Deliverance* to meet with Gates and Somers. Brewster had letters from De La Warre along with orders that made clear that the new governor had learned from men at Point Comfort that Gates planned to abandon the settlement and that he, De La Warre, fully expected all the settlers to turn around immediately and head back up the James to repopulate the town. Strachey—who, after all, wrote his narrative for consumption in England, where the Virginia Company wanted only good news published and who wrote it, too, with an eye to his own advancement—said that the news of De La Warre's arrival was met with "no little joys" on the part of the Jamestown colonists. In reality, the news that De la Warre was on the scene and that they had to go back to the charnel house of Jamestown was the cause of much grief and complaining, even if the complaints were muttered rather than shouted. In any event, as Strachey reported, "upon the receipt of His Honor's letters, our governor bore up the helm with the wind coming easterly and that night (the wind so favorable) relanded all his men at the fort again."[14]

Soon after that, De La Warre himself arrived at Jamestown with his ships and settlers and supplies. The English settlement in Virginia was saved, like a branch pulled from an open fire in the instant before it was consumed by flames. With De La Warre on hand, with new supplies and healthy settlers, Jamestown would never again face the terror of famine and the English foothold in America would be, though shaky, secure for the future. The role of the *Sea Venture* survivors in guaranteeing the survival of the settlement was made clear in a Virginia Company pamphlet printed later that year:

> If God had not sent Sir Thomas Gates from the Bermudos within four days, they had all been famished. If God had not directed the heart of that worthy knight to save the fort from fire at their shipping, they had been destitute of a present harbor and succor. If they had abandoned the fort any longer time [departed earlier] and had not so soon returned, questionless the Indians would have destroyed the fort.... If they had set sail sooner and had launched into the vast ocean, who could have promised that they should have encountered the fleet of the Lord La-ware?[15]

No doubt those sentiments are true. Had Gates and Somers and the others who survived the shipwreck in Bermuda not shown up when they did with their few supplies, all in Jamestown would have died of starvation or illness, been killed or captured by the native people, or fled the settlement long before Lord De La Warre arrived on the scene. If Gates had not stopped the angry settlers from setting fire to the town before their departure, the newcomers under De La Warre's command would have had a difficult time surviving in Jamestown with the native people at their throats and no safe haven. If Gates and the other settlers had left even a day or two earlier than they did, they might well have missed their meeting with De La Warre. In fact, William Strachey and Sir Thomas Gates and Sir George Somers and the others who survived the *Sea Venture* shipwreck, found salvation in Bermuda, then went on to sustain Jamestown so that De La Warre could arrive in the nick of time, rescued what was to be the first successful English settlement in the

New World and kept it from being nothing more than a second, slightly more notable "lost colony," no more than a footnote to history.

Jamestown's trials, however, were not over when Lord De La Warre arrived in the summer of 1610. And the roles played by survivors of the _Sea Venture_ shipwreck in guaranteeing the ultimate success of English colonies both in Virginia and Bermuda were far from ended.

9

The Buried Heart

Thomas West, Lord De La Warre, the governor for life and captain general of South Virginia, was a man who loved the pomp and circumstance that went with being a baron. One of the most powerful and most important men in the realm, he was a member of the Queen Elizabeth I's privy council and served the same role under King James I. Soon after the flagship named in his honor came to anchor off the palisaded little town on the banks of the James River, he made his way to shore, preceded by an honor guard of gentlemen—a group that included De La Warre's nephew Sir Ferdinando Weynman along with several other knights who had accompanied the lord on his voyage to Virginia. The settlers in Jamestown, having been alerted to the arrival of the new colonial governor, greeted Baron De La Warre with all the grandeur they could muster. The fort's soldiers—men William Strachey called the governor's "company in arms"—stood rigidly at attention on the narrow strip of land between the palisade and the river bank, halberds and muskets at the ready, forming an honor guard.[1] Almost certainly, though it is not mentioned in any surviving record, they fired a welcoming volley of small-arms shot that echoed over the river, stilling for a moment the birds and insects whose sounds filled the early-summer air. Strachey, proud of being assigned the duty of bearing Sir Thomas Gates's standard during the informal ceremony outside the town gate, stepped forward and lowered the colors at De La Warre's feet in a gesture of subservience to the baron and his command.

For his part, the highborn and powerful West surely must have been disappointed as he stood on the shore of the James and looked for the first time at the colony that comprised the heart of the vast territory he was to govern. No matter what he had been told, there was little chance he was prepared for the sight of the dilapidated palisade and the half-ruined collection of shacks that made up England's only holding in the New World of America.

According to Strachey, after passing into the palisaded town, West immediately "fell upon his knees and before us all made a long and silent prayer to himself."[2] Just thirty-three years of age when he arrived in Jamestown, West suffered from gout, almost certainly caused by a diet loaded with good English beef, red wine, and rich sauces. As a consequence of his ailment, which typically causes excruciating pain in the big toe or ankle, West must have limped as he made his way ashore, probably leaning against a servant to take some of the weight off his throbbing foot. He may well have dropped to his knees just to escape the pain of standing.

In any event, West eventually hobbled into Jamestown's little church—Strachey called it a "chapel"—where he heard a sermon by the Reverend Richard Bucke, the seemingly tireless preacher who had served the *Sea Venture* survivors in Bermuda, said the first prayer in Virginia after Somers, Gates, and the others arrived in the Chesapeake, and now was tapped to serve as the new governor's assigned preacher. After the prayer service, De La Warre had his commission from King James I read aloud to the settlers—those who had survived the Starving Time, those who had come from Bermuda, and the 150 or so newcomers who had sailed with De La Warre himself—by Master Anthony Scot, his "ancient" or standard bearer. The simple fact that a man of West's stature, a member of the king's privy council and hence a man accustomed to easy access to power and money, was now styled the lord governor for life of the colony must have made those who had struggled to survive in Bermuda and those who had faced such horrors in Virginia feel a certain sense of relief. Finally, they would have thought, the company in London is serious about providing us with what we need to thrive in this inhospitable world. Surely, they must have thought, with De La Warre at the colony's helm, their situation would improve.

For his part, De La Warre's disappointment at what he found in Jamestown soon turned to anger as he saw the settlement's tumbledown houses, the town gates hanging broken and half open, the lack of planted crops, the garbage-filled streets, and other obvious signs of disorder. And then there was the smell: the stench that filled his nostrils made him gag. In his first speech to the assembled settlers, instead of congratulating them for having survived what he must have known was a terrible time of illness and famine, instead of commiserating with them, he "delivered a few words unto the company, laying some blames upon them for many vanities and their idleness" and then went on to warn them that if they did not mend their ways he "should be compelled to draw the sword in justice to cut off such delinquents, which he had much rather . . . draw in their defense to protect them from enemies."[3]

De La Warre had reason to be upset. At the same time, the settlers had plenty of cause for anger at what many would have considered betrayal by the Virginia Company, which had never managed to provide adequate support for the Virginia settlement. The settlers knew full well that De La Warre was supposed to have sailed from England a full year earlier, not long after the *Sea Venture* and the other ships of the 1609 fleet had departed, bringing a few settlers and supplies to what was to have been a thriving colony with some six or seven hundred colonists. They had every reason to wonder why West and his supplies had not arrived in time to help avert the tragedy of the Starving Time.

In fact, it isn't easy to determine just why De La Warre's plans were altered. Perhaps his departure was delayed because of a desire on his part, or the part of the Virginia Company, not to send another fleet into harm's way, to avoid the height of the summer Atlantic hurricane season. Further delay ensued when, on November 9, Samuel Argall arrived back in England, having tested the new, fast route to the Chesapeake. Argall was the bearer of good news, of course, since he was able to report that he had made good time across the Atlantic and that he could have shaved an additional two weeks off the time if he had had better fortune with the winds. He also brought news that the fish in the Chesapeake "proved so plentiful, especially of sturgeon," that he could have "loaded many ships" and returned to England with a profitable cargo if a man sent on the voyage to "pickle it and prepare it for keeping" had not died somewhere in midocean.[4]

While this good news was heartily welcomed by Sir Thomas Smythe and Sir Stephen Powle and the other promoters and investors of the Virginia venture, there was other, much less welcome information: Captain Argall reported that while seven ships of the Third Supply fleet had arrived in

Jamestown, the *Sea Venture* and the small ketch had not yet made port in late August or early September, when he departed for his return voyage to England. It was not so very unusual for ships to go missing in midocean only to appear later, so while Smythe and others in England were troubled by Argall's news, they would not have immediately assumed that the *Sea Venture* and all her passengers were lost. They would have been more troubled, however, by Argall's news that, thanks to the lack of supplies—they were missing on the *Sea Venture*—the colony was in "necessity and distress . . . for want of victual." In typical Virginia Company fashion, though, Smythe and the other members of the Virginia Council eventually placed blame for the food shortage not on the company's lack of planning but on the laziness of the settlers and the "misgovernment" of Jamestown's leaders.[5] Still, it would have been natural enough for the leaders of the Virginia Company in London to put Lord De La Warre's plans on hold, at least temporarily, until they were able to learn more about what had happened to Sir Thomas Gates and Sir George Somers and the others who had left Plymouth bound for Virginia.

Soon enough, though, Sir Thomas Smythe and the other adventurers in London learned that there was little hope that either the *Sea Venture*, with Gates and Somers and Strachey and all the other passengers bound for Virginia, or the ketch would ever be seen again. Within just a few weeks of Argall's return, several ships of the great fleet—including the one that carried the badly injured Captain John Smith back to England—returned to port, bearing men who were all too eager to share their firsthand accounts of the terrible tempest—how they had watched the *Sea Venture* disappear into the maelstrom and how the flagship had never been seen again. Not surprisingly, the Virginia Company would have wanted to keep the bad news hidden as much as possible, just as all the company leaders kept all bad news hidden in an effort to guarantee continued support for the colony. While they could—and did—routinely censor printed material, there was no way to muzzle the mariners returning from the Chesapeake. As the news of the disaster spread from the docks in Plymouth and the Thames waterfront to taverns and inns and to the streets of London, it became common knowledge that the flagship of the fleet that had departed with such high hopes just a short time earlier had come to a sad, perhaps even a tragic, end.

Of course, the families and friends of those who had set sail in the summer of 1609—Lady Somers, Lady Gates, the friends of William Strachey, John Rolfe's family, and countless others—were hard hit by the news of the ship's demise. So, too, were investors like Stephen Powle who had backed the Virginia venture with their hard-earned pounds and who now faced the loss of their investments.

As word of the *Sea Venture* disaster spread, the company sprang into action, not to rush supplies and more settlers to Jamestown, but to print a propaganda brochure, *A true and sincere declaration of the purpose of the plantation begun in Virginia*, published on December 14, 1610. In twenty-six unsigned pages, the company explained how the difficulties in Jamestown arose from bad fortune and intransigence on the part of the settlers and the native people, from the form of the original charter, and from the danger of the ocean passage, but that all was repaired now so all should be well in Virginia. Then the "declaration" asked for more colonists and appended a list of men needed, including ministers, surgeons, fowlers, sturgeon dressers and "preservers of the caviary," and—with an eye to a prosperous future—silk dressers and pearl drillers.[6] The declaration also said that West should set sail no later than the last day of January 1610.

Still, the good intentions of the declaration aside, it was February 28, 1610, before West was given a royal commission to set sail for Virginia. With the *Sea Venture* gone, more than 150 mariners and would-be settlers presumed dead, and badly needed supplies thought to be sitting on the bottom of the ocean, West would have to resupply the colony, not simply show up as its new leader. The new governor's commission ordered De La Warre to "take into your charge our Fleet consistinge of three good Shippes with the Masters Mariners saylors and one hundred and fyftie landmen under your command with what speed conveniently you may unto Virginia and with the first wind to set sail for that place." Like Argall on his exploratory voyage and the ships of the Third Supply, West was instructed to avoid Spanish territories unless he was forced by bad weather to take refuge in some unfriendly port.[7]

Even after receiving his commission, it took a month for De La Warre to load his three ships, gather supplies and settlers, and sign on crewmen and soldiers for the voyage. Samuel Argall, as a measure of his new stature with the Virginia Company, was in command of West's flagship, named the *De La Warre* in honor of the new governor of Virginia. The other ships in the small fleet were the vice admiral, the *Blessing* (the same vessel that survived the hurricane that scuttled the *Sea Venture*), and the *Hercules*, the smallest of the three vessels, but given the ostentatious title "rear admiral." The fleet bearing De La Warre, his 150 settlers, and enough food to feed four hundred men for a full year set sail from Cowes on the Isle of Wight, just off the southernmost coast of England in the Channel, on April 1, 1610. Leaving the Needles and then the Lizard and the Scilly Isles astern, the three ships moved into the open ocean. For some reason—almost certainly the simple vagaries of wind and current—the ships did not follow the more southerly course made by Argall on his first voyage but instead took a more southwesterly track that carried them, by April 12, within sight of Terceira Island in the Azores. That night, the ships lay becalmed. In the morning, though, as the sun rose so "did the wind likewise rise west and west by south, a rough and loud gale" that forced the ships to seek shelter near Graciosa Island, the northernmost of the Azores.[8] As the wind howled and seas built, cables parted, anchors were lost or pulled free from the sea bottom. Sailors worked madly on the pitching decks of the three vessels, fighting for their very lives. With their anchors lost, the ships were forced to claw their way offshore to find sailing room or risk being smashed to kindling on a lee shore.

Somehow, thanks to good fortune or excellent seamanship, all three vessels were able to find open ocean. By the next day, they were beating their way into unfavorable winds just west of the Azores when the *Hercules* somehow became separated from the rest of the fleet. The other ships spent a day searching for the lost vessel, then—hoping she would reappear at some point—headed south, still forced to sail into contrary winds. Finally, on April 27, when the fleet was far to the south, at twenty-eight degrees south latitude, the same height at which Argall found friendly winds on his earlier voyage, the winds turned favorable. The *De La Warre* and the *Blessing* turned west and then north of west on a course that took them to anchor just off Cape Henry late in the day on June 5.

According to one narrative that was signed by De La Warre along with Gates, William Strachey, George Percy, and Captain Ferdinando Weynman, the new governor and his men went ashore on Cape Henry either on June 5 or June 6, "as well to refresh ourselves as to fish, and to set up a cross upon the point, if haply the *Hercules* might arrive there, to signify our coming in." While they were fishing, a group of friendly Indians showed up, apparently in need of food, and De La Warre "gave unto them of such fish as we took, which was in good store."[9]

This version of the narrative sent to the Virginia Company might well have been no more than propaganda. De La Warre, in a letter written to Lord Salisbury, the lord high treasurer of England, makes no mention of plentiful fish or trading with hungry Indians. In fact, the version sent to the Virginia Company raises several questions. Why were natives at Cape Henry suddenly willing to trade? Why could they not catch their own fish? Why, indeed, were De La Warre's men able to catch enough fish near Cape Henry to help feed the native people while settlers in Jamestown found it impossible to feed themselves no matter where or how often they cast their nets?

In any event, sometime on June 6, someone on one of the vessels spied a vessel moving away from the mouth of the bay. De La Warre, who must have thought the ship might be a Spanish vessel coming to investigate or even to attack the English colony, was overjoyed to see she was the *Hercules,* his "own consort that had been missing near eight weeks."[10]

The next day, the reconstituted fleet was able to move into the mouth of the Chesapeake, where the three ships came to anchor just off Point Comfort. There Lord De La Warre heard the news that Sir Thomas Gates and Sir George Somers were both safe and in Jamestown, news that undoubtedly made him, as he said, "most happy," since he would have known both men socially as well as professionally and would have, with justification, assumed they were both dead. It was a good thing he heard that happy news, he said, since what he learned of conditions at the settlement he was to govern was "sufficient to have broke my heart and to have made me altogether unable to have done my king or country any service."[11]

It was then that De La Warre made his way up the Chesapeake and James to anchor at Jamestown and to find the settlement in such a parlous state that he had to warn the settlers to either put their shoulders to the wheel or face his "sword of justice."

De La Warre's first order of business—after prayer and his speech of warning to the assembled settlers—was to name his council. William Strachey, the impoverished lawyer, finally found a place of note when West tapped him to serve as the colony's recorder, a position that guaranteed his name would be known not just in the colony but in England, by the officers of the Virginia Company and perhaps by King James I himself. George Percy, the inept gentleman who led the settlement during the Starving Time, was named captain of James Fort, in command of the settlement's soldiers; Sir Ferdinando Weynman, West's nephew, was named master of the ordnance, in charge of all weapons; and Edward Brewster, the son of one of the original colonists who had died in the settlement's first terrible summer, was chosen to lead Lord De La Warre's own company of soldiers. Samuel Argall was made a captain of a company of soldiers, as was George Yeardley, a veteran of the Dutch wars and one of the *Sea Venture* survivors.

Soon after naming his council, De La Warre set the sailors "a-work to un-lade ships" as he ordered the "landmen (settlers) to cleanse the town."[12] The town must have been in truly terrible shape. That night, and indeed for the first two nights of his stay in Virginia, Lord De La Warre refused to sleep in the settlement, instead returning to his quarters on the flagship to avoid the stench and filth in Jamestown. Meanwhile, as the settlers cleaned the town, it seems they dug a trench and shoveled or threw rusted arms and armor, some presumably useless knives and swords, broken pottery, the bones of wild animals and fish, and other refuse all together in a mix that was destined to bring joy to the hearts of archaeologists almost four centuries later.[13]

On June 13, the new governor called a meeting of his council—the *Sea Venture* survivors Gates, Somers, Yeardley, and Strachey along with Percy and the others—to discuss the situation in the settlement. To be sure, while the arrival of Lord De La Warre and his three-ship fleet laden with victuals meant the days when Jamestown's residents would be forced to eat snakes and rodents to ward off hunger were over—never to return—food, or at least fresh meat, was still in short supply. Most of the food brought to the colony in the holds of De La Warre's vessels was grain. The new leader was forced "to put his own people and the rest of the colony to a very mean allowance, which was seven pound of English meal for a man a week, and five pounds for every woman, without the addition of any victual whatever."[14] De La Warre knew that while English meal—this apparently included peas—would keep men alive—and women, too, despite their unequal share—it was not very appetizing or healthy as a steady diet. The colonists were in dire need of meat, any kind of meat.

As the council tried to figure out how to supply nearly four hundred colonists with fresh meat at a time when hunting and fishing were fruitless and trade with the natives seemingly out of the question, Admiral Sir George Somers surprised De La Warre and the others by announcing his willingness to return to Bermuda where, he said, he knew he could find plenty of fish and turtles and hogs, enough to supply all in Jamestown for six months, at least.

De La Warre and the others must have looked at the old admiral as if he'd taken leave of his senses. He was about sixty years of age by that time, ancient in Jacobean terms, and, though nobody says so, he must have been frail and tired, having weathered a storm, shipwreck, and ten months of toil in

Bermuda, followed by a small-boat voyage from the Bermudas to Virginia. Even a much younger man would have been exhausted by his experiences. The voyage back to Bermuda would be difficult and dangerous under the best of circumstances, but when Somers made his surprising offer, the season of summer storms—like the one that had wrecked the *Sea Venture*—had already started. What was more, Somers volunteered to sail back to the islands in the *Patience*, the little pinnace he had built on the beach in Bermuda, using just a single nail. West and the others were rightly impressed by what the *Sea Venture* survivor Sylvester Jourdain called the old salt's willingness "to do service to his prince and country without any respect of private gain."[15]

While Somers's offer must have appeared foolish, if not lunatic, given the dangers of any ocean voyage, Lord De La Warre jumped at it, issuing a commission to the admiral to proceed to the Bermudas without delay and to return quickly with supplies. He also assigned Samuel Argall as Somers's second in command, to sail in company with the admiral as commander of the sturdy old *Discovery*, the pinnace that had been doing steady duty ever since she served as smallest of the three-ship fleet that carried John Smith and the other original settlers to the Chesapeake in 1607.

On June 20, 1610, a Wednesday, Somers and Argall climbed aboard their small ships with their selected crews, ordered anchors hoisted and sails raised, and waved good-bye to Lord De La Warre and the settlers who stood on the river shore wishing them good fortune and Godspeed. The two vessels moved down the James on the ebbing tide after Somers promised the other settlers he and Argall would be back with their holds full of supplies "before the Indians do gather their harvest." That meant he and Argall fully expected to be back in Jamestown by mid-August or so, or about seven weeks after their departure, from the place Somers called "Bermooda . . . the most plentiful place that ever I came to, for fish, hogs, and fowl."[16]

Instead of the swift passage hoped for by Somers and Argall, the *Patience* and the *Discovery* ran into trouble almost as soon as they sailed out of the mouth of the Chesapeake. For three weeks—more than the amount of time Somers had figured it would take to sail to the Bermudas—the two ships were forced to tack to and fro in a dense fog and unfavorable winds, uncertain of their position since they would have been unable, for hours on end, to see the stars or sun. As they struggled to make headway, stores of food and water on the two vessels grew short, tempers frayed, and men grew fearful and impatient.

On July 16, Somers, obviously disgusted with the ships' lack of progress and growing desperate to obtain supplies for Jamestown, changed plans. Instead of sailing to Bermuda, he and Argall would head north for the rich fishing grounds off New England. As the ships bore north, they were once again enveloped in pea-soup fog. It appears likely that the *Patience* ran into trouble; perhaps the ship's planks, hand-hewn in Bermuda and fitted with treenails, started to open or there was some difficulty with the rigging that had been salvaged from the *Sea Venture*. Whatever the case, on the evening of July 26, Somers dispatched a ship's boat to Argall with instructions that the two vessels should "stand in for the River Sagadahoc"—the Kennebec River in Maine, known to the English since 1605, when an expedition under the leadership of George Weymouth visited the region just long enough to capture five Indians who were later taken to England.[17]

Argall followed Somers's instructions, but when he made Kennebec, the admiral and the *Patience* were nowhere to be seen. For roughly a week, as Argall waited for Somers to show up, he and his men fished the cod-rich waters off the river, filling their ship almost to the gunwales. Finally, thinking Somers and his men were lost, he headed south for the Chesapeake. On August 27, he sailed into a great bay where, he said, he found a "great store of people which were very kind."[18] Almost exactly a year earlier, the same bay had been visited by Henry Hudson on his ship the *Half Moon*, though Hudson did not bother to give the bay a name. Argall, not one to pass up an opportunity to curry favor with his boss, promptly christened the bay in honor of De La Warre. Then Argall headed south again, coasting his way just off the shore of modern-day Delaware and Maryland until he and his men came to anchor off Cape Charles on August 31.

Nobody knows for sure where Somers and his men—including his nephew, Matthew Somers, serving as the sailing master of the *Patience*—were while Argall was loading his ship with cod and investigating the bay he named in honor of the governor for life of Virginia. Assuming he tried to make landfall in what was then known as "north Virginia," he could have found safe harbor anywhere between Long Island Sound and Maine. Exactly where he went is a mystery that may never be solved. What is certain is that something, probably the need to repair the pinnace, delayed Sir George for several weeks. Perhaps, just perhaps, Somers and his men came ashore somewhere on the coast of what is now Connecticut to repair the pinnace or to replenish fresh water and food supplies for the voyage to Bermuda. An interesting hint that this may have been the case came to light in 1924, when a gold signet ring bearing Sir George's coat of arms was found on a Connecticut beach. In any event, Somers and the others on the *Patience* seem not to have set out across the Atlantic again until sometime in October.

There's no record of Sir George's journey or even of his arrival in Bermuda. Given what is known, however, it is safe to say that sometime in late October or very early November, one of the two *Sea Venture* mutineers who had remained in the islands when the other shipwreck survivors sailed on to Virginia, either Christopher Carter or Edward Waters, must have looked out to sea and spied the sails of a lone ship as she slowly made her way toward the island chain. The two men, practiced mariners who had probably helped build the *Patience* on the beach in Bermuda, would soon have recognized the approaching pinnace and rushed to the beach to watch as the little vessel came to anchor. Perhaps they launched a boat to row out to meet their old shipmates and Matthew Somers and, of course, their commander, the admiral. Somers, for his part, would have been overjoyed to see the two former mutineers. Though their clothes were tattered, they looked hale and healthy, sunbrowned but certainly no worse for wear after spending six months alone in Bermuda. In fact, Somers and the other men on the *Patience* soon learned that the two men were thriving, with an ample supply of salted turtle meat and plenty of plump birds, enough to fill the bellies of Somers and his crew and plenty, too, to take back to Jamestown to supply the settlers there.

Even before Somers had departed from the Bermudas for Virginia, he had been convinced that the islands were ripe for colonization. Now, as he stepped ashore in Bermuda for the second time and looked around at the lush scenery, smelled the fragrant air, and heard Carter and Waters chattering excitedly about their food supplies, his conviction was even stronger. It was only strengthened by what he'd experienced in his brief time in Jamestown, where hunger and death seemed constant companions. In fact, what he found when he returned to Bermuda "so inflamed him . . . that he resolved upon a plantation" even if it had to be financed "by the purse and meanes of himselfe and his friends."[19]

By that time, Somers was a sick man. He had lived for nearly six decades, a life filled with many difficult sea voyages. He had been exhausted even before volunteering to sail back to Bermuda and then physically strained by the difficulties he and Argall had encountered after leaving Jamestown. The long, uncomfortable voyage from the Atlantic Coast to Bermuda was more than Somers's tired, aging body could stand. Within days of coming ashore, his health was failing. Without a medical record of some sort it is almost impossible to know exactly what disease or diseases attacked the old sea dog. Perhaps the stress of the last year or so caused him to develop an ulcer. Perhaps he had stomach cancer. We will never know. What was clear to those who sailed on the *Patience* and to the two mutineers who had remained in Bermuda was that Somers was dying. It was also clear to the admiral. He was in pain, forced to take to his bed, maybe in the cabin he'd occupied during the ten months the *Sea Venture* survivors lived in the little settlement of thatched-roof cottages just off St. Catherine's Beach.

Somers called his nephew to his side sometime during the first week of November. He tried to prepare Matthew for his death, told him that he must, no matter what happened, gather the badly needed provisions for those in Virginia and return to the colony without any delay. He told his nephew that he would be happy to be buried in Bermuda, in the little garden he'd planted in the first weeks after the *Sea Venture* came to rest on the reef off the Bermudan beach. Then, it seems, he told Matthew to go to England as soon as he could following his return to Virginia, to tell Lady Somers of his death, and to raise money—through the Virginia Company, if possible, or by private means, if necessary—to establish a colony in Bermuda. Then, on November 9, 1610, Sir George Somers died.

It seems the old admiral's body was still warm when his nephew, who did not prove to be the most reliable of men, decided to forget his uncle's dying wishes. Instead of returning to Virginia with the much-needed supply of meat Somers had promised the settlement, he decided to head east, to England. Putting the best light possible on Matthew's actions, it is just barely possible to believe that he was forced to turn his back on Lord De La Warre and the other Jamestown settlers by his men, who forced him to sail east instead of west. However, it seems likely that if he'd been forced to return to England by recalcitrant mariners, he would have pressed charges or at the very least reported the mutiny to officials in London. Instead, he never said a word against any of his crew.

Matthew Somers also refused to carry out his uncle's wishes when it came to Sir George's final resting place. For reasons that can only be surmised, the young man decided to eviscerate his uncle's corpse and bury his heart and entrails on St. George's Island—perhaps in the admiral's garden—and carry his gutted body back to England.[20] According to John Smith, the younger Somers hid the body in a cedar chest, sneaked the chest on board the *Patience*, and secreted it someplace belowdeck. Smith, of course, was writing at a remove from the action, not reporting firsthand as he did when he wrote of his own adventures in Virginia. He may have passed on misinformation he received from some mariner or repeated what was no more than pure rumor. In any case, it is extremely unlikely that a cedar chest large enough to hold the admiral's body—gutted or no—could have been somehow brought on board a vessel that was certainly guarded without anyone knowing of it. It was even less likely that a cedar chest could have been hidden on a roughly thirty-foot vessel during the weeks it took to get from Bermuda to England.

Another story has it that the admiral's corpse was stuffed in one of the barrels routinely used to store food and drink, a type of barrel that would have certainly been stowed belowdeck on the *Patience*. To preserve the body, the story went, Matthew "pickled" the old mariner's remains, filling the keg with brine as if Sir George was a cod. If this was done—and it certainly seems more plausible than the cedar chest version of the story—all on board were undoubtedly aware that they were carrying Somers's body back to England. They may have grumbled and looked at the heavens for protection and maybe even crossed themselves furtively—after all, sailors were and are a notoriously superstitious lot—but Matthew Somers was their captain and, unless they were mutineers, they would have had to bow to his wishes.

It seems logical that Matthew took the body to England because he wanted to prove that his uncle was indeed dead. His later actions (he tried unsuccessfully to stake a claim to Sir George's not inconsiderable estate that included a manor house near Lyme—now Lyme Regis—on England's south coast as well as to his shares in any Virginia Company profits) indicate he had a vested interest in proving the old sailor was gone for good and always. Perhaps Matthew was more worried about proving Sir George's cause of death. It was not unusual in Tudor and Jacobean England for the death of any important man to be accompanied by a chorus of rumors about poisoning or foul play. Perhaps Matthew thought the knight's pickled body would serve as some proof that he'd died of natural causes. We'll never know.

When the mutineers, Waters and Carter, heard that the pinnace was returning to England, Waters gave at least passing thought to abandoning Bermuda. The draw of home with its inns and taverns and female companionship would have been strong for any man who'd spent two years marooned on an island, no matter how lovely the island. It seems, though, that his shipmate Carter talked Waters into staying, reminding him that as the first settlers of the previously unclaimed territory they stood to gain, perhaps grow wealthy, once the English determined to colonize the islands, as they surely would. Not only that, Carter also convinced Edward Chard, one of the men who'd sailed to Bermuda from Jamestown with Matthew Somers on the *Patience*, to remain behind as well.

By that time, Matthew Somers was surely determined to see Bermuda settled by the English, so determined that he was able to promise Chard and Waters and Carter that relief, in the form of additional settlers and supplies to plant the island, would quickly be sent from England. Meanwhile, Matthew and his shipmates were in no hurry to leave Bermuda, with all its pleasures, to begin the difficult and dangerous three-thousand-mile voyage to England. It was late March or early April 1611 when the *Patience* made her way through the Bermudan reef and turned her bow to the east, toward England, bearing her grisly cargo either in a cedar chest or stuffed and pickled in a wooden barrel. Sometime in early June, the pinnace that had been built on the beach on St. George's Island—later named not for Admiral Somers but for England's patron saint—sailed into the harbor at Lyme, Somers's hometown. The residents of the little seaside town were used to the comings and goings of ships from the open ocean into the well-protected harbor with its stone pier, but still, many would have watched the strange, weather-beaten vessel as she slipped through the harbor's waters to nudge gently against the Cobb, the stone mole or quay that served the town's residents and merchants. At some point, someone on the Cobb would have recognized Matthew Somers and the word must have rushed from hearer to hearer that Admiral Sir George Somers, the town's most famous son, was dead, his body on board the strange-looking vessel that had just edged into port.

Given his high rank, none on the vessel would have stepped ashore until Sir George's body was carried to land in something like state—not the easiest thing to arrange given the strange, even macabre, way his body had been transported. Still, messengers would have hurried to notify John Somers, the admiral's younger brother and a prosperous merchant, as well as Sir George's wife, Lady Joane, and the rest of Matthew Somers's relatives. Lady Joane, who lived in Berne Manor, a two-hundred-acre estate some ten miles from the port, would not have made it to the town until the following day, but other family members rushed to the dock to watch silently while a handful of musketeers stood at attention and fired a volley of small shot over the admiral's body as the barrel or cedar chest was taken ashore and muscled up a narrow flight of steps that led to the top of the Cobb. In all likelihood, Lady Joane made her way to Lyme on the second or third day of June and took possession of her husband's body. On 4 June, the admiral was buried in the small church of St. Wita's in the town of Whitchurch Canonicorum, not far from Berne Manor.

IO

Violent Proceedings and Villainy

By late June 1610, when Sir George Somers departed from Jamestown for Bermuda on what proved to be his last voyage, the Virginia settlement was a very different place than it had been in the Starving Time, just a few weeks earlier. With the arrival of the *Sea Venture* survivors, followed by the coming of roughly 150 settlers—and food supplies—brought to the Chesapeake by Lord De La Warre, the English colony in Virginia was on a firmer footing than it had been at any time since the first settlers came ashore three years earlier.

Though De La Warre's leadership and the influx of new blood revitalized the settlement and marked a turning point in Jamestown's history, the English colony in Virginia was to face continuing struggles during the next several years as illness, hunger, and ongoing conflicts with the native Powhatan people threatened the colony's survival. Never again, though, would Jamestown totter on the edge of the precipice as it had in the weeks just before the *Sea Venture* survivors arrived on the James River from Bermuda.

Still, life in the colony was harsh in the summer of 1610, harsher than any of the settlers had imagined in far-off England. While famine was held at bay thanks to a sufficient supply of grain and meal, meat was scarce and fish were rare and would be until late summer, when Samuel Argall returned with a shipload of cod from his unplanned voyage to Kennebec. As the summer deepened, the newcomers suffered from unrelenting heat and humidity and the ever-present biting, stinging insects. The work would have been back-breaking and constant. Men were kept busy clearing land, planting crops, building or repairing the dwellings and other structures within the enclosed town, or preparing clapboard and soap ash and other commodities for shipment to England. They stood guard and performed military duty when needed. Women, highborn ladies as well as the former tavern maids and servant girls, worked in the fields, washed and cleaned and ground meal and made candles, and, no doubt, fell into bed gratefully soon after sunset. The summer heat and the insects and the bad water, along with a poor diet and weakness brought on by overwork, made the colonists ideal targets for the deadly illnesses that lashed so many newcomers to the colony. While no exact reckoning is possible, it is safe to assume that dozens, maybe even scores, of graves were dug in Jamestown in the months following the arrival of the *Sea Venture* survivors.

Though life in Jamestown remained harsh, there were times when it achieved something like the normalcy of life in an English village. The town and its market square were cleaner than they had been in months; palings were repaired; dwellings were patched with clapboard and thatch; and, under the leadership of Lord De La Warre and Sir Thomas Gates, something like order was being imposed from above, an order that had not been seen in Jamestown since Captain John Smith had sailed away almost a year earlier. One of the first things De La Warre ordered was the repair of the small church inside the fort, described by William Strachey as a "chapel" roughly sixty feet long and twenty-four feet wide. When repaired, Strachey said, it was to "have a chancel in it of cedar and a communion table of the black walnut, and all the pews of cedar, with fair broad windows to shut and open." It was furnished with a pulpit and two bells and kept sweet smelling—on orders of the governor for life, who apparently had a sensitive nose—with "divers flowers." Once each Thursday and twice each Sunday, the settlers gathered in the chapel for services. On other days, the church bells were rung at ten in the morning and four in the afternoon, reminding all in the colony that it was time to pray. De La Warre's love of pomp and ritual was particularly apparent on Sundays, when he showed up in church "accompanied with all the councilors, captains, other officers, and all the gentlemen, and with a guard of halberdiers in His Lordship's livery, fair red cloaks, to the number of fifty, both on each side and behind him."[1] Surrounded by his subjects, the governor sat

on a green velvet chair or knelt on a velvet cushion as he prayed before troop-
ing back to his home with all his retainers.

Several of the *Sea Venture* survivors would, in this period, have enjoyed positions of authority and privilege in the colony. Sir Thomas Gates, of course,
had taken his place as lieutenant governor, second in command, once Lord
De La Warre arrived in Jamestown. In the summer of 1610, Gates and De La
Warre no doubt lived together in the best dwelling in the little settlement,
shared the best victuals, and rarely, if ever, got their hands dirty digging in the
fields. The Reverend Richard Bucke was fulfilling his duty to the Virginia
Company—and to God—in his service as the minister in Jamestown. George
Yeardley, who seems to have stayed in the background in Bermuda, was a cap-
tain of the soldiers in the settlement and probably ate at table with George
Percy and Edward Brewster and other officers.

Of all the *Sea Venture* survivors, none had risen any higher any faster than
William Strachey. The former poet must have relished his elevation to the
governor's council, must have felt particularly proud as he trooped into the
little chapel behind Lord De La Warre. He certainly had improved his lot in
life in the months since he climbed aboard the *Sea Venture* in England carrying
little more than his hopes, even if he was half a world away from his home
and family and the London he knew. No longer impoverished and an object
of pity, the colony's recorder would have been assigned accommodations in
one of the better dwellings in the town and relieved of the most onerous duties. No doubt most important to Strachey, he was now able to bask in the
unfamiliar respect of his fellows.

While Strachey—and Jamestown—were enjoying relative prosperity in
the summer of 1610, Wahunsonacock must have been dismayed. Of course,
he had been overjoyed when it appeared that the starving *Tassantassas* had
abandoned the Indian lands, then angry and downhearted just a few days later
when he learned not only that the coat-wearing people had not actually departed, but that their numbers had increased with the arrival of more of the
big ships from across the sea. From his headquarters in Orapaks, he sent word
to his people in the villages scattered throughout Tsenacommacah to refuse
trade and to continue sniping at the interlopers whenever possible. It is likely
that the paramount chief still held some hopes of convincing the English, as
he had convinced the tribes of the Tidewater, using ungentle persuasion—a
tactic Strachey described as "by force subdued . . . or through fear yielded"—

that their best course of action was to become his subjects, paying tribute in exchange for his beneficent protection.[2] At the same time, it is obvious that the English continued to hold on to their own hopes of turning the native people into English-speaking, Christian subjects of King James I. Sadly, particularly for the Indians of Virginia, these mutually exclusive goals guaranteed continued conflict between the two peoples and the ultimate eradication of the less technologically advanced Powhatans.

In any event, any hopes that Wahunsonacock or De La Warre had of achieving something like détente were soon dashed. Within just a few days of Somers's departure for Bermuda, the *Sea Venture* survivors and the other Jamestown colonists were in a state of war with the native people. It was, to be sure, what today might be characterized as a low-tech war of attrition between the *Tassantassas* and the Indians, but it was war all the same.

The first skirmish occurred when Sir Thomas Gates traveled south to Fort Algernon at Point Comfort, where he discovered that the longboat belonging to the fort on the point had loosed its mooring and been blown across the James, where it ran aground. Gates sent a man across the river in an old canoe to retrieve the valuable longboat. A group of Nansemonds on the south shore of the river spotted the man—his name was Humphrey Blunt—as soon as he reached the shore, surrounded him, and dragged him, screaming, into the woods where no doubt he met a brutal end.

According to Strachey, who in his new post as colonial secretary would have been in a position to know, Gates hoped to avoid open conflict with the Indians. He "would not by any means," Strachey said, "be wrought to a violent proceeding against them for all the practices of villainy with which they daily endangered our men, thinking it possible by a more tractable course to win them to a better condition." With Blunt's killing, however, the deputy governor's usually soft heart turned hard. He "proposed to be revenged."[3] On July 9, he led a force to Kecoughtan, the Indian village about four miles from the fort at Point Comfort, on the north shore of the James. Why the attack was launched on a group of natives who apparently had nothing to do with Blunt's murder isn't clear. Whatever the motivation, Gates led a flotilla from Jamestown to Fort Algernon at Point Comfort.

The raiding party included William Strachey, perhaps because of his position as one of the colony's governing council or perhaps because he volunteered so he could write a firsthand account of the raid. George Percy, as captain of the soldiers in Jamestown, was involved, as were the soldiers he commanded. Like Strachey, Percy wrote a description of the raid. The party also included a "taborer," or drummer, apparently brought along simply to serve as human bait. After landing near Point Comfort and advancing on the village, Gates ordered his men to disperse in the woods, then told the taborer—his name was Thomas Dowse—"to play and dawnse thereby to Allure the Indyans to come unto him."[4] According to Percy, the plan worked beautifully, probably because the natives in Kecoughtan had no reason to expect trouble from the English. Seduced by the taborer, the Indians came to investigate and the Englishmen fell on them, putting five to the sword, mortally wounding others, and causing the rest to flee the village in terror. Strachey, for some reason, did not find it worthwhile to talk about the playing, dancing drummer in his narrative; however, he did admit that the spoils taken by the English in the village did not amount to much, just "a few baskets of old wheat and some other of peas and beans, a little tobacco, and a few women's girdles of silk, of the silk grass, not without art."[5] Not much to brag about, to be sure, but at the end of the attack the Indian village and its cleared, planted acres were left in the hands of the English, who built a fort—named Fort Charles—on the site of the village.

After returning to Jamestown, Gates departed for England on board the *Blessing,* one of the ships of the *Sea Venture* fleet, to report to the Virginia Company about everything that had happened in the year since the fleet set sail from England and to attempt to gain more financial and logistical support for the colony. Packed in the vessel's hold when she set sail on July 20, 1610, was a cargo of lumber and a few samples of iron ore. The vessel also carried at least one copy of William Strachey's narrative of the *Sea Venture* shipwreck and his eyewitness account of events in Bermuda and Virginia up until the time of the attack on Kecoughtan. This 25,000-word narrative, with the weighty title *A True Reportory of the Wreck and Redemption of Sir Thomas Gates, Knight, upon and from the Islands of the Bermudas: His Coming to Virginia and the Estate of that Colony Then and After, under the Government of the Lord De La Warre, July 15, 1610, Written by William Strachey, Esquire,* was a long letter, addressed to an unnamed "Excellent Lady." While what is known today as Strachey's *True Reportory* is an engagingly written account of the *Sea Venture* disaster and the events that followed, the letter is a transparent attempt to curry favor with a patron. It is surmised by Strachey's biographer that the letter was sent to Lady Sara, the wife of Sir Thomas Smythe, the treasurer of the Virginia Company.[6] This makes sense, since Strachey still wanted to advance his own interests and Sir Thomas was certainly in a position to help him. In any event, this document seems to have been circulated, perhaps copied, by members of the Virginia Company's governing council and perhaps by at least a few of the London literati who had befriended Strachey before his departure for Virginia. At the very least, many in London's literary circles were aware of the gist of Strachey's remarkable story, with later consequences that Strachey could never have foreseen.

Meanwhile, not long after Gates—bearing Strachey's letter—left Jamestown for England, Lord De La Warre sprang into action, determined either to achieve something like peaceful coexistence with Wahunsonacock, or to bring the paramount chief to heel. The new captain general for life sent Wahunsonacock a message that was supposed to be an overture to peace but that the chief could only have considered as an insulting ultimatum. This message began with a litany of the Indians' crimes against the settlers and an accusation that Wahunsonacock was setting his "people to attempt us with private conspiracies and actual violence," followed by a halfhearted admission that De La Warre "did not suppose that these mischiefes were contrived by [Wahunsonacock] or with his knowledge" but were, instead, the acts of "his worst and unruly people."[7]

After paying this lip service to the idea of Wahunsonacock's innocence, De La Warre went on to warn the chief that if he did not tell his "unruly people" to stop attacking the settlers, "the lord governor and captain general should be compelled . . . to offend [injure] him, which he would be loath to do."[8] De La Warre then went on to order Wahunsonacock either to punish or to send to Jamestown any of his people who had assaulted the English, to return any Englishmen he was holding, and to send to the settlement any English arms he had in his possession—including some "two hundred swords, besides axes and poleaxes, chisels, hose to pare [prepare] and cleanse the ground."[9] Lord De La Warre closed his letter by reminding Wahunsonacock how he had received a cheap crown and other regalia from Captain Christopher Newport almost two years earlier, when John Smith and the other English had coerced him into what they took to be a promise of fealty to King James.[10]

But the Wahunsonacock who had submitted, however unwillingly, to his "coronation" by Captain Newport was no longer willing to submit to the English, even symbolically. If De La Warre could send an ultimatum, so could the paramount chief. The English, he told the two men who'd carried De La

Warre's message to Orapaks, could either remain at Jamestown, not leaving the island, or they could climb aboard their ships and go home. No more exploratory trips or trading voyages. And if the *Tassantasssas* were foolish enough to disobey his warning, he would "command his people to kill us and do unto us all the mischief which they at their pleasure could and we feared." And, he added, don't bother sending any more messengers unless "they brought him a coach and three horses, for he had understood by the Indians which were in England how such was the state of great werowances and lords in England, to ride and visit other great men."[11]

While at first glance this demand seems laughable—what use could Wahunsonacock possibly have for a coach and horses in the forests of Virginia?—there may have been more to it than that. According to John Smith, the mature forest that covered much of the Tidewater region was comprised largely of huge old trees with few of the young trees and little of the underbrush found in second-growth woodland. John Smith, describing the forests, said that it was possible for a man to ride a horse full tilt through the woods. Perhaps, then, there was even enough room for a coach and three.

While Wahunsonacock's demand for a coach may have been serious, it is more likely he was mocking what he viewed as De La Warre's over-the-top demands that he, the chief of chiefs, bend his will to the English. According to narratives written by settlers, Wahunsonacock had a good sense of humor—he'd been known to twit the English in his negotiations with them more than once and was known to enjoy a good joke, even when it was at his own expense. De La Warre, though, saw nothing funny about Wahunsonacock's request. What Wahunsonacock could not have known was that the English were by that time determined that they would have to punish him or force him into submission in retaliation for what they were convinced was his role in the murder, two decades earlier, of Sir Walter Raleigh's lost colonists.[12] Indeed, the instructions given by the Virginia Company in London to Sir Thomas Gates in 1609 and still in force for Lord De La Warre made specific reference to the "slaughter [by Wahunsonacock] of Roanocke, uppon the first arrivall of our Colonie"[13] and told the captain general of Virginia that "if you find it not best to make him your prisoner yet you must make him your tributary."[14]

Used to getting his way and determined not to be lorded over by a man he considered a savage, De La Warre laid the olive branch aside, picked up his sword, and wreaked a terrible punishment on the natives of the Tidewater—

a punishment that gained the Indians' everlasting hatred—by ordering George Percy to chastise the Paspaheghs and Chickahominies, the tribes responsible for many of the attacks on settlers who wandered outside Jamestown's palisade. On the night of August 9, Percy led a force of seventy men in two barges up the James to the mouth of the Chickahominy. Landing there, Percy forced a bound Indian—he "Bastinaded him with [his] Truncheon and threatned to cutt of his head," Percy later bragged—to lead the invasion party to the village of Wowinchopunk, *weroance* of the Paspaheghs.[15] Outside the village, Percy formed his men into groups, cautioned them not to attack until he was in position with his colors, then made ready. At the signal—a pistol shot—the English "fell in upon them putt some fiftene or sixtene to the Sworde and Almoste all the reste to flyghte."[16] With the Indians on the run or slain, Percy ordered a drum sounded to signal the end of the attack. His blood-spattered men gathered around the colors, hauling with them a warrior, the queen of the Paspahegh people, and her children, all prisoners. Percy ordered the male prisoner beheaded on the spot but took the queen and her children on one of his barges, apparently intending to carry them back to Jamestown. Then, preparing to leave, Percy ordered his men to cut down all the growing corn and set fire to the village, to guarantee its usefulness to the natives was at an end.

What followed was one of the most brutal events in a war with more than enough brutality to go around. Here's what Percy said:

> And after we marched with the quene And her Children to our Boates ageine, where beinge noe soener well shipped my sowldiers did begin to murmur becawse the quene and her Children were spared. So upon the same A Cowncell beinge called itt was Agreed upon to putt the Children to deathe the which was effected by Throweinge them overboard and shoteinge owtt their Bryanes in the water yett for all this Crewellty the Sowldiers weare nott well pleased And I had mutche to doe To save the quenes lyfe for thatt Tyme.[17]

Before heading back to Jamestown with the Paspahegh queen, who must have been in shock by that time, Percy ordered James Davies—the man who had served as commander of the *Virginia* when she sailed in the fleet of 1609 and who later commanded at Fort Algernon—ashore with about half his soldiers. After chasing some attacking Indians into the forest, Davies marched unopposed downriver, burning crops and razing and torching any building he found, including the Indians' "howses Temples and Ildolles and amongste the reste A Spacious Temple cleane and neattly kept."[18] Then, apparently satisfied that he and his raiders had wreaked enough havoc for one day, Percy signaled for Davies and his men to rejoin the main party and all made their back way to Jamestown.

By that time, De La Warre was suffering from a variety of maladies in addition to his gout, and was, on his doctor's orders, living on one of the ships away from Jamestown's unhealthy and noxious vapors. According to Percy, once he and rest of the raiding party returned to the settlement, he and Davies rowed out to De La Warre's ship where, for some reason, Captain Davies had a private meeting with the captain general—a remarkable meeting, given the fact that Percy, Davies's superior, had been the man in charge of the raid on the Paspahegh village. In any event, Percy later reported that Davies told him that while De La Warre was happy that all the English were safe, he "yett Seamed to be discontente becawse the quene was spared ... and thatt itt was my Lords pleasure thatt we sholde see her dispatched." Percy went on to state that De La Warre told Davies that they should burn the queen alive but that, he (Percy) demurred, having "seene so mutche Bloodshedd thatt day now in my Cowldbloode I desyred to see noe more." Burning the queen alive, Percy said, would not be "fitteinge." However, he added, killing her "either by shott or Sworde to give her A quicker dispatche" would not be overly offensive.[19]

Davies then took the queen into the woods, where he killed her, ideally in some way that gave her a quick and relatively merciful end. Percy, a man who would have been aghast at even a hint that he was not a gentleman of the first order, took great pains to distance himself from the queen's murder and the brutal killing of her children. The facts are, however, that this supposed gentleman was unwilling—or unable—to stop his men when they voted to kill the queen's children by throwing them in the water and shooting their brains out. He did not bother to check with his commander, Lord De La Warre, when Davies reported that the captain general wanted the queen murdered. Worse, Percy went along with the order even though he admitted that while "Davis towlde me it was my Lords direction yett I am perswaded to the contrary."[20] Ultimately, the brutal behavior of the English under Percy's command may have gratified their desire for revenge, but it was extremely shortsighted. While the raid put an end to the native threat at Point Comfort (in fact, following the raid the Paspahegh people scattered to live with other tribal groups in Wahunsonacock's kingdom), it filled the Powhatans, who did not kill women and children taken in war, with implacable and understandable hatred.

Following the attack on the Paspaheghs, the undeclared war between the Indians and the *Tassantassas* grew even more violent and open. Sometime in September 1610, Captain Samuel Argall—by that time back at Jamestown after loading his vessel with cod off the coast of New England—led an attack on the Warraskoyack Indians, who were probably responsible for killing the settlers' pigs on Hog Island during the Starving Time. The Indians were on guard, however, and by the time Argall and his men crossed the James and landed near the Indian village, all the natives had fled, leaving Argall no way to take vengeance but to sack and burn the village and destroy the Indians' crops.

This fruitless exercise was followed by an attempt to search north of the falls for the minerals that some in the colony and in England still hoped would be their ticket to riches. At the same time, De La Warre ordered a group of men to travel by boat up the James to the falls, where they were to reestablish the outpost that had been previously abandoned by Lord De La Warre's brother, Francis West, who had then sailed back to England with a boatload of corn. When the men sent by the captain general—the group included Dowse, the drummer who had played and danced to entice the Indians into the surprise attack at Point Comfort—arrived at the village of Appomattoc, ruled by a *weroawansqua* (queen) with the unwieldy name Oppossuno-quonuske, they were lured ashore by natives, who invited them to rest and fill their bellies. The men were, Percy said, "easely thereunto induced and after intysed by the Salvages upp to their howses pretendeinge to feast them butt our men forgetteinge their Subtellies lyke greedy fooles accepted thereof more esteameing of A Little foode than their own lyves and safety."[21] This queen of the Appomattocs had, in an earlier time, been a friend of the English and had in fact brought water to Captain John Smith so that he could wash his hands when he was a "guest" of Wahunsonacock in 1608, before his rescue by Pocahontas. Now, though, no doubt having heard of the murder of the Paspahegh queen and her children, she was a siren luring the English into an Indian trap. Once the settlers were ashore, the Indians fell on them, "Slewe dyvers and wownded all the rest who w'hin towe dayes after also dyed."[22] The only man to survive was Dowse, the tricky taborer, who escaped by running to the boat, where he was able to use the rudder as a shield that protected him from a volley of arrows as he somehow managed to make his way downriver.

Despite all the bloodshed, Jamestown was, by late 1610, in better shape

than at any time since the English stepped ashore in the Chesapeake. With a
get-tough policy in place and roughly three hundred armed men in the settlement, including a goodly number of men who had survived the *Sea Venture*
shipwreck, the settlers were, for the most part, free from fear of Indian attack,
unless they left the confines of the settlement. There were still waves of illness
that killed many of the newcomers before they became "seasoned"—had an
opportunity to acclimate to the Virginia climate—and hunger still threatened the colony, forcing the English to rely on the natives to supplement their
always meager food supplies. For their part, the native people knew that the
settlers, despite their increasing numbers, were unprepared to feed themselves.
The Powhatan people, with a few exceptions, refused to trade, knowing or at
least hoping that famine would eventually take its toll on the *Tassantassas*, at
which time Indian warriors and force of arms could finish the job. Still, the
famine that threatened the colony in its earliest days had abated and the pace
of the dying slowed somewhat.

Sometime around Christmas 1610, Samuel Argall, enjoying a position of
ever-increasing importance in the colony, got permission from De La Warre
to attempt trade with the Patawomeke Indians. This group lived on the banks
of the Potomac, far enough from Jamestown, and from Wahunsonacock's
control, to risk his displeasure. Hence, they had been willing to trade when
John Smith was still in Virginia. Argall made his way to the village, where he
was met by Iopassus, a Patawomeke subchief, in company with Henry Spelman, the English boy who had been "traded" to Wahunsonacock by John
Smith in 1609, along with some copper, for the Indian village below the falls.
By this time, Spelman was fairly fluent in the Powhatan language, a skill that
Argall knew would serve the colony well. Iopassus, who was to prove a greedy
and self-serving fellow, let Argall know he was willing to trade food—and
Spelman, who must have felt like a pawn—for a good supply of copper. Argall jumped at the chance. By the time he sailed back to Jamestown, he had
four hundred bushels of corn, some peas, beans, a fair number of furs, and a
translator. The Indians and the English were all smiling when they parted
company, seeming the best of friends. In the final analysis, though, while the
victuals were important and Spelman was handy to have around, what was
more important was the fact that Argall had made Iopassus a fast friend,
gained his trust, and started a relationship that would ultimately pay divi-
dends that Argall could not have dreamed of.

Sometime during this period, John Rolfe, the merchant's son who had

John Smith's map of Virginia, reprinted in Edward Arber's *Travels and Works of John Smith*. Contrary to current practice, geographic north is to the right on this seventeenth-century map. The Virginia Sea is the Atlantic Ocean. (AUTHOR'S COLLECTION)

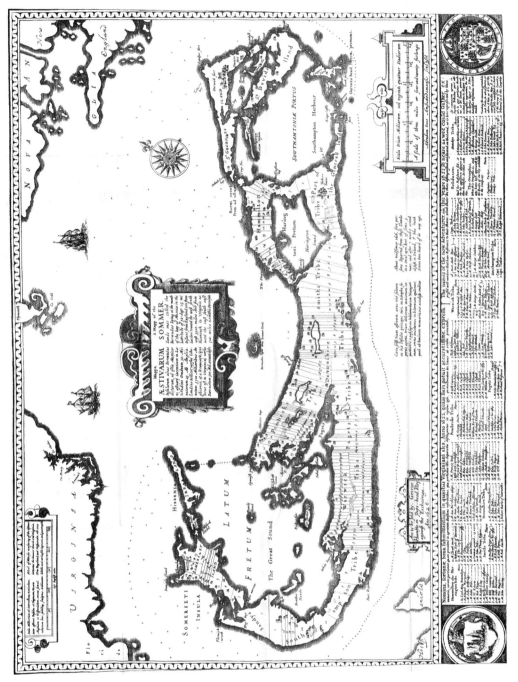

Map of Bermuda (called the Somers Islands by the English), by Richard Norwood, reprinted in *Memorials of Bermuda*. (AUTHOR'S COLLECTION)

THE PORTRAICTUER OF CAPTAYNE JOHN SMITH ADMIRALL OF NEW ENGLAND.

These are the Lines that shew thy Face; but those
That shew thy Grace and Glory, brighter bee:
Thy Faire-Discoueries and Fowle-Overthrowes
Of Salvages, much Civilliz'd by thee
Best shew thy Spirit; and to it Glory Wyn:
So, thou art Brasse without, but Golde within.

Portrait of Captain John Smith from an engraving by Simon van de Passe. This portrait is a detail from Smith's map of New England, reprinted in Edward Arber's *Travels and Works of John Smith*. (AUTHOR'S COLLECTION)

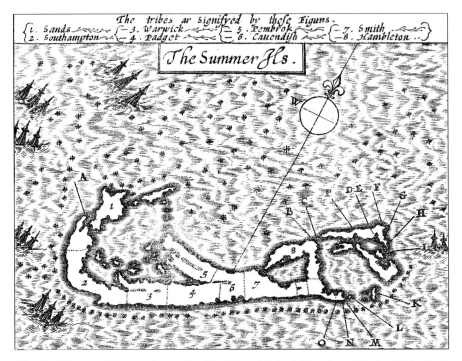

The tribes ar signifyed by thefe Figuns.
{ 1. Sands   [3. Warwick   [5. Pembrok   [7. Smith
{ 2. Southampton [4. Padget   [6. Cauendifh   [8. Hambleton

The Summer Hls.

John Smith's map of Bermuda, reprinted in Edward Arber's *Travels and Works of John Smith.*
(AUTHOR'S COLLECTION)

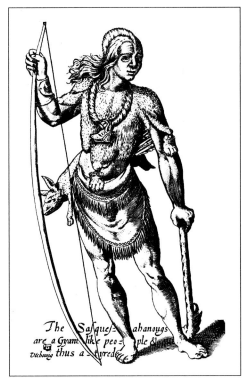

The Safque ahanougs are a Gyant like peo ple Vichowig thus attyred

A portrait of a Virginia Indian. Detail from John Smith's map of Virginia, reprinted in Edward Arber's *Travels and Works of John Smith.* (AUTHOR'S COLLECTION)

King Powhatan comands C: Smith to be slayne, his
daughter Pokahontas, beggs his life, his thankfullnes
and how he subiected 39 of their kings. reade y² history.
printed by Iames Reeve

The rescue of John Smith by
Pocahontas. Smith is the reclining
figure being protected by the
Indian maid kneeling by his side.
Powhatan is seated upper right.
Reprinted in Edward Arber's
Travels and Works of John Smith.
(AUTHOR'S COLLECTION)

POWHATAN
Held this state & fashion when Capt. Smith
was deliuered to him prijoner
1607

Appamattuck

Powhatan in state. Detail from
Smith's map of Virginia, reprinted
in Edward Arber's *Travels and
Works of John Smith.* (AUTHOR'S
COLLECTION)

The Abduction of Pocahontas, by Theodore de Bry. (PERMISSION BY THE VIRGINIA HISTORICAL SOCIETY, RICHMOND, VA.)

Portrait of George Percy,
by Herbert Smith.
(PERMISSION
BY THE VIRGINIA
HISTORICAL SOCIETY,
RICHMOND, VA.)

Portrait of Sir George
Somers, by Charles
Harris. (PERMISSION BY
THE VIRGINIA HISTORICAL
SOCIETY, RICHMOND, VA.)

Pocahontas, 1616. In this engraving by Simon van de Passe, the Indian princess is dressed as she may have been when presented at court. (PERMISSION BY THE VIRGINIA HISTORICAL SOCIETY, RICHMOND, VA.)

Sir Thomas Smythe, the Treasurer of the Virginia Company of London, in 1617. (PERMISSION BY THE VIRGINIA HISTORICAL SOCIETY, RICHMOND, VA.)

climbed aboard the *Sea Venture* with his pregnant wife and then had to bury his infant daughter, Bermudas, just a few days after her birth in the little camp on St. George's Island, had to stand by the side of another gaping grave in Jamestown when his wife died. Such deaths were so common that men routinely outlived two or three or more wives. Perhaps his first wife never fully recovered from what must have been a difficult childbirth in Bermuda. Perhaps she was one of the many colonists who succumbed to one of the diseases that ravaged the colonists during their first days or weeks in the Tidewater. In any case, her death, terrible as it must have been for John Rolfe, made it possible for him to remarry, an event that would later be linked to Argall's new friendship with Iopassus and be even more fortuitous for the English colony.

But that was in the future. In late 1610 and early 1611, while Argall was trading up the Potomac, Lord De La Warre was getting sicker by the day. By his own admission, he suffered from the "flux"—probably dysentery—and from gout and, he said, from scurvy, the deadly disease that usually afflicts mariners who are forced to eat a diet without sufficient vitamin C. At some point in late 1610, De La Warre, hoping his health would improve away from the swamps and marshes of Jamestown, moved his headquarters to the falls, where the colonists had finally been able to erect a fort at the site of what had been the Powhatan village. By early 1611, when the change of scenery did nothing to improve his health, De La Warre decided to leave Virginia for the island of Nevis in the Caribbean, where he could rest and take advantage of the island's medicinal hot springs. The man who had been named captain general for life of Virginia had been leader of the settlement for about six months.

De La Warre sailed from Jamestown on March 28, 1611. Amazingly, when he departed from the colony, he took roughly fifty men with him, a sizable entourage at a time when the little settlement could have made use of their services as soldiers or laborers. These men and De La Warre must have been expecting a pleasant voyage and something like an extended vacation in the West Indies. Instead, they were forced to weather their own nightmare at sea. Blown off course by unfriendly winds, the ship bearing De La Warre headed east for the Azores, where she finally arrived with most of the passengers almost dead from scurvy and heat prostration. De La Warre, who left Jamestown intending to return to Virginia after a period of recuperation in Nevis, instead landed in England on June 11. Not surprisingly, his return in ill health did little to boost confidence among English investors in the Virginia venture or among would-be settlers.

With Lord De La Warre's departure from Jamestown, George Percy once again took over the leadership of the settlement, but only briefly. In early May, Sir Thomas Dale arrived from London, accompanied by three hundred new settlers. Dale carried with him orders to serve both as marshal of Virginia, responsible for the colony's defense, and as De La Warre's deputy governor, replacing Sir Thomas Gates, who remained in London, trying to stir up interest in the settlement. Like most of the other leaders in Jamestown's early days, Dale was a professional soldier who had served with distinction in the Netherlands, the training ground for colonial service. Knighted for his services by King James in 1606, Dale was granted a leave from his duties on the continent and dispatched to Virginia where, with both De La Warre and Gates absent, he assumed the governorship.

Dale roared into the colony filled with righteousness and a willingness to impose discipline as it had never before been imposed in Virginia. After spending just a few hours inspecting conditions at Fort Algernon in the company of the well-seasoned, one-armed mariner Captain Christopher Newport, who brought him to the colony, Dale saw that the English "were not so provident, though once before bitten with hunger and penury, as to put corne into the ground," intending, instead, to rely on the food supply in the settlement's storehouse. According to Ralph Hamor, a survivor of the *Sea Venture* shipwreck who arrived with Gates and Somers and Strachey in 1610 and who ultimately became colonial secretary after William Strachey, Dale immediately put "all hands" at Point Comfort to planting corn sufficient to feed the colonists living at the point.[23]

A few days later, Dale moved on to Jamestown. After landing—it was a Sunday—he attended a church service and then immediately had William Strachey read his commission as deputy governor and marshal of the colony. Probably with a sense of relief, given his earlier experiences in the office, George Percy immediately resigned his commission, to be once again named captain of the fort.

At Jamestown, as at Point Comfort, Dale found "no corn set" other than a "few seeds put into a private garden or two."[24] Hamor was more colorful in his description, saying Dale found most of the settlers "bowling in the streetes."[25] Obviously, the orders to work that had been handed down by Gates and De La Warre had only limited effect on the indolent colonists. But

Dale soon fixed that situation, ordering the settlers to work on "the reparation of the falling church" (apparently the work on the chapel that had been described by Strachey had never been completed) along with a new "storehouse, a stable for our horses, a munition house, a powder house, a new well for the amending of the most unwholesome waters which the old afforded" and other projects, including a building for curing sturgeon, repairs to a brickhouse, a cattle barn, a blockhouse on the landward side of the narrow neck of land that at that time joined Jamestown Island to the mainland. In addition, Dale ordered the construction of a wharf outside the palisade's main portal, "private gardens for each man" and common gardens where "hemp and flax and such and other seeds" would be planted.[26] Even as this work was being undertaken, Dale—in accordance with his instructions from the Virginia Company in London—was planning to move the colony's headquarters away from Jamestown with its unhealthy conditions. He put the settlers at Point Comfort and at the main settlement to "necessary workes, as felling of Timber, repairing their houses, ready to fall upon their heads, and providing pales, postes and railes to impaile his purposed new Towne."[27] Already, the new leader was planning to expand the colony by constructing a strong town upriver, away from the swamps that surrounded Jamestown.

By that time, William Strachey, acting on instructions given to both Sir Thomas Gates and Lord De La Warre, had written at least a rough draft of the first formal legal code for the Virginia settlement. This code, *Lawes Divine, Morall and Martiall,* was quickly expanded and honed by Sir Thomas Dale. In the process, the legal code was given teeth or, more properly, fangs. Draconian in terms of its scope and aims, it replaced the guarantee of all rights, liberties, and immunities of all trueborn Englishmen that had been granted to the colonists in the first two colonial charters and established something very akin to martial law in the colony. Anything from murder to thievery of an ear of corn to blasphemy and disrespect to any colonial officer was punishable by death. Lesser offenses merited public whippings or worse. The theft of a shovel was punishable by a public whipping, and any man or woman who dared to discard dirty laundry water within the fort or within forty feet of the palisade or who dared "to doe the necessities of nature" within a quarter mile of the fort would be whipped "since by these unmanly, slothfull, and loathesome immodesties, the whole fort may bee choaked, and poisoned with ill aires."[28] This legal code, viewed as harsh even by English settlers who were accustomed to the brutal justice practiced in their homeland, forced the colonists to toe the line. They may have grumbled, but they obeyed, particularly after Dale first enforced the new laws. Several men who had been captured after fleeing the colony to join the Indians were executed. According to Percy, "some he appointed to be hanged, some burned, some to be broken upon the wheel, others to be [burned at the stake], and some to be shot to death." A handful of men who robbed the common storehouse were "bownd faste unto trees" and left there to starve to death, all, Percy said, "To terrefy the rest for Attempteinge the Lyke."[29]

Dale also turned his martial attention to the native peoples, without any of the softness of heart that both Gates and De La Warre had exhibited. Within just a few days of landing at Jamestown, and apparently without any provocation, Dale set out with about a hundred armed men to attack the Nansemonds near Point Comfort. The Indians mounted a spirited defense. Dale was wounded by an arrow that just missed his eye; Francis West, the cowardly brother of Lord De La Warre who had abandoned the colony in the Starving Time and returned, most likely with Dale, was shot in the thigh; and John Martin, the colonist who left Virginia in 1608 and then returned on the *Falcon* to bedevil John Smith in 1609, suffered a wound in the arm. While the Indians were able to wound a few of the colonists, they had no real chance against the English who, for the first time, were all protected by body armor that Dale had obtained from the armory in the Tower of London and carried to Virginia. Scores of native warriors were killed or wounded. The rest were terrified when their arrows failed to hurt the Englishmen. The Nansemond village was burned, crops were destroyed.

This raid was followed by others, apparently without any excuse other than to teach the Powhatan people to fear the English and to flee their lands. In late June or early July, Dale planned an excursion to the falls to investigate conditions or perhaps just to chastise the natives. A week or so before the excursion, Wahunsonacock, who had heard of the plan, sent a message to Jamestown, telling Dale not to trespass in his lands and to return two prisoners, apparently taken in an earlier raid. The chief also hinted that if the English came to the falls, he would cripple them with "drink"—apparently poison—and then kill them. Dale took the threat as a joke. Undeterred, he set out, without returning the two prisoners, and made his way upriver. While camped, the English heard a strange noise coming from a nearby cornfield. According to the Reverend Alexander Whitaker, a volunteer missionary in Virginia, the noise was "like an Indian 'hup hup' with an 'Oho Oho.'" Some of the English said they saw an Indian run into their camp, leap over the fire, and disappear into the corn while making the same noise. "At the which," Whitaker said, "our men were confoundedly amazed." They were so confused, in fact, that they grabbed their muskets by their barrels instead of the stocks to shoot at the already vanished Indian.[30]

The confusion lasted about fifteen minutes. When the English returned to their senses, they said it felt as if they were waking from a dream. It's tempting to believe that Wahunsonacock somehow managed to managed to slip a hallucinogenic herb to the English, perhaps spiking their food. However, what the Englishmen experienced may well have been no more than a kind of group hysteria, caused by the very real fear and uncertainty that can strike even the bravest and most rational of men at night in a strange place, surrounded by unseen enemies making strange noises.

At about the same time as all this action was taking place, a Spanish ship on a spying mission from Cuba entered the Chesapeake Bay. This ship was under the command of Don Diego de Molina, an adventurer who went ashore not far from Point Comfort, accompanied by one of his officers and a pilot, a man named Francis Lembry who was, it would turn out, a renegade Englishman masquerading as a Spaniard. On shore, the spies were surprised by a party from the fort under the command of Captain James Davies, the former commander of the *Virginia* of the 1609 fleet, and placed in irons. After Molina convinced the English on shore that his ship had simply strayed off course and that all he wanted was a safe anchorage, an English pilot was rowed out to the Spanish ship to take it upriver to Jamestown while Molina, his officer, and the pilot—who was unfamiliar with the Chesapeake—remained in English custody. As James Davies and the other English on the shore watched in amazement, the Spanish caravel hoisted sail and raced out of the Chesapeake for the open ocean. Enraged and surprised, Davies marched his prisoners to Jamestown, where they were clapped in irons and where, in fact, Molina would remain a prisoner for five years, spying all the while and smuggling reports to his handlers—in one case by passing a letter to a "gentleman from Venice" (no one knows who he was) who carried the message in the sole of his shoe.[31] The immediate effect of Molina's capture, however, was that the colonists were even more alarmed than usual at the thought of a fleet of Spanish caravels with their triangular, lateen sails moving into the Chesapeake to wipe out the English colony.

By mid-August 1611, Dale had formulated plans he hoped would guarantee the success of the English colony in Virginia. These plans, outlined in a letter written to Lord Salisbury, called for the expansion of the settlement to include four towns in addition to Jamestown: one—a "spacious and commodious town for a chief commander"—at Point Comfort; the second at a spot near Werowocomoco, Wahunsonacock's former headquarters; the third, to be called Henricus, in honor of Prince Henry, not far from the falls near the site of present-day Richmond; and the fourth about ten miles north of the falls. He also proposed a bold and ambitious—if somewhat foolhardy— plan to recruit some two thousand new settlers from among the men and women (and children) sentenced to death in the next nine months in England.[32] Such a plan, he promised, would "render the whole country unto His Majesty" and would "so overmaster the subtle, mischievous Great Powhatan (Wahunsonacock) that I should leave him either no room in his country to harbor in or draw him to a firm association with ourselves."[33]

While Dale was writing his letter, George Percy, the on-again, off-again leader of the Jamestown colony, was busy crafting a letter to his "singuler good Lord and Brother The Earle of Northumberland." This letter, saved in the Northumberland papers, tells a great deal about George Percy's view of himself, and about English society in the still danger-fraught wilderness of Virginia.

Percy humbly regretted that his service in Virginia during the last year "hath not bin a little Chargdgable [expensive] unto your Honnor" and went on to beg Northumberland to believe that he had not wasted his money. Now, though, the younger Percy found it necessary to ask his older brother for more financial help because of his need as "Govournour of James Towne to keep a continuall and dayly Table for Gentlemen of fashion aboute me." To this letter he attached bills that amounted to almost £75 ... or about $50,000 in today's money. But that was not all. Percy also ordered, at his brother's expense, several articles of clothing he deemed necessary to live in style in Jamestown. These included silk stockings and garters, gold lace, ribbons for "shoestringes," gold buttons, and a Dutch beaver hat, for a total of more than £14.[34]

Sometime around August 20, 1611, the two letters—Dale's and Percy's— were carried onboard a ship bound for England. This same ship also carried William Strachey, the *Sea Venture* survivor and author of the stirring account of the shipwreck, returning home after almost two years in the new worlds of Bermuda and Virginia. Strachey carried his own important papers—a copy of the *Lawes Divine, Morall and Martiall* that he would ultimately publish in London, and the notes for a lengthy book, *The Historie of Travaile into Virginia Britannia*, which would be published much later and display Strachey's strengths as an observer of nature and of the native people of the Tidewater. Strachey hoped, must have believed, in fact, that his services in Virginia would be rewarded by the Virginia Company and that, finally, he would find some financial ease. Perhaps, since it is believed he sailed on a ship named *Prosperous,* he saw an omen of good things to come in his native land.

However, before the ship dropped down the James, a longboat from Point Comfort arrived at the settlement with the frightening news that a fleet of as many nine ships had arrived in the Chesapeake. Since three of the ships had the triangular lateen-style sails that marked many Spanish vessels, the fleet was thought to belong to England's longtime enemy, come to attack the settlement. At the news, Jamestown's church bells rang, drums sounded, and men rushed to take up weapons. Even as the settlers prepared to repulse the Spanish invaders, word arrived that the fleet was English, bearing Sir Thomas Gates, the *Sea Venture* survivor, back to Jamestown to serve as the colony's governor. Gates brought with him several hundred new settlers along with arms, tools, food, and other supplies. He also brought firm orders to move the colony's headquarters from its original location upriver to some spot less vulnerable to Spanish attack.

Once Gates arrived in the settlement, Dale resigned his job as governor, reverting to his role as marshal of Virginia. The colony was soon reorganized under Gates's leadership, and plans were immediately laid, in accordance with Virginia Company instructions, to establish a new colonial headquarters near the falls. In early September, Dale set out by boat for the satellite settlement that would be named Henricus (today Henrico), while a company of laborers and soldiers under the command of Captain Edward Brewster headed overland. During the march, Brewster and his company were attacked several times by natives led by a chieftain named Nemattanow (sometimes Munetute), but called Jack of the Feathers by the Englishmen because he typically entered the field of battle "covered over wᵗh feathers and Swans wings fastened unto his showlders as thowghe he meante to flye."[35] Ultimately, Brewster and his men made their way to the site of the new township. Under Dale's stern leadership, steady progress was made at Henrico even in the face of steady Indian attacks that wounded and killed many of the colonists who stepped outside a hastily constructed palisade.

During this period, Sir Thomas Gates ran the colony in Jamestown with a much firmer hand than he had displayed with the *Sea Venture* survivors in Bermuda. Perhaps some of Dale's harshness had rubbed off on Sir Thomas or perhaps the rigors of colonial life had convinced him that justice had to be sharp if the colonists were to survive. In any event, when Indians came to Jamestown to trade, Gates, convinced they had come to the settlement to spy or to steal, had some arrested and put to death "for A Terrour to the Reste to cawse them to desiste from their subtell practyces."[36]

By early 1612, as the English colony in Virginia achieved something like stability despite continuing and often brutal conflicts between the natives and the settlers, George Percy was determined to return to England. By that time he was ill, almost certainly with malaria. Just as certainly, he must have been heartily sick of life in Virginia where, he must have known, while he would be allowed to serve as interim governor if no other qualified man was available, he would never be given the position or recognition he felt he deserved. On April 22, 1612, after spending almost five years in the Tidewater, Percy set sail from Jamestown on a ship named the *Trial*. The voyage home must not have been easy, for the *Trial* did not drop anchor in England for twelve weeks, sometime around July 21. While Percy's vessel was anchored in the port of Dover, the former governor met with Samuel Argall, now the admiral of Virginia in place of Christopher Newport, who had left the service of the Virginia Company earlier that year.

At that time, Argall had just been given command of the *Treasurer*, a hefty frigate of 130 tons, armed with fourteen guns. According to Percy, the two men stayed together a few days in Dover, apparently to keep Argall company as the newly appointed admiral waited for unfavorable winds to change. The two men must have frequented some waterfront tavern or inn where they swapped tales about life in Virginia before Percy, weak and sick after his time in Virginia and his trying sea voyage, mounted his horse and rode to London. At about the same time, the *Treasurer* hoisted anchor and made for Jamestown, where Samuel Argall would, almost on the spur of the moment, kidnap the paramount chief Wahunsonacock's daughter and, in the process, guarantee the survival of the English colony.

II

To Populate and Plant the Islands

By mid-1612, when George Percy, the former governor of Jamestown, returned to his native England and Samuel Argall set sail for the Chesapeake to keep what was to be a history-making rendezvous with Wahunsonacock's daughter Pocahontas, Virginia was no longer the sole focus of English colonial efforts in the New World. The Bermudas, once terrifying to mariners, were becoming familiar to the English as the Somers Islands. In the process, the chain of tiny islands scattered across the face of the Atlantic roughly three thousand miles from England was transformed in the English imagination from a dangerous and frightening place to an Edenic spot, ripe and ready for profitable English settlement.

Until that time only the Spanish had evinced anything like real interest in the island chain that lay almost athwart the route the great treasure ships took on their return from the West Indies. Even they saw the islands only as a potential refuge for passing vessels in need of food and water. By 1612, however, the pamphleteering Reverend William Crashaw, the same churchman who wrote and preached so optimistically about the Jamestown venture in 1607 and again in 1609, was able to wax almost poetical in writing about Bermuda. Prior to their "full discovery" by Sir Thomas Gates and Sir George Somers, the islands, Crashaw said, had been seen by the world "as inaccessible, so not inhabitable, but so fearful, hideous, and hateful as it seemed a place abandoned of God and man, and given up to the devil's power and possession . . . a very hell upon earth rather than a place for man to dwell in." Thanks to Somers and Gates and the others who survived in Bermuda following the loss of the *Sea Venture*, Crashaw said, it was now known that the Bermudas were a place "so goodly, so rich, so plentiful, so healthy, and so temperate . . . a habitation of such safety and security . . . , of such plenty of all things for life and of so good temper for health, and fraught with so many rich commodities for satisfaction of the adventurers, as for the present they be even as a new life and a seminary [training ground or place for nurturing settlers] to Virginia." The Bermudas, he added, would "prove a matter of greater consequence than most men think of, and of more worth than any islands or continent discovered in our age."[1]

This transformation of the Bermudas started roughly two years earlier, in the fall of 1610, when the *Sea Venture* survivor Sir Thomas Gates arrived in England on board the *Blessing*. The former governor of Virginia had returned to London to report on the state of affairs in Jamestown, to advise officials of the Virginia Company of London about the *Sea Venture*'s accident, and to bolster support for the Jamestown venture.

Not long after his return to England, Sir Thomas would have made his way to the company headquarters at Sir Thomas Smythe's mansion.[2] Gates, of course, was no stranger to the rambling mansion on Philpott Lane. In the months leading up to the departure of the *Sea Venture* fleet in 1609, he must have been a frequent visitor to the company offices as he checked on the progress of obtaining supplies and recruiting sailors and settlers. He would have been familiar with the souvenirs displayed in the quarters, including an "Esquimaux" canoe (it was undoubtedly presented as a gift to Smythe by some early English voyager who sailed in search of the fabled Northwest Passage) that hung suspended from the ceiling of the home's great hall, a silent reminder of dashed hopes and unrealized dreams.

Of course, on his earlier visits, the old soldier must have been filled with excitement and expectation as he thought of the adventures he would face as one of the leaders of the greatest colonial expedition ever mounted in England. Smythe and Samuel Purchas and the other leaders of the Virginia Company would surely have treated him with all the respect due a man who had earned his knighthood as a brave soldier in the service of his queen. He was, after all, one of the men the London investors had trusted to guarantee the success of the great Virginia venture. In 1610, however, after Gates returned to England, he came to Smythe's home not as a conquering hero but as the bearer of bad news, terrible news, not just about the wreck of the *Sea Venture* but also about the horrors of the Starving Time and of the deaths of hundreds of the men and women who had been dispatched to the New World by the leaders of the company.

While there are no reports of what Gates said to the Virginia Company adventurers who gathered to hear his report firsthand—a group that no doubt included Smythe and the Earl of Southampton and perhaps Sir Richard Powle, the man who invested £50 in the Virginia fleet in 1609—it is not difficult to imagine their shock and dismay as Sir Thomas told of the *Sea Venture*'s trials, the murder and mutinies, the necessary execution of Henry Paine in Bermuda, and, worst of all, the ghastly conditions he and other shipwreck survivors had found waiting on the banks of the Chesapeake.

Even before Gates's return to England, some report to the company had probably been made by Francis West, Lord De La Warre's younger brother who fled from Jamestown in the midst of the Starving Time, stealing a boatload of Indian corn that might have kept a few settlers alive in the process. If, indeed, Francis West had made some sort of report to the company, he would certainly have been careful to protect his reputation (and his skin) by avoiding anything like a true recounting either of conditions in the colony or of his own cowardly decision to abandon the starving colonists in Jamestown.

If there was any good news in what Gates had to report—and the adventurers surely would have wanted some good news—it was in his tale of what he and the other *Sea Venture* survivors discovered in the Bermudas. Just as it is easy to imagine Smythe and Southampton and Powle and other adventurers listening aghast as Gates told his harrowing tale, it is easy to picture them leaning forward in their seats, listening intently as he spoke of the felicity and fertility of the islands they had previously known, if at all, only because of their fearsome reputation. At that time, though, it seems none in the company publicly expressed any interest in colonizing the Bermudas, perhaps because Smythe and the others were too busy toting up the huge cost of the disappointing Jamestown venture. If any of the London adventurers heard what Gates had to say about Bermuda and thought of risking any more of their money across the Atlantic, they appear to have kept their thoughts to themselves.

In fact, even as Gates met with the adventurers in London, the company was seriously considering cutting its losses in Virginia, simply abandoning the

Jamestown colony. By this point, Smythe and the other investors in the colonial venture had hoped that profits would be rolling in and that further investments would not be necessary. Instead, "finding the smallnesse of that returne which they hoped should have defrayed the charge [cost] of a new supply," the company "entered into a deep consultation and propounded amongst themselves whether it were fit to enter into a new Contribution, or to . . . send for [the colonists in Virginia] and to abandon the action." The concerned company officials "adjured" Gates to "deal plainly with them" and made him swear a "solemn and a sacred oath" to tell them the unvarnished truth about conditions in the Virginia colony.[3] While Gates certainly described the horrible conditions in Jamestown, he also argued that the colony could be profitable, given time and financial support, as a source of valuable commodities, including sugar, wine, sturgeon, timber, rice, and iron. Perhaps he also reminded the adventurers that those who were still alive in Jamestown had crossed the Atlantic and faced terrible difficulties because they had been promised support by the company's financial backers and that to abandon them—and the colony—would be a betrayal. Whatever he said, he was ultimately able to count his journey to England a success: the adventurers promised to send fresh supplies of settlers and provisions—promises they lived up to when they dispatched Sir Thomas Dale and, later, Sir Thomas Gates himself for a second stint in Jamestown.

Meanwhile, at some point soon after his return to London, Gates delivered William Strachey's *True Reportory*, the long letter recounting the story of the *Sea Venture* shipwreck and the events that followed in Bermuda and Jamestown, to its addressee, whoever that "Excellent Lady" was. Though there is no way of determining for sure, it is thought that the recipient may have been Lady Sara Smythe, the wife of the treasurer of the Virginia Company of London. If that is the case, Gates may well have given the letter to Smythe when he first visited the company headquarters soon after his return to England.

While the letter seems to have been written as "private" correspondence, Strachey would have known—indeed, he would have fully expected—that it would be read by Sir Thomas Smythe. He would also have expected that Smythe would pass the letter on to other Virginia investors. Given Strachey's ties to the London literary scene, he also must have hoped most heartily that his writing would eventually be read by his friends and acquaintances, including Ben Jonson and Michael Drayton. It is easy enough to picture Strachey in the wilds of Virginia imagining his literary reputation soaring after the crowd at the Mermaid Tavern read his account of the *Sea Venture*'s sinking. And, in fact, it was a common practice for colonists and adventurers and travelers to write letters to patrons and friends knowing and intending the letters to be published. Captain John Smith's first report on conditions in Jamestown, known as the *True Relation,* carried the note that it was "Written by a Gentlemen of the said Collony [Virginia], to a worshipfull friend of his in England."[4] This seemingly private letter was in fact published in August 1609, placed on sale at the same time, and widely read by an audience hungry for news from the New World.

While Strachey's *True Reportory* was not published until 1625, when it was included by the Reverend Samuel Purchas in his weighty collection of travel narratives, *Purchas his pilgrimes,* it is safe to assume that the letter passed from reader to reader and that copies of Strachey's report were made and circulated. There is certainly no denying there would have been an audience avid to read what happened to the Virginia fleet that had departed with such fanfare and such high hopes in 1609. One who would have snatched up a copy of the letter at his first opportunity was the Earl of Southampton, a heavy investor in the Virginia Company and other colonial ventures and a fairly regular visitor to Smythe's house.

Southampton—born Henry Wriothesley (pronounced to rhyme with "grisly") on October 6, 1573, in Sussex—counted among his friends and patrons some of England's most powerful men and women. Succeeding to his title in 1581 at the age of eight, following the death of his ne'er-do-well father, Southampton became a royal ward under the care of William Cecil, Lord Burghley, one of the most powerful peers in England and a favorite of Queen Elizabeth. Educated at Cambridge and at Gray's Inn, like many of England's most powerful men, Southampton was presented at court at the age of seventeen and quickly became a favorite of the queen and of the powerful royal favorite, Robert Devereux, the Earl of Essex.

Southampton, like most men of his class and age, was active in wars against the Spanish. He accompanied Essex to Cádiz, the Azores, and Ireland. He served, of course, in the House of Lords and was an active investor not only in the Virginia Company but in the East India Company. Perhaps his greatest claim to fame, however, was his patronage of some of the leading literary lights of his times, including—and most notably—William Shakespeare.

In 1509, Southampton, than about twenty-five years of age, was thrown in

1598

the Tower of London following his quick, secret marriage to Elizabeth Vernon, one of Queen Elizabeth's ladies–in–waiting. He soon gained his freedom thanks to the good offices of Sir Robert Cecil (later Lord Salisbury), William Cecil's son.

Southampton later got in much more serious trouble when he became involved in the abortive Essex plot to overthrow the queen. This plot was hatched in early 1601 after Essex—a headstrong, egotistical man whose notable good looks and charm far outweighed his good judgment—lost favor with the queen, in large part because he failed miserably when he was dispatched to Ireland to quell a rebellion led by Hugh O'Neill, the Earl of Tyrone. Finding himself on the outs with the aging queen, Essex disobeyed orders to remain in Ireland and stole back to England. Without bothering to wash himself or change his traveling clothes, he rushed to Nonesuch Palace, where he forced his way into the queen's privy chamber to plead his case. Stunned by his effrontery, the queen ordered him confined to his mansion, where he began conspiring with a group of young gallants who hoped to force Queen Elizabeth to remove the Cecils—William and Robert—from power and to invest the leadership of government in Essex and his followers. By early February 1601, the plot was ready for hatching. On the night of February 8, Southampton and some other men of noble birth, all backers of Essex, paid Shakespeare's players at the Globe a bonus of forty shillings to stage a revival of *Richard II*, the drama built around the deposition of an unpopular king.[5] It was their delusional hope that the performance would arouse the people of the city to join the rebellion. It did not work. When, on the following day, Essex and his followers took to the streets, they found themselves alone except for soldiers loyal to Elizabeth. Essex was captured, imprisoned, and ultimately beheaded. According to Sir Walter Ralegh (who would later lose his own head, with much less reason), Essex was so loved by the queen that he might have survived even this foray into treason had he not, shortly before his arrest, said that the "Queen's conditions [for his return to the court and favor] were as crooked as her carcase."[6] This insult—Elizabeth was old enough to be Essex's mother—was more than her pride could bear.

Southampton himself was arrested, and with good reason since he had unwisely allowed the conspirators to gather for strategy sessions at Drury House, his dwelling. Southampton, along with Essex, was assigned the duty of actually capturing the queen and, it seems, the two may well have been prepared to commit regicide. Southampton could well have lost his head. Instead, he lived. Tried for treason in 1601, he had to forfeit his titles and lands and was condemned to death, but this sentence was later commuted to life imprisonment, at least in part because he did not, at that time, have an heir, and the queen would not have wanted to kill the last male in a line of peers of the realm.

Held in the Tower of London for two years, Southampton, like Sir Thomas Smythe, was freed when James I took the throne. Under the new king, Wriothesley quickly regained his titles and lands and took his place at court, where he was made a Knight of the Garter. By 1603, Southampton was enough in favor with the crown—and close enough to William Shakespeare—that he staged a performance of *Love's Labour's Lost*, put on by Richard Burbage and his company, to which Shakespeare belonged, as an entertainment for theater-loving Queen Anne.

It certainly seems likely, given Southampton's involvement with the Virginia Company (an involvement that would have whetted his interest in Strachey's *True Reportory*) and given his links to Shakespeare and the theater, that the earl would have read Strachey's letter and, soon after reading it, would have passed it on to Shakespeare. There's no doubt that Shakespeare would have been interested in the tale if for no other reason than it would have made engrossing reading. He may—though there's no proof of this—have known Strachey personally. Perhaps he had met the poet and theater habitué at the Blackfriars Theatre, where Strachey lived for a time before leaving for Virginia and where Shakespeare would have visited Burbage, a resident of Blackfriars and the Bard's most famous actor. At the very least, it seems logical that Shakespeare would have known of Strachey and been intrigued by his tale of the *Sea Venture* shipwreck.

What is known, with a fair degree of certainty, is that by mid-1611, Shakespeare was captivated by the story of the *Sea Venture* shipwreck and by the tale of the Isle of Devils. By that time, either at his home in Stratford or in his lodgings in London, the playwright was putting quill to parchment, creating the play he would call *The Tempest* and, in the process, making full use of Strachey's narrative.

In June 1611, at about the same time that Shakespeare started writing *The Tempest* and Sir Thomas Dale came roaring into Virginia with his love of discipline and hatred of laziness, Matthew Somers would likely have made his way to Smythe's mansion in London from Lyme, where he'd just buried the gutless, heartless body of his uncle, the admiral. Sunburned from his long months at sea and from his time in the Bermudas, walking with that rolling gait, almost a swagger, that mariners seem naturally to adopt on land, Matthew undoubtedly cut quite a figure as he pushed his way along the narrow, crowded streets of the old city not far from Tower Hill. Like Sir Thomas Gates before him, Matthew would have been called upon to report on the loss of the *Sea Venture* and the situation both in the Bermudas and in Jamestown. He certainly would have been grilled about his uncle's death.

From later events, though, it seems that by the time Matthew Somers returned to London, the Virginia Company's officers, thanks to Sir Thomas Gates's report and to William Strachey's letter, were starting to recognize the Bermudas as a likely spot to establish an English colony that might return them profits they had certainly not found in Virginia. What Matthew had to report could only have heightened their interest. Perhaps he carried with him a copy of his uncle's Bermudan map so he could point to where the *Sea Venture* survivors established their little camp just above St. Catherine's Beach as he told of the hogs and tortoises and birds on the islands, of the fish that seemed almost willing to jump into cookpots, and of the seeds his uncle had planted that had sprouted in a matter of days. Whatever he said, he surely captured the attention and imaginations of Smythe and the other investors.

Matthew Somers was not the only man in England talking about how wonderful and welcoming the Bermudas had proved to be to the shipwreck survivors. Within days of their arrival in England, even as Sir George's body was being lowered into its grave, the twenty or so sailors who manned the *Patience* on her journey from Jamestown to Bermuda and then on to Lyme—also men who had spent ten months in the Bermudas—were telling their friends and family members and tavern maids and anybody they could find about the beautiful islands with their white-sand beaches and deep blue waters and about the plentiful game and fish and the fine weather. To those who listened, it must have sounded like a paradise. As the "home minded company" told of their adventures in Bermuda, one of the island colony's first governors later reported, "it came to be apprehended by some of the Virginia Company, how beneficiall this Island might be for that colony of thers."[7]

Even as Sir Thomas Smythe and Southampton and others at the helm of the company "apprehended" the value of the Bermudas as a potential colony, they knew it would be difficult to convince English adventurers to risk money on yet another colonial venture. English investors were, by this time, growing tired of throwing good money after bad in Virginia. They'd been willing to finance the first venture in 1606, then to back the *Sea Venture* fleet in 1609, to pay Lord De La Warre's expenses the following year, and to finance further shipments of supplies and colonists at Gates's urging, but they were disheartened by constant bad news from across the sea and by the lack of anything even resembling a financial reward. After all, they'd been promised gold and pearls, and all they'd gotten were a few shiploads of clapboard and soap ash and worthless ore. So bad was the situation that the Virginia Company was unable to collect subscriptions (contributions) that had been promised—but never paid—by adventurers in exchange for shares of company stock.

Yet the company's leaders—men described as "divers of eminencye and ranck"—could not simply discount Bermuda out of hand. Instead, mindful of "the aydefull vicinitie of the place [Bermuda] to that colony of thers . . . [they] began not only to hearken to the reportes, but at last to propound a course of experiment" to settle Bermuda.[8] By the fall of 1611, many of the Virginia Company's most influential leaders and wealthiest backers— including Smythe, Southampton, Sir Edwin Sandys, and the famous Jacobean diarist John Chamberlain—were busily putting together plans to send colonists to the Bermudas.

At this time, the leaders of the Virginia Company, little concerned with such niceties as geography, considered the Bermudas part of Virginia, at least as far as colonization was concerned. These company leaders knew that if they wanted to sustain Virginia and take advantage of any opportunities of-fered by the Bermudas, the Virginia Company would need more money and more willing settlers. To whip up interest in the Virginia colony, including Bermuda, the company's leaders—guided by Smythe, the masterful propa-gandist who promoted the 1609 voyage—once again urged friendly preach-ers and writers to produce sermons and pamphlets singing the praises of Virginia. Among others, Robert Johnson, the pamphleteer who had written *Nova Britannia* in praise of Virginia not long before the *Sea Venture* and the other ships of the hurricane fleet set sail in 1609, swung into action yet again, writ-ing a long-winded treatise entitled *The New Life of Virginia*. This report on "the former sucesse and present estate of that plantation" is pure public relations, touting Virginia without mentioning any of the difficulties that still beset the colonists.[9]

Ultimately, though, it was Gates and Matthew Somers and William Stra-chey and other survivors of the *Sea Venture* shipwreck who carried good news about Bermuda to England who provided the real spark needed to reignite the fires of colonialism, and a willingness to invest, among the adventurers in London and across England. Where once Virginia and the Chesapeake were the hot topics of conversation on the docks of London and Plymouth and in waterfront taverns and in the London Stock Exchange, the dreamers of big profits and new opportunities now spoke of the place they knew variously as the Summer Isles or Somers Isles or the Bermudaes.

In the midst of this new excitement about the distant islands he knew so well, William Strachey, the bankrupt lawyer, would-be wordsmith, and former secretary of the Jamestown colony, returned to England. Strachey had every reason to be hopeful about his future when he stepped ashore, in Plymouth or perhaps in London. His prospects were certainly better than when he had boarded the *Sea Venture* more than two years earlier. He had performed well as colonial secretary in Virginia, attracting the attention of Sir Thomas Gates and Lord De La Warre and, no doubt, of leaders of the Virginia Company in London. He had written the lively *True Reportory* about the loss of the *Sea Venture* and of events in Bermuda and Virginia, and he would have expected his writing to bring him to the attention of even more powerful men in England. He had contributed—at least through his skill as a penman and compiler—to the creation of the *Lawes Divine, Morall and Martiall,* promulgated to bring order to the disorderly Virginia colony. He was, even as he disembarked, in the early stages of writing what would become *The Historie of Travaile into Virginia Britannia,* a lengthy history of the English presence in Virginia. He had every reason to expect this book would add to his reputation. Sad to say, even as the *Prosperous* came to anchor and William Strachey climbed down to the dock, one of his creditors, a man named Jasper Tien, was preparing to take Strachey to court to recover £30 he had lent the impoverished Strachey four years earlier. In fact, despite Strachey's hopes and best efforts, his financial woes were destined to continue almost unabated for the rest of his life.

Of course, Strachey had no way of knowing what awaited him in London. Perhaps, as he made his way from the *Prosperous* to his lodgings in Blackfriars, he heard talk of the Somers Isles and realized that the desolate yet lovely place where he and the other *Sea Venture* survivors had found succor after their shipwreck was about to be populated by Englishmen and -women. Or perhaps he heard talk of a new play, *The Tempest,* written by William Shakespeare, about a storm and a shipwreck. Certainly someone in Blackfriars—that combination residential district and theater that was home to Richard Burbage and so many other actors and playwrights—would have told the newly returned Virginia colonist of the play and of the role his letter had played in its creation.

The Tempest had its official debut on November 1, 1611, right about the time that Strachey disembarked in England. How fitting and just it would have been if Strachey had been invited to attend the play's first performance when it was staged before James I and the court at Whitehall Palace's Banqueting Hall. But of course Strachey would not have received an invitation from the privy council to sit in the audience when the play was presented at Whitehall. Those invitations were reserved for members of court and highborn visitors. And so, even if Strachey was in London, he most certainly was not in attendance at Whitehall when King James and Queen Anne took their seats beneath the cloth of state on a raised platform at one end of the rectangular banqueting hall. He was not one who listened as the play started with what Shakespeare had described as "a tempestuous noise of thunder and lightning" followed by the voice of a ship's master urging the boatswain to put the mariners to work to keep the storm-tossed ship, the setting for the play's first scene, from running aground.[10]

James I, a man who was every bit as scholarly as he was physically ungainly, may himself have read Strachey's narrative. He certainly would have been aware of the gist of Strachey's letter, touching as it did at the heart of a colonial venture that was expected to provide funds for the king's badly depleted royal treasury. As he listened to the play's dialogue and watched the fantastic story unfold on the raised platform at one end of the rectangular banqueting hall that had been renovated in 1609, he may well have noted the striking similarities between Strachey's letter and Shakespeare's comedy.

In *The Tempest*, a fleet of ships carrying Alonso, the king of Naples, is on its way to Naples when (just like the *Sea Venture* fleet) the vessels are battered and dispersed by a terrible storm. Alonso's ship, the flagship of the small armada, is separated from the balance of the fleet and, again like the *Sea Venture*, is assumed lost. The other ships in Alonso's fleet make it safely to port. So did the other ships that set sail with the *Sea Venture* in 1609, save, of course, the unnamed and ill-fated ketch.

The fact that both Strachey and Shakespeare wrote about storms and shipwrecks is nothing like proof that the playwright used the colonist's words as the basis for the play. Storms at sea were no more rare in 1611 than they are today, and fleets were dispersed and ships lost with alarming regularity. But there are other parallels between the *Sea Venture* story and Shakespeare's work. Shakespeare's language in describing the storm itself is more than simply reminiscent of Strachey's; it almost mirrors what Strachey wrote in 1610. Most notable, perhaps, are the parallels between Strachey's description of the St. Elmo's Fire that so amazed Sir George Somers on the storm's third day and Shakespeare's description of Ariel as he boarded Alonso's ship (Ariel is the spirit who serves Prospero, the magician who rules the island that is the main setting of the play). In his narrative, Strachey wrote, "Sir George Somers . . . had an apparition of a little round light, like a faint star, trembling, and streaming along with a sparkling blaze, halfe the height upon the main mast, and shooting sometimes from shroud to shroud . . . running sometimes along the main yard to the very end, and then returning . . . but upon a suden, towards the morning watch, they lost the sight of it, and knew not which way it made."[11]

And Shakespeare, almost as if he was looking over Strachey's shoulder, described how Ariel, in his words, "boarded the King's ship; now on the beak . . . now in the waist, the deck, in every cabin . . . . Sometimes I'd divide, and burn in many places . . . on the topmast, the yards and bowsprit, would I flame distinctly . . . then meet and join."[12]

There are parallels, too, in the authors' descriptions of the roaring storm. Strachey writes, "Fury added to fury . . . . Prayers might well be in the heart and lips but drowned in the outcries of the officers."[13] And Shakespeare writes, "A plague upon this howling! They are louder than the weather or our office."[14] William Strachey writes of the "glut" of water.[15] Shakespeare, in the first scene of the first act, uses the same word to describe his storm, the only instance in his writings that he makes use of the word *glut*. All the *Sea Venture* passengers survive, as do all the passengers in *The Tempest*. Just as Bermuda, the Isle of Devils, is enchanted or haunted, so is the island in Shakespeare's play, where Ariel claims, "All the devils are here."[16] Then there's a direct reference to the "still-vex'd Bermoothes" in Shakespeare's play, more than a hint, it might be thought, of the source of much of his material.[17] The parallels are so numerous, and the language so similar, that many scholars have decided that it seems beyond arguing that Shakespeare took inspiration and more from Strachey.[18]

Meanwhile, as Strachey came home in late 1611 and as Shakespeare's players, the King's Men, rehearsed their lines for their play before the king and court, a group of the London adventurers, including Sir Thomas Smythe and Southampton, petitioned King James for another charter—the company's third. This charter, granted on March 12, 1612, reorganized Virginia's government yet again by stripping the council in Virginia of some powers and granting more power to the general assembly of adventurers in London. This can only be viewed as an attempt to foster renewed interest in the colony by giving its financial backers a stronger voice in the operation of its affairs. The new charter also included two provisions that addressed in dramatic form the parlous state of the company's finances. The first gave the company the right to raise money to support colonial efforts by running lotteries, offering cash prizes to ticket buyers (the first of many attempts in America's history to turn gamblers into public-minded supporters of worthy causes). The second confirmed that the law courts would support the Virginia Company in lawsuits against shareholders who defaulted on payments. But the most telling of the new Virginia charter's provisions was the one that enlarged the colony's territories. The second charter (of 1609) had specified that Virginia's territory was limited to a hundred miles from the coasts (both the Atlantic and Pacific, since it was still believed, or at least hoped, that the "Other Sea" lay not far beyond the mountains to the west). This was not suitable in 1612, when the adventurers wanted to make the Bermudas part of Virginia, for purposes of colonization. So the charter of 1612 specifically extended the bounds of the grant to three hundred leagues (roughly nine hundred miles) at sea, to include "divers islandes lying desolate and uninhabited, some of which are already made knowne and discovered by the industry, travell, and expences of the said Company, . . . all and every of which itt maie importe the said Colony [Virginia] both in safety and pollecy of trade to populate and plant."[19] In plainer English, the Isle of Devils, lying some six hundred miles from the mouth of the Chesapeake, was, with a stroke of the king's pen, made part of Virginia and opened to colonization.

With the charter in hand, the leaders of the Virginia Company then created what might be called an "under company"—a subsidiary joint stock company within the larger Virginia Company—to finance the settlement of the island chain. At this time, even the name of the new colony was not determined. Some of the adventurers who were paying the tab for the settlement wanted to call the islands Virginiola, indicating they were a part of the larger colony. Fortunately, more forward-looking heads prevailed. The islands were christened the Somers Islands in honor of Sir George Somers. Soon enough, and apparently out of a desire to praise the island chain's temperate climate, the place once known as the Isle of Devils was being called the Summer Islands and Summer Island and Somer Islands and so on. Somehow, though, the name that stuck was Bermuda or the Bermudas.

By mid-March 1612, when the new charter was signed by the king, plans were firmly under way to send a ship and some sixty colonists to Bermuda. Events would later show that—as had been the case in every earlier attempt at colonization—the colonists recruited for the Bermuda venture would include some of the least suitable of men, and a few women. Colonists included a few well-born troublemakers and layabouts as well as a few hard men who had spent more than one night sleeping in jail. But, within six weeks of obtaining their charter, the company had signed on a full complement of settlers willing to establish a colony in the Bermudas. These colonists were placed under the command of Richard Moore, a master carpenter who had been tapped to serve as the first governor of the Somers Isle colony. Moore was, according to one of the early colonists, "a man ... who, had he but bin educated answerably to the capacitye of his mind and speritt, would have expressed himself very worthily," since he "left behind him in thoes partes [Bermuda] many testimonyes, both of his sufficiencye and honesty."[20] Indeed, though Moore suffered from pride and a lack of foresight, he was—compared to some of the early leaders in Jamestown—a paragon of leadership. That, though, was in the future.

By the last week of April, the *Plough*, a small vessel leased by the company, was taking on passengers in London. There's no record that the ship was sent on her way with any of the fanfare that had accompanied the departure of the *Sea Venture* fleet almost three years earlier. On April 28, the *Plough* fell down the Thames.

I2

A Most Pious and Noble End

It was sometime around mid-September 1612—not long before William Strachey returned to London—when Samuel Argall, the newly named admiral of Virginia, sailed his well-armed frigate the *Treasurer* into the Chesapeake Bay and up the James to anchor off the English settlement that was, at that time, more than five years old. By that time Jamestown had grown to include several "pleasant, and beautiful howses" along with blockhouses and some farm buildings located outside the palisade, in a rough line that ran parallel to the river south of the original enclosed triangular fort. Inside the palisade, according to colonist Ralph Hamor, the *Sea Venture* survivor who took over as official secretary after William Strachey's departure, there were "two faire rowes of howses, all of framed Timber, two stories, and an upper Garret, or Corne loft high, besides three large and substantiall Store-howses, joyned togeather in length some hundred and twenty foot, and in breadth forty."[1] No longer were the dwellings cramped one-room structures of wattle and daub; they were tall and made all of framed wood. Not only that, but there were some real touches of relative luxury in the colony, including a new and larger church outside the fort and a fine garden planted at Sir Thomas Gates's house in Jamestown where, Hamor said, there were "many apple & pear trees come up."[2]

While the colony was boasting signs of civilization, hunger remained a worry, necessitating continuing trade between the settlers and Indians, and it was to trade that Argall turned most of his attention in the months following his reappearance in Virginia. Sir Thomas Gates had arrived in Jamestown just a few months earlier with a fleet bearing, Hamor reported, "men, provisions and cattle."[3] Still, with winter drawing near, it remained clear that something would have to be done to obtain more food to last during the coming cold weather. In December 1612, Argall set out with a small army of men on board the *Treasurer*, bound for the lands of the Patawomeke Indians on the Potomac, near the site of present-day Washington, D.C. These were the same Indian people who had, when John Smith was the governor of Jamestown, shown a willingness to truck with the *Tassantasssas* even if it meant risking Wahunsonacock's anger and the same people with whom Argall had established friendly relations on an earlier trading expedition. On this voyage, Argall was greeted as a friend by Iopassus, the Patawomeke *weroance* who had earlier proven his willingness to trade with the English. Once again Iopassus was ready to barter. The *weroance*, Argall said in a letter to a friend in England, "told me that all the Indians were my very great friend, and that they had a very good store of corn for me."[4] In short order, Argall sailed the *Treasurer* to Iopassus's village and quickly loaded the ship with more than a thousand bushels of corn. At the same time, as a sign of goodwill, he left a junior officer, identified only as an ensign named Swift, behind as a hostage, intermediary, and spy. To be sure, the grain was welcomed in Jamestown, but it only lasted a few months, and, in the spring of 1613, Argall set out yet again to visit his friend Iopassus on the banks of the Potomac.

Unknown to Argall when he left Jamestown sometime in late March or early April 1613, headed down the James, and steered *Treasurer* up the York in the direction of the Potomac, Wahunsonacock's daughter, the princess Pocahontas, was in the territory of the Patawomeke people, acting as her father's representative. The Indian princess, by that time fifteen or sixteen years of age, had not been seen at the English settlement for three years, ever since her friend Captain John Smith left for England and the settlers told her, untruthfully, that he had died. Though Argall, like most of the English who had come to Virginia after Smith's departure (and that was almost everybody in the colony), had never seen the princess, he certainly would have known of her by reputation. Perhaps he had heard stories of how she entertained ship's boys by turning cartwheels in the town's market square and brought food to the colonists in some of Jamestown's earliest, most trying times. No matter how much or how little he knew of her history, though, he certainly would have immediately understood Pocahontas's value as a hostage, should she fall into his hands. It isn't difficult to imagine Argall's glee, then, when he arrived in the lands of the Patawomekes to learn that Wahunsonacock's daughter was nearby.

Argall, no doubt, had read the instructions given to Sir Thomas Gates before his departure with the *Sea Venture* fleet in 1609 as well as those given by the Virginia Company to Lord De La Warre before he set sail from England in 1610. In both cases, those instructions called upon the leaders of the colony to further the cause of Christianity by removing the Indian priests from the Powhatan villages so that the priests could be converted, either in Virginia, where they were to be held prisoner, or, if they remained recalcitrant, in England, where they might be more willing to accept the tenets of the English faith. More important, Gates, De La Warre, and their successors were advised to "indeavor the conversion of the natives and savages to the knowledge and worship of the true God and theire redemer Christ Jesus"— this was called "the most pious and noble end" of the English colony—by capturing "some of their children to be brought up in our language and manners."[5] The idea of abducting young people to further the cause of colonization was in fact very popular with the Virginia Company and its backers. The company instructions went so far as to advise that the kidnapped children should be of royal blood, ideally successors to the chief *weroances* of the native people. "You must seise into your custody . . . their Werowances and all their knowne successors at once whom if you intreate well and educate those which are younge and to succeede in the government in your manners and religion, their people will easily obey you and become in time civill and Christian."[6]

Though there's no way of knowing for sure, it seems reasonable that Argall was instructed to keep his eyes open for any worthy kidnap targets, if for no other reason than it is unlikely that he would have taken upon himself any decision to kidnap the powerful paramount chief's daughter without tacit preapproval from Dale and Gates. And that is exactly what Argall did. As soon as he learned Pocahontas was nearby, he hatched a plot to make the princess his prisoner, not so much in the hopes that she would convert to Christianity but to use her as a bargaining chip, to force her father to return to the English captured arms and tools along with a few settlers he was holding hostage.

Within hours, Argall met with his friend Iopassus. By promising Iopassus that the English would protect him from the wrath of Wahunsonacock and convincing him that taking Pocahontas hostage would guarantee good relations between the *Tassantassas* and the natives, he was able to enlist the *weroance's* help in his plot to kidnap the princess. If Iopassus had any lingering doubts, Argall removed them by bribing him with gifts of "a small Copper kettle and som other les valuable toies so highly by him esteeemed, that doubtlesse he would have betraied his owne father for them."[7] For obvious reasons, Iopassus wanted to guarantee that Wahunsonacock would have no reason to doubt his loyalty, so the Englishman and the Indian devised a subterfuge that would keep his treachery hidden. The plan required Iopassus and his wife to go walking with Pocahontas and to guide her down to the creek where the frigate *Treasurer* was anchored. Once at the creek, Iopassus's wife (her name is not recorded) pretended that she had a sudden, uncontrollable desire to visit the English ship, claiming that she had never been on board one of the big vessels before. Iopassus, according to plan, refused to allow her to visit the English unless accompanied by another Indian woman. At that, the *weroance's* wife broke down in tears, at which point Iopassus relented, provided Pocahontas accompanied his wife on her visit to the ship.[8] At first, Pocahontas was unwilling to go on board, perhaps sensing a trap or at least aware that she was putting herself in danger. Finally, however, she gave in to her friend. The three natives were rowed out to the *Treasurer*, where they were met by a gleeful Argall, who showed them around the vessel and served a fine meal, probably in his cabin. According to Hamor, once they were seated at Argall's table, Iopassus and his wife kept stepping on Argall's foot under the table as if to signal, " 'Tis done, she is your own!"[9] After the meal, Argall convinced the three to rest for a time on the vessel and showed them to the gunner's room, a private spot almost as fine as his own great cabin.

Pocahontas may well have been suspicious before the meal ended. Maybe she saw some conspiratorial glances pass between Iopassus and his wife when they were stomping Argall's foot under the table. In any case, she woke early and begged Iopassus and his wife to leave the ship. When she and her traitorous companions climbed on deck and asked to disembark, Argall sprung his trap, telling Pocahontas that she was his prisoner. Iopassus, of course, acted surprised and angry while Pocahontas, not surprisingly, became, in Hamor's words, "exeeding pensive, and discontented."[10] Still, the deed was done. Iopassus and his wife left with their gewgaws and copper kettle and Argall, while going to great pains to treat Pocahontas kindly, sent messengers to her father, alerting him to the fact that the princess was being held hostage and that she would be freed as soon as the paramount chief ransomed her by returning "eigh[t] of our English men, many swords, peeces, and other tooles, which he had at severall times by treacherous murdering our men, taken from them."[11] It is believed that Wahunsonacock was residing in the village of Matchut, far up the Pamunkey River, about forty miles overland from the scene of his daughter's kidnapping. For two days, Argall tarried, waiting for the messengers to return. When they did, they carried a message from Wahunsonacock stating that he hoped the English would treat his daughter well and promising that if Argall brought his ship up the Pamunkey to his village he would pay the ransom. At that point, Argall may have wanted to get some official approval for his actions, or he may have feared that Wahunsonacock was setting a trap to capture the *Treasurer* and retake his daughter by force, for, instead of setting out for Matchut, he set sail for Jamestown, with Pocahontas, no doubt, confined to the gunner's room in the ship's stern.

At the time of her capture, Pocahontas, though still a teenager, was certainly a mature young woman. By that time, she had in fact been married for roughly two years to a warrior named Kocoum. Marriage at what would today be considered a young age was typical among the Powhatan people. Pocahontas would have been physically adult by the age of thirteen or so and would have learned from the women in her family and village all she needed to know to fill her role as an adult woman. At that age, she would not only have been ready to marry, she would also have been expected to take her place in society as a married woman.

All we know of Pocahontas's Indian spouse was written by *Sea Venture* survivor William Strachey, who said that at the time of her abduction Pocahontas was "married to a private captain called Kocoum some two years since."[12] The term "private captain" seems to have meant he was a warrior who commanded other men in battle but who was not a man of recognized public stature like a *weroance*.

As Wahunsonacock's daughter, Pocahontas was of course an important figure among the natives of the Tsenacommacah. However, since her mother—one of Wahunsonacock's many wives—had not been of noble birth, the line of succession did not run through Pocahontas. As a consequence, she would have been free to choose the man she married instead of having her father select a husband to strengthen a political alliance with a minor *weroance*. Given the fact that Pocahontas could have had her choice of husbands, including any one of a number of young subchiefs, it is easy, and tempting, to assume that the marriage between the princess and Kocoum was a love match.

The couple's courtship would have been like that of other Powhatan couples: Kocoum would have begun by wooing the paramount chief's daughter with gifts of venison, fish, or plant foods, not only to impress her but to prove to her and her family that he was a good provider. Once he found his attentions to the lively, pretty girl were not repulsed, he would have asked her if she wanted to become his partner. When she agreed, he went to Wahunsonacock and they negotiated "bride wealth"—the goods Kocoum and his family agreed to pay to the chief to compensate him for the loss of his daughter. After the price was agreed upon, both families gathered for a feast, presumably arranged by the bride's family. The groom would then, with his family's help, gather the bride wealth and prepare a house with sleeping mats and pots and a mortar and pestle and other items needed to start housekeeping. When everything was prepared, Kocoum would have taken the bride wealth to Wahunsonacock and returned to his new home to wait for his bride. Soon Pocahontas would have appeared, almost certainly accompanied by her father. The marriage ceremony itself was simple. The old chief stood in front of the couple and joined their hands together. Kocoum's father, or a close friend if his father was dead or absent, then produced a string of worked beads, held it high to show it was as long as his spread arms, then broke it forcefully over the couple's joined hands, after which the beads belonged to the bride's father. With the breaking of the beads, the couple was married. The bride and groom then joined friends and family members in a celebration that lasted for several days.

After the marriage, Pocahontas would have allowed her hair, cropped in front when she was unmarried, to grow out. Then she world have cut it all to a common length, either shoulder length or long, as she wanted, and decorated it with flowers or perhaps with feathers. Though no tattoos are visible outside her clothing in a portrait painted of her later, she, like most Powhatan women, probably had her arms or legs or both tattooed with what Strachey described as "flowers and fruits of sundry lively kinds, as also snakes, serpents, efts (beastes), etc."[13] As a married woman, her daily life would have been filled with toil. After visiting the river or creek closest to her village (wherever that was) to bathe each morning, a practice the English were all too willing to forego both in Virginia and in their native land, she would have made a ritual prayer with her eyes toward the sun, then, after eating a morning meal, she would have turned her attention to planting and harvesting crops; gathering edible foods, including the tuckahoe root (*Peltandra virginica*), which had to be laboriously dug by hand in the shallows of freshwater marshes; sewing clothing; hauling water; and cooking for her husband, whose job it was to hunt and fish and, when necessary, go to war. When the day's work was finished, she may well have joined other young women and boys in a game much like soccer or traded stories with other women around a communal food pot.

Apparently, the marriage ended by the time Pocahontas was abducted. She and her husband may simply have drifted apart and divorced, since that was perfectly acceptable behavior among the Powhatan people. If, as is certainly possible, he came from a distant village, he may have abandoned her to return to his own people in a sort of *de facto* divorce. He may have been dead by the time Pocahontas was abducted. As a warrior and a "private captain" in command of other warriors, he may well have been killed in battle with some of the very Englishmen who became her captors. We will never know. We also will never know if Pocahontas and her Indian husband had any children, though it is unlikely since she seems never to have mentioned a child.

The English, of course, cared little about Pocahontas's marital status when she stepped ashore in Jamestown. To them, she was no more than a savage girl, notable only because of her relationship to the man they knew as Powhatan and because of her value as a bargaining chip. As she was rowed from the *Treasurer* to the dock built on Sir Thomas Dale's orders just outside the fort's main gate, she must have looked around wide-eyed at the *Tassantassas* who flocked to the riverfront to greet the ship on its return and to gape at Argall's prisoner as she walked into the fort. No doubt she held her head high, kept her gaze level. She was, after all, the daughter of a great chief. Inside, though, she must have been terrified. She, like all Powhatan women, had grown up knowing that her capture by an enemy war party was always a possibility and that capture meant she might never go home again. She also knew that the native people treated their women captives kindly, allowed them to marry into their new tribes, if for no other reason than to take advantage of their intrinsic value as producers of valuable crops and commodities. At the same time, she knew that the *Tassantassas* were different—they had killed women and children in their raids on native villages—and she surely would have heard of the brutal murder of the Paspahegh queen and her children by the men under George Percy's command.

As she walked into the palisaded fort she must have searched for a friendly face. John Smith, of course, was gone; dead, or at least so she had been told. Only a handful of the original settlers, whom she might have recognized, were still in the town, so many had died in the settlement's earliest days or in the Starving Time or in the skirmishes with the natives. Perhaps she spied Samuel Collier, one of the few boys she had frolicked with in the fort's open square, and perhaps he smiled at her. For the most part, though, nobody would have smiled. The faces that looked back at her were not only unfamiliar, they were also closed.

She saw, too, that Jamestown itself was changed as well, grown larger than Wahunsonacock's largest village. The houses inside the fortification were more substantial, covered with clapboard that would have looked to her like tree bark. As she walked into the town's small market square, she saw pigs and a few horses and goats in enclosed areas and ducks and chickens that roamed the dusty streets and men dressed in shiny metal corselets and helmets, carrying the swords and muskets her father valued so highly. She might also have seen a few native women who had chosen to live with the *Tassantassas* as servants and may have noted that there were no Englishwomen in the fort. She would later learn that the women lived up the river in the place the whites called Henrico.

Word of Pocahontas's capture would have reached Jamestown long before the *Treasurer* sailed back up the James River from the lands of the Patawomeke. It is likely that Pocahontas was greeted soon after her arrival by Governor Sir Thomas Gates, his marshal Sir Thomas Dale, or both. These English worthies, born and bred to be caste conscious, would have been fully aware of her position as the daughter of the paramount chief and would have seen to it, as Ralph Hamor reported, that she was "very well, and kindly intreated."[14] Soon enough, she was taken to the governor's residence with its garden or Dale's home, where she was treated like the royalty she was, but royalty under house arrest.

Amazingly, there are hardly any references to Pocahontas's captivity in Jamestown in the narratives written by the English of the time. There is no record of how she felt or how she responded to her abduction and imprisonment in an enemy camp, where she was unable to see her family or any of her people. It isn't difficult, however, to imagine her discomfort as she was stripped—almost surely by Indian women who resided with the English—of the comfortable clothing she wore in the forest and dressed in itchy, hot, multiple layers of clothing: a long petticoat and heavy overskirt and chest-compressing, laced-up bodice and socks and maybe even shoes in place of her moccasins. It is easy to imagine, too, her loneliness when she realized that there were none of her own people to talk to about the strange customs of the *Tassantassas*; her confusion at all that had happened to her; and her growing fear as days passed with no hint that her father was taking action to win her freedom. Since Gates and Dale would have worried that she might try to escape, she was almost certainly not allowed outside the dwelling where she was an unwilling guest, certainly not outside the town or near the forest or the river. Such confinement would have been torture for a free-spirited young woman used to living her life in the open.

Wahunsonacock, meanwhile, waited several days for the *Tassantassas* to sail their ship up to his village. He had told the messengers sent by Argall that he would ransom his daughter and still they did not appear. Finally, he decided to take matters into his own hands and send the seven captive white men home to Jamestown along with a canoe full of corn, a handful of old tools, and a few broken and useless guns. He instructed the freed hostages to tell Gates that the other guns he had taken were either broken or lost but that he would send an additional five hundred bushels of corn to the settlement as soon as his daughter was freed. Gates responded in the negative. As Hamor reported, "We could not beleeve that the rest of our Arms were either lost, or stolne from him, and therefore till he returned them all, we would not by any meanes deliver his daughter, and then it should be at his choice, whether he would establish peace or continue enemies with us."[15]

That exchange, brief as it was, ended negotiations between the paramount chief and the English. It seems that Wahunsonacock decided he would simply wait out the *Tassantassas,* as if he expected them to tire of their prisoner and release her. The English, equally recalcitrant, dug in their heels and waited for Wahunsonacock to accede to their desires. And that's the way matters stood for roughly nine months.

If Wahunsonacock expected the English to cave in to his demands— perhaps thinking that hunger would, as it had so often in the past, force them to trade—he was to be disappointed. Perhaps, though, his inaction stemmed from the fact that he simply found his options too horrible to contemplate. On the one hand, he faced the loss of his favorite daughter; on the other, he had to face the loss of the weapons he valued so highly and considered necessary for his people's survival. The English, meanwhile, were in a stronger bargaining position than ever. With a strong settlement established at Henrico and adequate supplies, they had no real need to free their captive to gain food or in fact to recover the weapons held by the Powhatans.

During this period, news of the kidnapping of Pocahontas made its way to England, carried by one of the several ships that by that time made more or less regular voyages between the Chesapeake and English ports. John Chamberlain, a raconteur and gossip whose letters provide a lively portrait of life in Jacobean England, reported on the abduction in a letter he wrote on August 1, 1613, to a friend, Sir Dudley Carleton, in the Netherlands. "There is a ship come from Virginia with newes of their well-doing," he wrote, "which puts some life into that action, that before was almost at the last cast. They have taken a daughter of a king that was their greatest enemy, as she was going afeasting upon a river to visit certain friends, for whose ransom the father offers whatsoever is in his power." An investor in the Virginia Company who, like most, was heartily sick of not seeing any profits, Chamberlain then went on to complain that, as good as the news was about the capture of Pocahontas, the ship "brought no commodities from thence, but only these fair tales and hopes."[16]

At about this time—perhaps even by the time Chamberlain was writing his letter to Carleton—Pocahontas was taken from Jamestown to Henrico, the new colonial headquarters created on the direction of Sir Thomas Dale about ten miles south of present-day Richmond. By that time, Henrico was a thriving community with a population of about 350 men, women, and children. Dale, following instructions given to Gates by the Virginia Company in London, had placed his city upriver, on high ground, where settlers would be less vulnerable than in Jamestown to either Spanish or Indian attacks. By this time, too, Sir Thomas Smythe and the other leaders of the Virginia Company in London were firmly convinced that the low-lying site chosen for the first settlement was unhealthy. It was hoped the air upriver would be more wholesome than that found around the insect-infested swamps and marshes that surrounded Jamestown.

Dale was the ideal man to build a wilderness city in record time. Once Governor Gates provided Dale with a large workforce of his choosing and all the tools he needed, it took the old soldier, Hamor said, only "ten daies" to oversee the erection of a palisade on a plot of high land on the north side of the James River. Soon, a blockhouse was erected on each corner of the palisade and inside the palisade a church, several storehouses and "convenient houses, and lodgings for himselfe and men." In four months, Hamor reported, Dale had "made Henrico much better and of more worth than all the work [accomplished] ever since the colony began."[17]

By the time Pocahontas arrived in the town—it was erected on a site she would have known well, not far from the spot where her old friend John Smith had tried to establish an outpost on land he had been given by her father—it had expanded to include about twelve square miles of land across the James. Five small forts, more like blockhouses than substantial fortifications, had been erected, along with a palisade that enclosed several dwellings, plots of cleared land, and enclosures for hogs. One of these dwellings, a frame structure, was the parsonage of the Reverend Alexander Whitaker, the man who had volunteered for the important task of converting Pocahontas in the Christian faith.

Born at Cambridge in 1585, Whitaker was the son of the Reverend Dr. William Whitaker, the master of St. John's College, Cambridge University, and Susan Culverwell, related to some of London's wealthiest men. He attended Cambridge in the early 1600s, at the time when the university professors and scholars and divines were busy writing and rewriting what was to become the King James Bible and, in the process, redefining English Protestantism and creating a generation of dedicated churchmen. Whitaker himself was ordained as a minister in 1609, at about the same time as the *Sea Venture* and the other ships of the Third Supply set sail from Plymouth. Given his background—his friend Rev. William Crashaw called him "a scholar, a graduate, a preacher, wellborn and friended in England"[18]—he could easily have guaranteed himself a prosperous living in his homeland. Instead, in 1611, after just two years as a minister in the north of England, he turned his back on what would have been a life of ease to serve God by converting the native people of Virginia to the Protestant faith. His dedication was notable, even at a time when religious fervor was less remarkable than today. He fully accepted what he viewed as the godly charge to carry the faith to the poor Indians of the New World and, in *Good Newes from Virginia*, he wrote that it was the duty of his fellow Englishmen to give liberally to the colony, "to lay their helping hands to it, either with their purse, persons or prayers,"[19] to further the salvation of the Indians and the establishment of a Protestant, English settlement in the Americas.

If Whitaker sounds like a religious zealot, he was. But he was a zealot with a liberal bent. Unlike many of his fellow seventeenth-century religionists whose avid Puritanism could and did lead them to unreasoning intolerance, Whitaker saw the natives of Virginia as intelligent children of God, no more savage than his own ancient ancestors before the Romans and then the Christians came to civilize the blue-painted Britons. Even before he began tutoring Pocahontas, an experience that almost certainly would have softened the heart of almost any English tutor, Whitaker was convinced that the Virginia natives were intelligent, quick learners, open to ideas. "One God created us," he said. "They have reasonable souls and intellectual faculties as well as we. . . . They are of body lusty, strong, and very nimble. They are an understanding generation, quick of apprehension, sudden in their dispatches, subtle in their dealings, exquisite in their inventions, and industrious in their labor."[20] Believing Pocahontas both worthy of saving and teachable, Whitaker, imbued with the passion of his convictions, was the perfect teacher.

Pocahontas could have remained in Jamestown, to be tutored by the Reverend Richard Bucke, the *Sea Venture* survivor, but her conversion was the special project of Sir Thomas Dale, whose headquarters were upriver in Henrico. In fact, Dale, in a letter to a friend in London, was happy to take credit for her conversion, though it is not likely he had much of a hand in her Christian education. "Powhatans daughter I caused to be carefully instructed in Christian Religion," he wrote, adding, "Were it but the gayning of this one soule, I will thinke my time, toile, and present stay [in Virginia] well spent."[21]

Whitaker's landholding—the manor was called Rocke Hall—was a one-hundred-acre glebe farm (a parcel of land assigned to Whitaker as partial payment for his services as Henrico's resident minister) well protected by one of the nearby blockhouses. It may have been chosen as a suitable residence for the Indian princess because it was virtually impregnable to Indian attack and, as well, an isolated location where Pocahontas could be watched during her imprisonment.

In the months that followed her move to what was fast becoming the colony's most prosperous city, Pocahontas found the twenty-eight- or twenty-nine-year-old Whitaker to be a kindly but stern teacher. Though we don't know for sure how she spent her days, it is safe to say much of her time was devoted to the study of English, study that would have been made easier by her relative youth, by her obviously quick mind, and by the fact that she had some familiarity with the language from the days when she visited Jamestown and conversed with Captain John Smith. As a princess, she would not have been required to do much in the way of work around the bachelor Whitaker's house, but she undoubtedly had talks with his housekeeper, who was probably married to one of the minister's servants or employees, and with other women of the household. At the same time, she had myriad social rules to learn: how to eat at a table at set times instead of dipping food from a communal pot whenever she was hungry, how to move and sit properly in her new clothing, how to sleep in one of the English beds instead of on furs on a sleeping platform or the ground, all the things that were so new and strange to her.

Then there were the daily lessons with Whitaker, memorizing the catechism, learning the tenets of the Christian faith by rote, repeating her teacher's words, slowly and haltingly, trying to mimic his sounds even as she struggled to remember the meaning of the strange-sounding words. Though it seems unlikely, given the fact that so few Englishwomen could read or write, she may even have learned to make a few letters and to decipher a few words in Whitaker's ornate Bible, probably a copy of the Geneva Bible, filled with elaborate maps and illustrations of beasts and birds and ancient people, illustrations that Pocahontas would no doubt have found fascinating as she turned the book's fragile pages, marveling at the printing, unlike anything she'd ever seen.[22] Slowly, under Whitaker's tutelage, she learned what it meant to be a Christian, about one God and about the devil instead of the four deities of the Powhatan people—Ahone, the creator; Oke (probably pronounced *okee*), the punishing god; the Sun, to whom the people swore oaths and to whom they prayed each morning; and the Algonkian Great Hare believed by the natives to be the creator of the first people, the land, water, fish, and deer.[23] She learned to say the Lord's Prayer and the confession of faith and to give thanks at each meal. Slowly, she left her Powhatan ways and became more and more an Englishwoman.

Each Saturday, Whitaker and Pocahontas and other members of the household traveled the few miles down the James to the plantation of Sir Thomas Dale, where the marshal hosted a prayer meeting for the colonists who lived nearby. At these gatherings, Pocahontas would have met other Englishmen and -women and probably would have been shown off—and gawked at—as Whitaker's star pupil, proof positive that the English hopes of converting the "salvages" of the New World could indeed be realized. Then, on Sundays, she and other members of the minister's household spent the day in Henrico, where Whitaker performed his churchly duties, preaching in the morning and teaching a catechism class in the afternoons. If Pocahontas found this schedule trying—and there must have been times when she wanted to tear off her confining English clothing and run into the forests, to feel the wind in her hair and against her skin, to be alone, to be free again—she also found reason to enjoy her visits to Dale's plantation and Henrico in the person of the *Sea Venture* survivor John Rolfe.

By that time, Rolfe, who had embarked in Plymouth in 1609 with his pregnant wife in tow, must have often wondered why he had ever left his native land for the Chesapeake. His life as an immigrant had been marked by tragedy. He and his wife had buried their infant daughter, Bermuda, just days after Mrs. Rolfe gave birth in Bermuda. Then, sometime not long after arriving in Jamestown, Mrs. Rolfe herself had died and been buried somewhere, perhaps inside the fort. As Rolfe stood by his wife's grave, he must have felt almost cursed. It would have brought him little comfort that it was not unusual, in those times, for children to die before they celebrated their first birthdays or for staggering numbers of young and otherwise healthy women to die following childbirth. Then, at one of the Saturday night prayer meetings at Sir Thomas's house or some Sunday service in Henrico, he met Pocahontas.

In 1613 Rolfe was in his mid- to late twenties, roughly the same age as Whitaker. Almost nothing is known about his background with anything like certainty. It is thought that he was the son of John and Dorothy Rolfe of Heacham in Norfolk, on the North Sea coast. John Rolfe the elder (at least the John Rolfe believed to be the father of the John Rolfe of Virginia fame) was a merchant: his tombstone read, "He increased his property by merchandise. By exporting and importing such things as England abounded in, or needed, he was of the greatest service"[24] It is this epitaph, as much as anything else, that makes a convincing case that John Rolfe was indeed one of the Rolfes of Heacham, for he, like the man buried beneath that epitaph-bearing stone, found his way in the world and "increased his property" by sending to England such things as were needed. And, of course, by marrying the most famous Indian princess in Virginia.

Like so much of the early Virginia story, not enough is known about the meeting and courtship of Rolfe and Pocahontas. John Smith says that Rolfe was one of the worthies of the colony who helped Pocahontas with her English lessons and with her catechism. Perhaps it was during these lessons at Rocke Hall that the widowed Englishman and the once-married Indian girl— still only about sixteen or seventeen years of age— first felt the stirrings of love. What a story that would make if it were known. Unfortunately, all we know is that by the end of 1613 he had fallen in love with Pocahontas, and she with him. Around that time, perhaps as they studied the Book of Common Prayer together or walked the fields around Whitaker's home, their eyes must have met and they must have known they wanted to be together always. By early 1614 they were thinking about and then discussing the unthinkable: that they would marry.

What was it in Pocahontas that made her so ready to accept the English way of life, embrace Christianity in place of her own vibrant beliefs, and ultimately fall in love with and then agree to marry a man so unlike the men she had known all her life? It is possible that once she had been told that John Smith was dead (a lie that was not untold until she went to England several years later), she began grieving and that in her grief she unconsciously wanted to cleave to another way of life, the life of the *Tassantassas,* and to cleave to another foreign man, John Rolfe, in place of the bearded Englishman who had played such an important role in her girlhood. Then, too, it was possible that in her time in captivity she began to relate to her captors, the way hostages sometimes identify with, even fall in love with, their captors, behavior now recognized by psychiatrists as the Stockholm Syndrome.[25] Then, too, the explanation might have been simpler, more mundane. Pocahontas had seen how women were treated by the Powhatans. Her own mother had been the wife of the paramount chief for a brief period, only long enough to bear and give birth to Pocahontas herself. Then she was shunted aside for a new wife, reduced in stature from that of a chief's wife to that of a commoner, and then stripped of her daughter as soon as Pocahontas was old enough to take her place in Wahunsonacock's household. The princess herself had been married and perhaps divorced. To be sure, John Rolfe was not a chief like her father. He was neither a warrior nor a hunter like Kocoum and the other young men she knew; but, it seems, he was thoughtful and gentle. His few surviving writings show he was intelligent and cultured. Perhaps the Indian girl, alone and lonely, was attracted to this Englishman simply because he was different.

Then there may well have been the political motivation. Pocahontas was an intelligent, perceptive young woman, surely smart enough, as she lived with the English, to understand that the scope of their resources and their technological superiority would spell ultimate doom for her people unless an alliance between the two groups was forged. Perhaps she saw herself as the agent who could forge this alliance in the way that the Powhatan people often brought about alliances, by marrying one of the enemy and bearing him children who would serve as links between the two cultures. This raises the intriguing idea that Wahunsonacock, who during this period made no move to ransom Pocahontas even though he must have heard reports that his daughter was becoming more English with each passing day, was perfectly happy to sit back as his daughter forged this link between the *Tassantassas* and the natives of the Tidewater. That certainly would explain why he made no attempt to buy or gain her freedom and would explain why, later in her captivity, he would quickly give his approval to her marriage to Rolfe. Maybe without even realizing it, or perhaps as some Machiavellian plan, Pocahontas's capture was exactly what the old chief wanted. After all, he was no fool. By 1614, he, like his daughter, must have known there was no way the natives could stem the flow of *Tassantassas* to the Chesapeake.

None of this is to say that Pocahontas did not truly love John Rolfe. Whatever her motivation, Pocahontas at the very least seems to have truly cared for Rolfe, enough that she wanted to marry him and enough that she was willing to renounce her old life for a new one with him.

Rolfe, meanwhile, struggled mightily with his feelings for the Indian girl. He was fearful that his love for a native would demean him in the eyes of his fellow colonists. More than that, though, he was afraid that his love for Pocahontas was rooted in carnality, was somehow sinful. As a churchman familiar enough with the Bible to tutor Pocahontas, he knew full well the Old Testament stricture against "marrying strange wives."[26] He was insightful enough to wonder if what he felt for Pocahontas was nothing more than desire for the strangeness of the forbidden, dark woman of the New World. And so Rolfe agonized even as he fell in love, and when he was away from Rocke Hall and away from her presence, he prayed to be relieved of his love, thinking as he prepared to sleep, or to toss and turn in his dwelling downriver from Henrico, that his feelings were "wicked instigations hatched by him who seeketh and delighteth in man's destruction."[27] But no matter how hard he tried, he could not put Pocahontas out of his mind or his heart.

Meanwhile, during these months, Dale and Gates waited for some word from Powhatan, but the chief remained unwilling to meet the English demands that he give up his weapons. In March 1614, when Pocahontas had been a captive of the English for nearly a year, Sir Thomas Gates, the *Sea Venture* survivor who took charge of the colonists in Bermuda, left his post in Virginia for England, leaving Dale in command, again, as deputy governor. While Gates had been willing to allow Powhatan to drag his feet, Dale was less patient. Almost immediately, he ordered Samuel Argall, Pocahontas's kidnapper, to make his ship, the *Treasurer,* ready for action against the Indians. The English and the Indians, after all, were still at war, and Dale was not the type of soldier to allow Wahunsonacock simply to ignore English demands. Matters, in fact, had been made worse by the fact that some of the Englishmen the paramount chief had released soon after his daughter's kidnapping had chosen to return to the Indians, where the living was easier than under Dale's iron rule. In late March, on Dale's orders, the *Treasurer* took on supplies, crew, and roughly 150 armed men with orders to find Wahunsonacock and convince him to submit to Dale's commands that he return weapons and provide the colony with corn. John Rolfe was tapped to accompany the expedition, probably because by that time he was trusted by Dale. Ralph Hamor, the colony's secretary, went along to keep a record of events. Pocahontas was recruited as an unwilling participant in Dale's campaign and forced to board the ship that had been the scene of her kidnapping and where she was now being used as a pawn in the chess game between Dale and Wahunsonacock, threatened with death if her father did not accede to Dale's wishes.

Sometime in late March, the *Treasurer* set sail, accompanied by several other small vessels that had been commandeered by Argall. Unfortunately, the two surviving eyewitness accounts of what happened on the expedition—one by Hamor and the second by Dale—do not agree in all matters. It seems, though, that the flotilla, led by the *Treasurer,* made its way down the James and then up the York to Werowocomoco, Wahunsonacock's former headquarters, where the English vessels dropped anchor and waited. Soon enough, some Indians on shore demanded to know what the English were doing in Indian territory. The English answered that Pocahontas was on board and that they were ready to exchange her for weapons, men, and a ship full of corn. If the exchange was made, Dale added, "we would be friends; if not, burne all."[28] According to Dale, the natives then asked for time to get a message to the paramount chief, who was upriver. Hostages were exchanged—routine in dealings like these—and the English settled down to wait.

The next day, Dale and the others learned from the Indians that Wahunsonacock was three days' journey distant, almost certainly at Matchut, high up the Pamunkey River, but that his younger brother, Opechancanough, could act in the paramount chief's stead. This Indian was one of the fiercest Powhatan warriors and the man who would eventually take Wahunsonacock's place as leader of the Indians of the Tidewater. Dale called him Wahun-sonacock's "chief captain" and said that he could command the Indian warriors as readily as the old chief himself.[29] He and John Smith had bumped heads several times during Smith's time in Virginia—in fact, it was this brave warrior who captured Smith in 1607—and he had no love at all for the *Tassantassas*, as he would later prove in particularly bloody fashion. For now, though, he was willing to try to win his niece's freedom. Over the next few days, as negotiations hit one snag after another, tensions rose and then boiled over. The English went ashore and a skirmish broke out. "They shot at us," Dale reported. "We were not behinde hand with them: killed some, hurt others, marched into the land, burnt their houses, tooke their corn, and quartered all night ashore."[30]

Following this skirmish, the flotilla moved farther upriver making its way closer to Matchut. Finally, to hurry negotiations along, Argall sent Pocahontas ashore to meet with a group of her own people. What must she have thought and felt as she stepped off the vessel after nearly a year in captivity, suddenly free—no matter how temporarily—and surrounded by men and women she had known all her life, perhaps even some of her distant relatives? Was she tempted to run, to try to escape? Apparently not, for, Dale reported, she "would not talke to any of them scarce to them of the best sort, and to them onely, that if her father had loved her, he would not value her lesse than olde swords, peeces, or axes." Even across the centuries and obscured a bit by Dale's twisted prose, Pocahontas's anger fairly crackles. Shunning her countrymen, she was willing only to talk to "the best sort"—presumably her father's councillors or perhaps a close relative or two. And she made her anger plain. If her father did not want her, did not value her, she would, she said, "still dwell with the English men, who loved her."[31]

Hamor's story is slightly different. According to the colonial secretary, Pocahontas spoke with two men he described as "Powhatans sonnes... very desirous to see their sister." These two—they could have been any of scores of Pocahontas's half brothers sired by Wahunsonacock—were so pleased to see the princess that they promised the English they would "perswade their father to redeeme her, and to conclude a firm peace" with the settlers.[32] Though it is not clear from Hamor's narrative, it can be assumed that Pocahontas at this time told her relatives of her intention to marry John Rolfe, news that would quickly have been carried to Wahunsonacock. In any event, after the meeting between Pocahontas and her people, Rolfe and a young man named

Rob Sparkes, who had earlier been left with the Patawomekes and who there-fore knew something of the Powhatan language, were dispatched to talk to Wahunsonacock. It seems that it was also about this time that Hamor gave Dale a long letter that had been written by Rolfe, in which he declared his love for Pocahontas and asked the deputy governor's permission to marry the Indian princess.

Apparently, Rolfe was nervous enough about Dale's response that he did not want to face the old soldier's wrath. Rolfe's letter is a remarkable docu-ment. He took great pains to make it clear that his primary motive in marry-ing the young Indian was to spread the Christian faith among the savages of Virginia. In pleading his case, he came very close to insulting the woman he claimed to love, professing that if his only goal was to satisfy his base desires he could do so "with Christians more pleasinge to the eie."[33] Perhaps, in writing these words, he was remembering his wife, the dead mother of his dead child, and paying her homage more than he was disparaging his new love. Or maybe, to be charitable, he was overstating his case in hopes that Dale would be so firmly swayed by his arguments that he would speedily grant his blessing.

Rolfe also claimed to be well aware that he was considering a step that could do his reputation little good in Virginia or in England. A gentleman, he claimed he knew he was running the risk of being looked down upon for marrying beneath himself. A bit of a snob, like so many of his fellows, Rolfe apparently had no idea that many in England—including, it was later said, James I—would consider that Rolfe had married above himself by taking a princess as his bride. In any case, he said he was willing to risk alienating his family, his friends, and all who heard of his marriage "for the good of this plantation for the honour of our countrie, for the glory of God, for my owne salvation, and for the converting to the true knowledge of God and Jesus Christ, an unbeleeving creature, namely Pokahuntas. To whom my heartie and best thoughts are, and have a long time bin so intangled, and inthralled."[34] No matter what the cost, he said, he wanted to marry Pocahontas.

However, he continued, he would bend his will to Dale's (not that he had any real choice in the matter). "I freely subject my selfe to your grave and ma-ture judgment, deliberation, approbation and determination, assuring my selfe of your zealous admonitions, and godly comforts, either perswading me to desist, or encouraging me to persist ther in."[35]

As it turned out, Rolfe need not have worried about Dale's reaction to the news that his young friend was in love with, wanted to marry, an Indian girl. Dale immediately assented to the match, perhaps even before he issued orders that Rolfe head upriver with young Rob Sparkes to talk to Wahunsonacock.

Events speeded up suddenly, after almost a year of inaction in which Pocahontas was a prisoner of the English, however willing, and during which her father took no action to gain her freedom. Unfortunately, the two accounts of what happened over the next few days—the one by Dale and the other by Hamor—are again rambling and often contradictory. Neither Rolfe nor Pocahontas, sadly, left a record. It seems, however, that Rolfe and Sparkes never did get to see Wahunsonacock. Instead, the paramount chief, perhaps hearing of his daughter's love for the Englishman, sent a message to Dale saying that the guns, swords, and tools in his possession would be sent to Jamestown within fifteen days, along with some corn. He also promised that any runaway *Tassantassas* would be returned to the settlement and that if any of his people hurt any colonists or killed cattle or stole, he would turn them over to Dale for punishment. Furthermore, he named "such of his people and neighbor kings"—subordinate tribes and leaders—that he wanted to include in a general peace between the native people and the *Tassantassas*. Even the warlike Opechancanough got into the act, declaring that since "he was a great Captaine, and did alwaies fight" and that Dale, too, was "also a great Captaine," therefore the two would be friends forever. Dale, who would later say that the "God of battles" had a hand in delivering this remarkable peace to the English in Virginia, quickly accepted Wahunsonacock's offer of peace and headed back to Jamestown and then on to Henrico, carrying Pocahontas and John Rolfe, now formally engaged.[36]

It is likely that the news that Pocahontas wished to marry an Englishman came as less of a surprise to Wahunsonacock than it had been to Dale, given the tradition that Indian women who were taken hostage often wed one of their captors. It certainly seemed, from the old chief's ready willingness to strike a treaty with the invading *Tassantassas*, that he viewed the marriage as a welcome opportunity to guarantee amity between the two peoples.

By the first week of April, Pocahontas was once again in Jamestown. There, having announced her intention to marry Rolfe, she openly renounced her old faith and accepted Christianity. At her baptism, the girl whose given name was Amonute, made it known that she had another name, Matoaka. This was her private name, a name that was known only to members of her family since it was believed by Algonkians, like many other native people, that this private name could be used by evil wishers to hex victims. Now, as a Christian, she took yet another name when she was christened Rebecca.

The name—it was likely chosen by her tutor, Whitaker—would have seemed ideal to the minister. Rebecca, the wife of Isaac, was the mother of twins who struggled within her womb, forcing her to question the Lord who told her:

> Two nations are in thy womb,
> And two manner of people shall be separated from thy bowels.
> And the one people shall be stronger than the other people;
> And the elder shall serve the younger.[37]

Eventually, when the biblical Rebecca's twins were born, the first—Esau, a cunning hunter and outdoorsman—was red, while the second—Jacob, an indoorsman—was pale. Rebecca, in the course of things, came to favor the pale son, going so far as to trick Isaac into giving his birthright and blessing to the younger, paler, more acceptable son. The New World symbolism that could be superimposed on this tale would have been almost enough to transport Whitaker. Pocahontas, like the Rebecca of the Old Testament, would have children that were both red and white, both Indian and Christian. But, like Rebecca, she would favor the younger people, the whites, who were newer in Virginia and younger on the land. If Rebecca/Pocahontas gave much thought to her new name and its symbolism, she never made that known. She may simply have accepted her Christian name as she had accepted her Indian names, as part of life's routine.

What is known is that Pocahontas and John Rolfe married on April 5, 1614, almost certainly in the church in Jamestown. It seems likely that the ceremony was performed by Richard Bucke, the minister who survived the *Sea Venture* shipwreck and who had christened little Bermuda Rolfe and then buried the baby in Bermuda. Dale would have been in attendance, and Ralph Hamor, of course, and at least a few of the other *Sea Venture* survivors who were still living in Jamestown almost five years after their arrival in Virginia. Other guests included two of Pocahontas's uncles, sent to represent Wahunsonacock at the event. The church was decorated, no doubt, with spring flowers and fragrant herbs. There would have been music, perhaps songs provided by the dancing taborer, Thomas Dowse.

The service would have been little different from a modern-day marriage in any Episcopal church. Bucke began with a reading from the English Book of Common Prayer. Perhaps one of the bride's uncles gave her away, or perhaps Dale filled that role. Eventually, rings were exchanged, the bride and groom plighted their troth each to the other, Pocahontas promised to obey her husband (a promise no longer required of most brides), and Master Bucke pronounced the couple married.

The marriage of John Rolfe, the *Sea Venture* survivor, and Pocahontas, the paramount chief's daughter, marked the beginning of a period of peace in Tidewater Virginia, a period of relative calm that enabled the English colonists to plant their feet firmly on American soil. Despite setbacks, including a bloody Indian attack that killed hundreds of English, Virginia's survival was never again seriously called into question.

13

"Our Hoped and Desired Ilands"

By the time William Shakespeare's company of actors staged the first production of *The Tempest* in the Banquet Hall of Whitehall Palace in late
1611, the three *Sea Venture* survivors who remained in Bermuda when Matthew
Somers carried his uncle's pickled body back to England had established a
mostly comfortable life for themselves in the place the English had long
known as the Isle of Devils. The three—Christopher Carter, Edward Waters,
and Edward Chard—settled on what is now known as Smith's Island. One of
the smallest of the Bermudan Islands, Smith's (it was named, despite its
spelling, for Sir Thomas Smythe of Virginia Company fame) sits nestled just
south of St. George's Island in the shelter of a roughly egg-shaped, almost
completely enclosed harbor between St. George's Island and St. David Island.
There, the voluntary castaways cleared land, built thatched cabins, and
planted corn, peas, pumpkins, beans, and wheat using seeds left behind by Sir
George Somers. They managed, somehow, to cultivate tobacco, perhaps from
plants left behind by some earlier Spanish mariner. Hogs were plentiful, or
plentiful enough to more than sustain three men, and they soon salted a plentiful supply of pork. Fish were easily hooked and birds were as easy to club
and as tasty as they'd always been. The men must have counted themselves
lucky indeed as they thought of what they might have been facing in
Jamestown or, for that matter, London.

Though the men surely found plenty to satisfy them in the Bermudas, they would naturally have spent countless hours on the top of one of their island domain's high points, steadily scanning the horizon, hoping to spy a friendly sail that marked the arrival of some ship from home. But day after day, all they saw was the empty sea, a sea broken only by wave tops that marched endlessly to the distant horizon.

When they were not busy tending their crops, hunting hogs or birds, fishing in the shallows of the harbor, or keeping watch, they often went exploring, rowing a small boat—perhaps the one Richard Frobisher built for Admiral Somers to use as a fishing skiff—to nearby islands, where they walked the shore, looking for pearls or Spanish coins or other valuables that might have washed ashore from some stricken and long-lost vessel. On one such trip, as the three men wandered along the beach just above the high-water mark, they spied a man-sized grayish white chunk of material wedged in the rocks that fronted the beach. As soon as the three men—all mariners—spotted the mass, they immediately recognized it as ambergris, a naturally occurring substance that is created in the intestines of sperm whales and found floating on the sea or cast ashore on beaches. They would have known, too, that the roughly 180-pound chunk of ambergris, along with a few other smaller chunks, were worth a not-so-small fortune in England, where the substance was used in the manufacture of perfume.

While Chard would later claim he was the first to spot the ambergris, all three immediately laid claim to it and, no doubt, set to dancing and shouting gleefully on the beach, imagining themselves living the good life in London town or perhaps sailing the seas as the owners of their own ships. Of course, reality soon set in. They must have wondered how on earth could they possible get a chunk of ambergris—a chunk described in a letter as "a piece . . . as big as the body of giant [with] the head and arms . . . wanting"[1]—off the Bermudas and to England, where they could sell it and pocket the proceeds. How could they keep it out of the hands of the adventurers of the Virginia Company who would, if they knew of its existence, claim it as their own?

The first thing the three men did was hide it, perhaps in one of the many caves that mark the Bermudas. Then they began to argue. Chard claimed the bulk of the ambergris belonged to him since he had discovered it. Waters and Carter, not surprisingly, disagreed. The three argued, then fought, for the better part of two years. At one point, while fishing together in their little boat, they started bickering and the bickering escalated into open combat. They had at each other with fists and teeth and oars and anything else they could use as weapons. Snarling and bloody, they fell overboard, where they kept fighting until, exhausted, they dragged themselves ashore. Things were so bad that a dog that had remained on the island with the three sailors—perhaps it was the same hunting dog that had helped the *Sea Venture* survivors capture wild swine—waded into the middle of a particularly noisy fracas, biting Waters in an apparent attempt to make them stop. Eventually, Chard and Waters were prepared to fight to the death with swords or pistols rather than share the ambergris. Carter, though, was determined to avoid bloodshed and not happy at all at the thought of spending years—perhaps the rest of his life— alone in the Bermudas with no company other than the dog. He hid the weapons so that an uneasy peace settled over the little camp on Smith's Island. And time passed.

By the summer of 1612, nearly three years after the *Sea Venture* was swept to the Bermudan reef by the wind and waves of the hurricane and more than two years after Matthew Somers departed for England bearing his uncle's body, the three men who had chosen to hold the Bermudas until the English sent colonists to inhabit the island chain began to think they might have been abandoned. Of course, as they counted the slow passage of time they had no way of knowing that the Virginia Company in London had grown enthusiastic at the thought of establishing a colony in the place that had given succor to the *Sea Venture* survivors and that by mid-1612 the first boatload of settlers was bound for the islands. Day after day they waited for relief to come from home, counting days and fearful that with each passing sunset their chances of ever seeing an English sail grew smaller. For all that the three men on Smith's Island knew, Matthew Somers and the others on the *Patience*, the pinnace jury-built in Bermuda, might have been lost at sea. Perhaps open war had broken out again between Spain and England, as it had in the time of the Armada, and all ships were once again needed for the protection of the homeland, making their rescue impossible. That's what had happened to Ralegh's people on Roanoke Island a quarter century before, so it was certainly possible. Fearful of ending their lives alone in Bermuda—wealthier than they ever believed possible but unable to enjoy their good fortune—they determined to build a small vessel and bring their ambergris to Newfoundland, where they could expect to find a fishing vessel to carry them home. By that time, as Captain John Smith wrote in his history of the Bermudas, "Their hopes of any forraine releefe [were] as naked as their bodies."[2]

By late June or early July, the three men set about the task of felling straight, strong trees and hewing them into planks they could use to fashion a vessel. They must have had canvas for sails and some rope for rigging—supplies salvaged earlier from the *Sea Venture*—but they, like Somers and the other mariners who built the *Patience* with found materials, must have carved treenails to fasten the vessel's planks and searched the beaches for wax and tar swept ashore from some wreck and for seashells they could crush for lime to fashion oakum.

On July 11, one of the three—it is not known which one—was climbing a ridge when he spotted a sail on the horizon, moving steadily toward the islands. His voice almost certainly trembling with excitement, he called to his companions. In moments, all three, dressed in tattered rags that barely covered their nakedness, would have been staring to seaward, straining to discover if the approaching vessel was English or belonged to the hated Spaniards, come to recover the islands they believed were theirs. At some point, one of the men must have spied the white and red cross of St. George flying from the vessel's masthead. She was English. And she was headed right for the large, almost circular bay known today as Southampton Harbour.

The *Plough*, carrying Richard Moore and the men, women, and children recruited to turn the Somers Isles into an outpost of English civilization and a stepping-stone to Virginia, moved into the large harbor in midafternoon of that day. According to one of the passengers, after the ship took on passengers in London in late April, she then lay anchored at Tilbury, across the Thames from Gravesend about three-quarters of the way between London and the English Channel, until May 5, when she headed to the Downs where she was forced to once again lay at anchor, probably waiting for favorable winds. This was the same spot where Captain John Smith and the first settlers dispatched to the Chesapeake had been forced to take anchor on board the *Susan Constant*, the *Discovery*, and the *Godspeed* for six weeks as their ships were battered by savage storms before they were able to move into the open waters of the Atlantic. Those on board the *Plough* were more fortunate. After just four days, on May 9, they were able to unfurl sails and leave England in their wake. The voyage was quick and apparently eventless. "Wee had a faire and comfortable passage, and by God's blessing found so direct a course, that on the eleventh of July in the morning betwixt nine and ten of the clocke wee descried our hoped and desired Ilands, and in the afternoone of the same day about three a clocke wee arrived in a very safe harbour," wrote the passenger, described only as a "companion of Governor [Richard] Moore."[3]

As the *Plough* inched her way into Bermuda's Southampton Harbour—one settler later said the channels leading from the southeast into the anchorage were "so narrow and curious, as ships must come in very leasurely"—her master, Captain Robert Davies would have stood at his place by the helm, alert to the dangerous reefs and shallows all around and shouting orders to the helmsman in response to soundings being taken by a mariner up forward.[4] The fifty or sixty settlers on the vessel, a number that included Governor Moore's wife and two children, stood on deck, looking at the islands that ringed the harbor, at tree-cloaked hills and sandy beaches. For almost an hour before reaching the islands, the *Plough* had been surrounded by a "company of Fish" that had followed the vessel as it moved into the harbor and now, as the ship came to anchor somewhere near St. David Island, south and east of St. George's, as sailors scurried aloft to strike sails and passengers and crew prepared to disembark, the waters around the little vessel teemed with grouper and mullet and snapper and other sea life.[5]

For some reason—perhaps they wanted to check the hiding place they had chosen for their ambergris one more time or perhaps they wanted to see if they recognized any of those on board the *Plough*—the three castaways did not immediately make their presence known to the newcomers. Instead, they remained hidden, no doubt watching as the ship's company and the settlers made their way to shore. They observed, silent, as the settlers and mariners gathered on the beach, then dropped to their knees, as one colonist said, to give "thanks unto the Lord for our safe arrivall."[6]

Those who were on the beach praying must have known that three Englishmen had been left in Bermuda when Matthew Somers sailed away more than a year earlier. They would, of course, have wondered what happened to the three men. While they were praying, Chard, Waters, and Edwards came rowing up to the beach. The settlers were amazed to see how healthy the three were, though their clothes were so tattered that they were almost naked. After greetings were exchanged, the whole company, led by Master George Keith, the minister dispatched to serve the new colony's spiritual needs, sang a psalm and, in the words of the passenger, "praised the Lord for our safe meeting, and went to supper."[7]

That first night those on the beach must have had something like a party.

Governor Moore and the others aboard the *Plough* would have been naturally overjoyed to feel solid ground beneath their feet, to be free of the crowded, smelly, damp, always swaying confines of the vessel. Chard, Edwards, and Waters—forlorn just a few hours earlier—would have been equally overjoyed to see their countrymen and -women. They would have happily, with a certain pride of ownership, shared their pork and fish and turtle with the settlers and seamen who had been eating the rough diet of the sea for the last month. They would also have shared tales of their time in the islands with the new-comers. The one thing they did not share was the news that they'd found a big chunk of valuable ambergris since, by that time, they had already decided to try to find someone to smuggle the ambergris back to England on board the *Plough*.

It did not take Moore long to realize that Smith's Isle was far too small to serve as the site for the thriving colony he envisioned. Soon after that wel-coming banquet on the beach, he ordered the settlers, including the three cast-aways, on board the *Plough*, this time for a short sail to the lee side of St. George's, the island lying at the northeast end of the Bermuda chain. This is-land, shaped roughly like an inverted V with its western leg roughly twice as long as it eastern leg, had been the site of the camp established by Gates and Somers and the other *Sea Venture* survivors. It was probably chosen by Moore because it was small enough to allow for easy defense, had cliffs ranging along its northeastern shore that provided a natural fortification, and provided a large, safe anchorage in Southampton Harbour.

Like the *Sea Venture* survivors before them, the newcomers were amazed at what they found in the place the Spanish knew as the Isle of Devils. As soon as the vessel was unladed, a few of the men set out with "a hooke and line" and quickly "tooke more [fish] than our whole company was able to eate." They found huge and tasty turtles—called "turkles...of a mightie big-nesse" by one witness—and, of course, the Bermuda cahows, birds they could capture in their bare hands. The hog population, diminished in the months the *Sea Venture* survivors lived in the Islands, had replenished itself, too, enough so that within a few days of landing, the settlers were dining on swine sweeter than the sweetest mutton found in all of England. "I am loath to write that which I have seene," said the anonymous reporter in a letter appar-ently carried back to London on the *Plough* when she made her return voyage, "by reason you would condemne my writing (as I feare) and thinke to be but false reports." The only reason he felt free to describe what he and the others

found in the Bermudas, he said, was that "all our company will or may ap-
prove [verify] it."[8]

The adventurers of the Virginia Company in London were used to receiving hearty, positive reports from their correspondents in Virginia and had nobody to blame but themselves when those reports proved misleading, or
downright false, since they made it plain they wanted to read only positive
news. However, they must have been heartened by what they read in this early
report.

"And whereas it is reported that this Land of the Barmudas, with the
Ilands about it . . . are inchanted and kept with evill and wicked spirits: it is a
most idle and false report," the letter sent to London on the *Plough* read. "God
grant that we have brought no wicked spirits with us, or that there comes
none after us, for we found none there so ill as ourselves."[9]

Then the writer continued, with a promise that would have brought cheer
to the heart of even the most skeptical investor sitting in far off London.
"But this I say to them that have adventured in Virginia, especially to such as
thinke they shall lose by that worthy action: let them do the like to us [sup-
port us as well as they have supported Jamestown], and I make no doubt but
wee shall in short time give them satisfaction.

"For our Inchanted Ilands, which is kept, as some say, with spirits, will
wrong no friend or foe, but yeeld all men their expectations."[10]

Before leaving England, Moore, who had been appointed to serve as governor for a term of three years, was given two sealed boxes by the Virginia
Company. One of the two boxes contained the name of the man appointed to
serve as Moore's successor in the event—not completely unlikely, given the
uncertainty of ocean voyages in the early seventeenth century—that Moore
should be taken "out of this life" before his term in office ended. The second
box held the name of a third settler in case both Moore and his successor "be
depted [departed] out of this world." In addition, in its commission granted
to Moore on April 27, 1612, the company named a council of seven men to
provide "ayde and assistance" to the governor.[11] This council was comprised
of Master Keith, the preacher; Edwin Kendall, a cousin of Sir Edwin Sandys,
one of the foremost investors in the Bermuda venture and a man who would,
in later years, take over the reins of the Virginia Company; Chard, one of the
three men who had remained in the islands; and three lesser-known men, John
Adhe, John Collabar, and Richard Garrard.

Sometime soon after the settlers landed on St. George's, Moore put the men to work digging a well and erecting thatched dwellings, including one for the governor and his wife and children. While these dwellings were being built, the newcomers used palm fronds for shelter, one beneath them for protection from biting insects and one above as protection against the rain. Moore set some of the men to hunting and fishing and fowling. Others were put to work making salt, under the guidance of Ralph Garner, a saltmaker sent as part of the company. John Collabar, the settler named to Moore's seven-man advisory council, was tapped to serve as "clarke of the stores."[12] As such, he would have been responsible for a storehouse where he watched over provisions that had been carried to the islands as well as turtle meat and pork and fish and any other commodities that the settlers were able to gather. Each single settler was allotted one rood (about a quarter of an acre) of arable land for planting; each married couple, twice that amount, along with seed, in the hopes that the company would be relieved of the expense of supplying the new colony with victuals. Soon the site of the little settlement on the island was bustling with activity. Each morning and evening, in accord with the company's instructions, the settlers and mariners, before they departed on the *Plough*, gathered for prayers, using a good supply of prayer books—copies of the Book of Common Prayer and the Geneva Bible— provided by the company.

Religion seems to have been important to Moore, at least as important as it was to the Virginia Company's leaders. One of his first official acts was to set some of the colonists to erecting a frame church, named St. Peter's, of hewn cedar, on a hill overlooking the little settlement. Despite that fact that Moore was himself a master carpenter who must have overseen the church's construction, this frame structure did not last long, being almost immediately destroyed by a strong wind, so Moore oversaw the construction of a thatched church in a sheltered spot in the town the settlers may already have been calling St. George's.[13] The lumber that had been hewn to build the church was used instead to construct a sturdy house for the Moore family.

Sometime during these very early days on St. George's Island, Governor Moore called Edward Chard, elevated in status from castaway to member of the governor's council, to his quarters. There, Moore asked Chard if he and his companions had found anything of value during the time the three men had been alone in the Bermudas. It is tempting to think that Moore somehow knew of the ambergris, but the evidence is that he was simply following what proved to be insightful orders from his bosses in England. In fact, in his commission Moore had been directed to keep a sharp eye out for anything of value he could send back to England on the *Plough*, "to give encouragemt to the adventurers" and, in that way, to guarantee that the new colony's financial backers would be willing to keep needed supplies and additional colonists flowing across the Atlantic. He was ordered especially to look for "Ambergreece wch wee doubt not but you shall finde readye gathered by those three who weare left by the last shipp."[14] Anyone finding the valuable substance, the company said, should be rewarded with payment of 13 shillings 4 pence per troy ounce. At that rate, figuring the 180-pound chunk of ambergris would tip the scales at roughly 2,625 troy ounces, the company was willing to pay almost £1,750 for the ambergris found in Bermuda. To get an idea of what that meant in buying power, consider that, at that time, a single shilling—one-twentieth of an English pound—would purchase roughly eight pounds of good English beef in a Southampton butcher's shop and 2 pence (there were 20 pence in a shilling) would purchase a pound of the best cheese. The ambergris, in other words, represented a fortune to working men like Chard and Carter and Edwards. Given the fact that it would have been worth much, much more on the open market in Europe, it is not surprising that Chard, even when asked a direct question by Moore, denied that he had found anything of value other than "the fruits of the Ile," but that he could not speak for his friends.[15] Further dissembling, he said he would surely let Moore know if he discovered that Edwards or Waters was hiding anything of value.

As John Smith later reported, Chard's assurances were nothing more than a delaying tactic. As soon as he was questioned by Moore, Chard ran to warn his cronies that the deputy governor was on the prowl and to swear them to secrecy, promising them that he would find a way to get the ambergris on board the little vessel that rode at anchor just off the beach and to get the three of them off the islands, as well. Of course, Chard was canny enough to know that he and the others had to act fast if they wanted to make good the plan to smuggle the ambergris out of Bermuda. "Till this was effected," Smith wrote, "they thought every houre an age."[16] Chard also knew that he and the others would never be able to ship the ambergris home without the connivance of someone aboard the *Plough*.

To forward their plans, Chard and his co-conspirators soon met with Captain Robert Davies and whispered to him of the wealth they had discovered on the beach. By promising him a portion of the proceeds of the sale of the ambergris in England, they convinced him—quickly, it seems—to help them. "Without further ceremony the match was accepted," Smith wrote, "and absolutely concluded, the plot laid, time and place set downe to have it aboord."[17]

It is a testament to the seductive power of the smelly chunk of whale refuse that Davies even considered joining the plotters in what was, after all, the theft of Virginia Company property, an act that would make him little better than a pirate. He was a seasoned mariner with a long history of service to the company, having served in the expedition that attempted to establish a colony in New England in 1606 and as co-captain, along with his brother Captain James Davies, of the pinnace *Virginia* that sailed in the *Sea Venture* fleet in 1609. Still, when Captain Davies thought of what the ambergris represented in terms of wealth, he quickly forgot his duty to the investors and leaders of the company in London.

For some unknown reason, perhaps because he needed help concealing the ambergris on the *Plough*, Davies decided to let Edwin Kendall, the settler who just happened to be both a member of Moore's governing council and a cousin of Sir Edwin Sandys, in on the plan. Despite his distinguished family ties and responsibilities to the colony, Kendall, like Davies, quickly joined the plotters.

When Carter learned that Captain Davies had involved Kendall in the plot, he must have been enraged, if for no other reason than the thieves, if successful, would now have to cut the profits five ways instead of four. Perhaps because of his anger, or maybe because he simply became frightened at the idea that a man like Kendall, close to Governor Moore and to the Virginia Company, might betray them all and that Moore would learn about the ambergris, Carter went to Moore himself and disclosed the plot.

Moore, for obvious reasons, was furious that Kendall, a trusted member of his council, would become involved in a plot to steal the ambergris. He was just as angry that Chard had told a bold-faced lie when he claimed he had found nothing of value in his months in the Bermudas. The governor knew, however, that he had to proceed cautiously. Getting his hands on the ambergris and sending it to the company in London would work to his personal benefit and gain him favor with the company's directors. However, it would be no easy matter to obtain the ambergris without destroying his council since two of the seven men named to serve as his assistants were among those plotting the theft. Forcing the plotters to give up their riches could, Moore knew, start a war that might destroy the settlement on St. George's Island in its infancy. Yet he knew he could not simply allow Chard and Davies and Kendall and the others to simply sail away with a fortune that rightly belonged to the Virginia Company and its investors. He decided to take whatever steps were necessary to spike the plotters' plans even if it meant "hazarding a mutiny." He confronted Kendall, in what Smith described as "faire tearmes," reproving him for dishonesty.[18] Kendall apparently answered with contempt and Moore responded by throwing both Kendall and Chard, the chief plotter, into what Smith called "prison," probably one of the dwellings on the island.

By this time, Captain Davies, blinded by greed, was fully committed to the plot to steal the ambergris. Involving his crew, he and his men determined to free Chard and Kendall, steal the ambergris, turn pirate, and sail off with a fortune. If he and his crew had acted swiftly, they probably would have been able to overpower those on the island—mariners were a hard lot, as a rule—but, for some reason, Davies and his men remained on the *Plough*, anchored offshore, beyond the reach of Moore and his followers.

Moore, meanwhile, was smart enough to be wary of Davies and his men. He supplied trustworthy settlers with weapons and told them to be ready for action at his signal. The men did not have long to wait. The following Sunday, when Davies and his crew came ashore, Moore was waiting. Using language unsuitable for the Sabbath, Moore accused the captain of treachery, of violating his obligations to the Virginia Company and to the Bermuda colony. He threatened to lock him in irons if he did not immediately give up his plans. Davies, it seems, did not even answer Moore's charges but instead pushed past the governor and made his way with his followers into the thatched church not far from the waterfront. The church service that Sunday morning must have been tense indeed, with Moore and his loyalists probably on one side of the little church and Davies and his tough crewmen on the other and all, seamen and settlers alike, with their hands on their knives or hidden pistols.

At some point before the service ended, Captain Davies rose and signaled his men. Without a word, he stomped out of the church, followed by his crewmen. At that, Moore called his men to action. There's no description of exactly how the confrontation unfolded, but it is easy enough to imagine the two armed groups—there were perhaps twenty or thirty men in each party—facing each other on the beach, snarling and cursing and inching closer to what Smith called "an uncivill civil war."[19] Suddenly, Captain Davies seems to have realized that Moore was a more formidable opponent than he had thought—if he had bothered to think—when he came up with his short-sighted plan to commit treason and steal away as a pirate. Davies told his men to stand down and then capitulated to Moore, begging his forgiveness.

As soon as Davies bent his knee, Moore allowed the *Plough's* captain his freedom and, at the same time, freed Kendall from confinement. Chard, however, was another matter. Because he was the ringleader of the plot to steal the ambergris, or perhaps because he'd lied blatantly, Chard was sentenced to hang for his crime. A gallows was soon raised on the waterfront. The company of settlers and all the mariners were called together, probably with the beating of a drum. Chard would have been freed from his place of confinement and dragged to the gallows by a cadre of armed men, all watched by the silent settlers and sailors as Master Keith, the preacher, read from the Good Book.

Even in imagination, the scene is dramatic. It was meant to be since it seems to have been staged by Moore as a way to strike fear into the hearts of the settlers and sailors. At the last moment, perhaps even as Chard stood on a ladder of some sort with the noose round his neck, Governor Moore ordered the execution stopped. Instead of dying, Chard was, John Smith said, "kept . . . a prisoner all the time he staied in the Country."[20] In all likelihood, Chard was forced to do some sort of hard labor—perhaps to serve as the governor's oarsman—since holding him under guard would have been almost impossible.

If, as seems likely, Moore's cleverly orchestrated quasi execution of Chard may well have been staged as a way to force the former *Sea Venture* crewman to turn the ambergris over to the governor. If that was the case, it worked beautifully, for Moore did take ownership of the valuable ambergris and was able to use it, during the next year or so, as a bargaining chip to convince the company in London to continue supporting the little colony on St. George's Island.

Soon after this period, when, as John Smith later reported, "this disturbing brabble passed over," Moore put the settlers to work erecting a series of forts designed to protect St. George's from the Spanish, who were still viewed as a threat to England's tenuous grasp on the Bermudas.[21] Fortifications—some of stone, others of planks laboriously hewn from the island's cedar trees—slowly took shape. The first were erected on Paget and Smith's Islands, guarding the entrance to St. George's Harbour, the body of water lying immediately to the south of St. George's Island. Other fortifications included King's Castle and Charles Fort on Castle Island (the western point of land commanding the entrance to Southampton Harbour); Pembroke Fort on Cooper's Island on the eastern side of the harbor's mouth; Gates' Fort and St. Catherine's Fort on the seaward coast of St. George's Island; and Warwick Castle overlooking the settlement and the water supply on St. George's. It was backbreaking work to build the forts and even more difficult when Moore sent a party of men to salvage artillery from the *Sea Venture* wreck. Slowly, the forts—they were not much more than square enclosures large enough to hold a few men and arms—took shape. Two cannon were hauled ashore: one was placed in Smith's Fort, the second in Warwick Castle. Settlers, on Moore's orders, also salvaged a few—very few—cannonballs that might be used in the ordnance. Meanwhile, Moore, who was described by Captain John Smith as "a good Gunner, very witty [wise] and industrious," set about training a corps of gunners to load and aim and fire the weapons.[22]

Sometime during this period, the *Plough* departed for London carrying news of the arrival of the ship and settlers in the Bermudas and what was the abundantly welcome report that ambergris had been discovered.[23] It is safe to assume that neither Davies nor Kendall—who abandoned his post in Bermuda to sail home as soon as the *Plough* headed east, probably without any regrets on Moore's part—reported on the attempted theft of the ambergris or on their complicity in the plot. In fact, the two men managed somehow to smuggle a few small pieces of the ambergris out of Bermuda—Smith said it was "either by the ignorance or connivency of the Governors" (members of the governing council)—and haul them back to London.[24] There, the two men sold the little chunks they had managed to steal for £600, or about $120,000 in today's money. In England, though, the two men—who seem to have hoped to purchase a ship either to enter the merchant trade or, more likely, given their personalities, to turn pirate—had a falling out, apparently over the proceeds of their theft, and their behavior called the company's attention to their newfound wealth. Company directors had a warrant for their arrest issued and they were forced to flee. Davies left England for Ireland and Kendall simply faded into obscurity.

In England, meanwhile, the company had concerns other than the theft of ambergris. The Spanish, having discovered that the English were settling the islands they thought belonged to them by right of discovery, grew concerned. Once again, Philip III was advised to take some action and—just as he had in 1609 when advised that England was sending a huge fleet to resupply Virginia—the king seemed determined not to do anything. Others in Spain, however—including the Duke of Medina Sidonia, Spain's highest-ranking admiral—were determined to dispatch ships to discover exactly what the English were doing in the Isle of Devils. The English, of course, were every bit as aware of what transpired in Seville as the Spanish were of decisions made in London, and even as Medina Sidonia grew concerned, the Virginia Company's leaders learned of the duke's plans to send a fleet to Bermuda. A diplomatic message received in London in early 1613 carried the news that a fleet would leave the port of Cádiz to "goe unto the Bermudas, there to inhabit."[25]

Made nervous by these reports, the Virginia Company almost immediately dispatched the *Elizabeth* carrying thirty settlers, provisions for the colony, and warnings about the Spanish plans. The ship also carried company orders to "have all the ambergreece."[26]

Moore, not without cause given the dearth of support given to Jamestown in its earliest days, was afraid that if he sent the entire chunk of ambergris back to the adventurers in London it might spell the end, or at least a waning, of support for the little colony. "Perceiving," as John Smith later wrote, that the ambergris "was the chiefest cause of their comming, and that it was the onely loadstone to draw from England still more supplies," Moore sent back roughly one-third of the ambergris, holding the rest out as a kind of ransom to be exchanged if the company sent more supplies.[27]

Of course, the Virginia Company's warning that the Spanish were sending a fleet to dislodge the English from their tenuous perch on St. George's Island had to be taken seriously in Bermuda. Moore put all the able-bodied men in the colony to work on the fortifications. In keeping with company orders, he maintained a record of the days each man worked so they could receive their fair pay. The adventurers in London had authorized Moore to pay skilled workers 22 shillings per day, while laborers were paid 12 shillings per day. Though there was no money on hand in Bermuda, the company promised to send coin to meet the payroll. This coin, created specially for use in Bermuda and shipped to St. George's sometime around 1616, was the famous Bermudan "hogge money," coins minted with the likeness of a ship on one side (presumably the *Sea Venture*) and a wild boar on the obverse.[28]

As work progressed on the forts, other important tasks were neglected. Men who could have hunted or fished for food for the colony were busy felling trees and hauling stones to the fortifications. Planting was forgotten in the rush to finish the fortifications. The colonists were driven to eat stores that had been brought on board the *Plough* and the *Elizabeth* and to kill the remaining hogs that had sustained them and the *Sea Venture* survivors before them. Forced to labor long hours and beset by hunger, some of the settlers— John Smith called them "drones that grew weary of their taskes"— complained to Master George Keith, the minister, that Moore was overworking them and that conditions in the colony were too hard to be tolerated. The chaplain apparently found the settlers' complaints credible, for one Sunday he took it upon himself to berate the governor from the pulpit in St. Peter's, saying that the governor "did grinde the faces of the poore" and oppressed them with what he called "Pharaohs taxes."[29]

Moore was not one to allow such a challenge to his authority, even from the colony's minister, to go unanswered. This was the man, after all, who faced down the mutineers who wanted to steal the ambergris. Soon after the church service he called a meeting of the settlers and ordered Master Keith to attend. At the meeting, almost certainly held in the church, Moore stood before the settlers and demanded that they explain just how he had mistreated them. It seems that even if the accusations were true, none of the settlers who were so willing to grouse to the chaplain wanted to voice their complaints in front of Moore, since Smith records that "with a universall cry they affirmed the contrary."[30] Keith himself immediately fell to his knees before the deputy governor and begged his forgiveness. Moore—as he had with Captain Davies—quickly forgave the minister, though he did urge him in future to watch his tongue.

While Smith's record of those days—the only record available—is sometimes confusing, it seems to indicate that sometime not long after that confrontation in the little church two of the settlers, presumably men who joined in the "universal cry" praising Governor Moore in the church, continued complaining, constantly upbraiding Moore. Moore, of course, knew that a few complainers could, as John Smith said, "breed ill bloud." It seems he warned the discontented settlers that he would be forced to impanel a jury to investigate their behavior and, if they were found guilty of making what amounted to treasonous comments, they might well be sentenced to death. The complainers took Moore seriously, so seriously that one of the two, Smith reported, "fell into a dead Palsie." Apparently, Smith meant the settler actually died of fright, since he goes on to say that "the other [settler] was set at libertie" and reformed himself, becoming a valuable worker.[31]

Though Moore seems to have been able to stop the complaining in the little colony, all in Bermuda was certainly not well. Since planting had been put off while the forts were being built, hunger was soon a problem. Not long after the *Elizabeth* sailed away with one-third of the ambergris—she sailed to England by way of Virginia—another vessel sailed slowly into Southampton Harbour. The *Martha* carried sixty settlers and, it seems, not much in the way of provisions. That raised the population in the Bermudas to roughly 150 persons, all living in the little settlement on St. George's. This ship also bore the company's firm orders to Moore telling him to hurry the ambergris to England without delay. Once again, though, Moore chose to ignore the company's orders, sending instead a second one-third of the treasure.

Meanwhile, as pleasant as the surroundings were in the Bermudas, the colony was having trouble, as much trouble as Jamestown, producing salable commodities to please the adventurers in London. A French specialist dispatched to the islands to try to produce silk failed, claiming that the mulberry plants native to the Bermudas were not "the right Mulberies he expected."[32] Tobacco, likely planted by Chard, Edwards, and Carter using seeds harvested from a few plants they found growing on the islands in their time alone there, was spoiled when the settlers tried to dry it for use.

As soon as the *Martha* made her way back to London, bearing the second one-third of the ambergris, the company dispatched the *Elizabeth* again, this time carrying an additional forty settlers and a command to send the remaining ambergris without delay. Moore had no more excuses and had to stand watch as the precious ambergris was removed from his house, where it was almost certainly stored, down to the waiting ship for transport back to England. In London, the ambergris, broken into chunks, sold for roughly £3 per ounce, with the largest pieces bringing even more. All told, the ambergris that made it into the company's possession was sold for roughly £10,000 pounds. It is safe to assume that at least some of the valuable material that Chard and Waters and Carter found on the beach in Bermuda never made it to the company's hands in London and that the total value was much higher than that. Still, the £10,000 return—about $2 million in today's terms—was enough to cover the adventurers' initial costs for the Bermuda settlement and to encourage additional outlays.

When the Spanish learned of the not-so-small fortune recovered on the Isle of Devils, they became even more determined to send ships and men to investigate. Medina Sidonia's original plans had come to nothing, partly because of Philip's lack of interest in the far-off Bermudas and partly because of intransigence on the part of individual Spanish mariners. Finally, though, in the late summer of 1613, in the wake of reports of the discovery of the ambergris, Philip III ordered Captain Diego Ramirez, the man who had been marooned with his shipmates on Bermuda in 1604 and who wrote such a glowing report of the islands, to take ship to investigate the situation and then to travel on to Havana to report to the governor there.[33] Still, the Spanish— this was more than two decades after the defeat of the Armada, decades in which the great empire of Spain was sliding into disarray—couldn't seem to take the steps necessary to reconnoiter the little settlement in Bermuda. By the time Ramirez received the king's orders, it was winter, certainly no time to send a ship to the dangerous waters around the Bermudas.

As the Spanish dithered, life for the settlers in Bermuda—including Christopher Carter and Edward Waters, the two *Sea Venture* survivors who were included among the first residents of the island chain, and, of course, Edward Chard, the *Sea Venture* crewman being punished for trying to steal the ambergris—remained difficult. Though there was no dreadful famine like that experienced in Jamestown, hunger was fairly constant in the colony's early days. It must have seemed like a godsend to the colonists, then, in mid-1613 when an English captain, Daniel Elfrith, sailed a Spanish prize, a caravel, loaded with grain into the harbor off St. George's. Spain and England were not at war, of course, so in the eyes of the law Elfrith was a pirate, but the Bermuda colonists were much more interested in food than they were in legal niceties. They quickly and happily traded what goods they had, perhaps fish or turtle meat of which they would have been heartily sick, for Elfrith's grain. Even as the colonists baked the first loaves of bread they'd eaten in long months, the Bermudans found that Elfrith's visit was not without unintended consequences: a horde of black rats swarmed ashore from the moored vessel. They soon bred and spread throughout the little colony, nesting in palm trees and in the thatched roofs of the cottages and church and storehouse. The pests dug holes in the soft coral, ate the colony's corn and wheat, devoured young plants as soon as they sprouted, and generally made life miserable. According to Smith, "within two yeeres" the rats "neere ruined all."[34] Despite the colonists' valiant attempts—they built traps, hunted with dogs, and loosed cats that themselves grew feral—it took several years before the rats (they were not native to the Bermudas and hence had no natural enemies—other than the settlers) were brought under control.

During this time, the adventurers in London made good their promises to supply the Bermudas with plenty of settlers. Two months after Elfrith off-loaded grain and rats, the *Blessing,* the same vessel that suffered through the

1609 hurricane after leaving the *Sea Venture*'s company, delivered a hundred settlers to St. George's. Two days after the *Blessing* arrived, the *Starre* sailed into the harbor, bearing 180 more colonists. These ships were followed just a few days later by the *Margaret* and what Smith described as "two Frygats," bearing a total of 160 settlers.[35] By late 1613, then, the colony's population stood at more than five hundred persons, including a good number of women and children (there's no way of knowing how many with any degree of certainty). The ships carried some supplies, to be sure, but nowhere near enough provisions to keep all the colonists fed for any length of time. At the same time, it appears that Moore kept many of the men working on finishing the fortifications, a course of action that limited the food produced in the colony. This, coupled with the population of voracious rats, meant that starvation loomed, as it had for so long in Jamestown.

Here's what John Smith wrote about that time.

> Master More ... followed the building of these Forts so earnestly, neglecting planting of Corne, till their store was neere all consumed, whereby they became so feeble and weake, some would not, others could not goe abroad to seeke releefe, but starved in their houses, and many that wen abroad, through weaknesse were subject to be suddenly surprized with a disease called the Feagues [fugues?]: which was neither paine nor sickenesse, but as it were the highest degree of weaknesse, depriving them of power and ability from the execution of any bodily exercises, whether it were working, walking, or what else.[36]

When the *Elizabeth* called at St. George's almost a year earlier with orders to haul the last of the ambergris back to England, her captain had delivered some Irish potatoes to the settlers along with some other needed supplies. The settlers, displaying the same level of ineptitude that so haunted Jamestown for so many years, planted potatoes, watched happily as they flourished, and devoured them with gusto, but improvidently neglected to save any seed potatoes for the next season. When the time came to plant, they found that the potatoes remaining in their storehouse were rotten. Only because a few that were thrown on one of the town's garbage heaps were salvaged after they took root was the potato saved as a viable crop in the Bermudas; from there, it eventually spread to the Americas. But in the time of famine, there were no potatoes to feed the hungry and those, Smith said, who "found not present succour, died."[37]

On March 14, 1614—in the middle of this travail—a dozen or so men who manned the two forts on Castle Island, guarding the mouth of Southampton Harbour, saw the sails of two vessels approaching the island. Apparently, the ships were quite close before they were spotted, for one of the two vessels was being towed by its skiff and both ships, proceeding slowly, were sounding as they picked their way through the shallow, dangerous waters. The men in the forts, hungry as they were, must have been overjoyed to spot the sails, hoping they were English ships full of food and other provisions.

As was custom, a boat manned by men from the fort set out from shore to meet the strange vessels and guide them to an anchorage. When those in the boat hailed the strange ships, they soon discovered that the vessels were foreign, most likely Spanish. In minutes, the boat was back on shore and a messenger was speeding to St. George's to alert Governor Moore of the arrival of the ships. Moore must have been almost ecstatic as he and a few of his soldiers rushed back to Castle Island. Finally, the enemy had arrived! All the work that had been done on the fortifications would finally pay off.

The Spanish later said that "in both" the forts on Castle Island "there [were] some ten or twelve pieces of artillery."[38] It's not clear whether that means there was a total of at least ten pieces between the two forts or whether there were as many as twenty-four pieces in all. It's more likely that there were fewer than ten or maybe twelve pieces of ordnance scattered through all the forts erected under Moore's direction and only four on Castle Island. Of course, the Spanish—and the English, too, for that matter—were not above overstating the strength of any enemy they faced, knowing that they had better hedge their bets in case they failed and had to answer to an irate ruler in Seville or London. In any event, if the Spanish had known the weakness of the forts on Castle Island, things might have turned out differently. But they didn't.

On the little island, now uninhabited except for some ruins, Moore sprang into action. He had no doubt that the vessels had been dispatched by Philip III to steal the Bermudas from him, and he and the other settlers were not about to let that happen without a fight. Moore barked orders and, it is safe to assume, the settlers ran to man one of the fort's cannon. Moore himself aimed the piece and put a shot near the lead Spanish ship, as a warning and as a gauge of the range. Still the ship moved closer. On his order, the men reloaded the cannon. Moore aimed again and ordered the cannon fired. With a roar, the cannon belched fire. The heavy cannonball, according to one witness, "passed through and through" the Spanish vessel. At that, "both the shyps, cutting their maine-sayles, cast about and made quite awaye, and thus ended that fraye."[39]

Why did the Spanish flee so quickly? Perhaps, as John Smith later reported, they thought they "might be received as friends" or, at least, "durst not be resisted as enemies" and once they discovered "the ordinance to speake more loud and hottly" than they thought possible, they simply did not want to risk any further confrontation. Smith himself thought it possible that they turned cowardly, explaining that, "the Spaniard although a good soldier generally, yet abhorres to march upon the cannon."[40] The fact that the Spanish fled in the face of what was nothing more than a show of resistance was something of a miracle, for what happened in the little fort was almost laughable—and almost tragic. In the excitement of the "battle," one of Moore's gunners kicked a barrel of gunpowder, which spilled all over the floor yet failed to ignite even though the working cannon fired directly over the powder. What was more, if the Spanish had pressed on, Moore and his men would have been quickly at their mercy since, after firing two shots at the approaching vessels, the little garrison on Castle Island had only one cannonball left.

Meanwhile, the discovery of the ambergris and what seemed to be the providential retreat of the Spanish were the only good news the colonists were able to enjoy in the colony's early years. One of the settlers, a man named William Millington, perhaps suffering from the ill-defined tiring illness described by John Smith, hooked a fish so large that it dragged him into the sea and he was "never after ever seene."[41] And the promise of riches to be made from pearls found in the islands proved a myth when Richard Norwood, a diver sent by the company, discovered that "there were but few pearls and amongst them very few that were precious and of worth." They were, he added, in "no ways equivalent to the time and labour that must be bestowed upon them."[42]

The hunger continued unabated during this period. Unfortunately, there was no scribe like George Percy to record the happenings during Bermuda's "starving time," no reporter like William Strachey to write a lively report of the dying, and hence no record of how many settlers succumbed. However, it is safe to say that dozens perished from hunger and from the illness, perhaps a tropical fever, described by John Smith. Matters were so bad that Moore allowed the settlers to stop work on fortifications and to spend all their time searching for edibles. He also—like Smith when he served as governor in Virginia—dispersed settlers, sending about 150 to Cooper's Island, in the mouth of Southampton Harbour, where cahows were still plentiful. By this time, the Reverend Lewis Hughes had been dispatched to serve the growing colony in Bermuda. In a report Hughes wrote in 1621, the minister had little compassion for the hungry, saying that as the population of the colony increased, so did "sin and disorder," which angered God "so as divers did perish very miserably." But, he added, most that died "were ungodly, slothfull and heartlesse men" who deserved nothing better.

"I cannot but wonder," he wrote, "when I think upon the nastinesse & loathsome lazinesse, wherin, too many of them died, crying night and day for meat, notwithstanding they had meat enough of not too much, for they did nothing night and day but dresse, and eate, and so greedy...more like dogges than Christians ...."[43]

Hughes went along to Cooper's Island when Moore dispersed the 150 settlers—the minister described them as a "lazie starving crewe" fleshed out with some industrious, honest persons—and described how the hungry settlers ate so many cahows that many fell sick from overeating.[44] Perhaps at Hughes's urging, Moore then moved the settlers to Port Royal, on the southwest coast of the main island now known as Hamilton Island. There, the settlers acted in ways that certainly gave some credence to Hughes's seemingly unkind words, killing a bull and some cows owned by the company, then claiming the animals, which had been placed there to graze, had drowned after they ran into the sea to cool off. Eventually, after several of the settlers sent to Port Royal had died, either of starvation or, as Hughes said, "with meate in their mouthes crying for more," most struggled back to St. George's Island, though a few refused to return, instead choosing to hide in the woods rather than work for Moore in what amounted to the colony's capital.[45]

During this period, Moore sent constant pleas to England that the colony be supplied with food. Of course, the adventurers had hoped and planned that Bermuda, certainly described as a land of plenty, would be self-sustaining, and they viewed its failure to accomplish this end as a failure on Moore's part. It was, to a degree, but mainly because he focused all his attention on protecting the islands from Spanish invasion. Still, Moore was self-willed, almost pigheaded, in his refusal to send the ambergris to England when ordered to do so, and he had done himself no good by failing to discover any marketable commodities.

In 1615, in answer to an urgent request from Moore, the company dispatched a heavily laden ship, the *Welcome*, with plenty of supplies for the colony. It also carried no dispatches for the governor, not even a word of thanks for his stand against the Spanish or for his—by that time—three years of work on the company's behalf. When Moore learned he was not being reappointed to the colony's leadership, he must have breathed a sigh of relief. He packed his sea chest and prepared to leave the islands.

Before leaving, Moore named a six-man council to fill out the remaining months of his term as deputy governor, with each man to serve one month. Those named to the council were Captain Miles Kendall, Captain John Mansfield, Thomas Knight, Charles Caldycot, and the two *Sea Venture* survivors, Edward Waters and Christopher Carter.

To be sure, Bermuda's beginnings were not what must have been imagined by Sir George Somers or his nephew Matthew or, it is certainly safe to say, the adventurers who heard tales of the island chain's fertility. Though the company was able to pocket profits from the sale of the ambergris found by the *Sea Venture* survivors, expected riches were not found. As in Jamestown, starvation was an almost everyday companion in the Bermudas. However, by the time Moore left Bermuda, the colony was on solid enough ground: there was no reason to doubt that it would ultimately be successful as an adjunct to Virginia. The fact that there were English settlers at all in the little colony in the middle of the Atlantic Ocean was the direct result of the *Sea Venture* shipwreck and, ultimately, of the vision, the determination, and even the greed of the *Sea Venture* survivors Sir George Somers, Matthew Somers, Edward Chard, Christopher Carter, Edward Waters, and others whose names have been lost in history.

14

The Virginian Woman

Not long after their wedding in April 1614—just a few weeks before the two Spanish ships mounted their halfhearted assault on the Bermudas—John Rolfe and the Indian princess Pocahontas set up housekeeping on a grant of land he had been given by the Virginia Company, on Hog Island, across the James River from Jamestown. There, the couple lived in a relatively comfortable half-timbered dwelling similar to the brick-and-timber structures common throughout England.[1]

By the time the couple—Rolfe was about twenty-eight years of age, and his wife, Pocahontas (we shall continue to refer to her by her best-known name), was perhaps aged eighteen or nineteen—settled on Hog Island, Rolfe was a man of some importance in Virginia. He was a protégé, even a friend, of Sir Thomas Dale. He had, by that time, found some success with agricultural experiments that brought him to the favorable attention of the colony's leaders in Virginia and in London. And, most important, he was married to the daughter of the most powerful Indian leader in the Tidewater.

As a man of substance, a man who could expect to entertain Governor Dale and the Reverend Alexander Whitaker as well as any individuals of note who wanted to meet his Indian wife, Rolfe would have had servants who helped Pocahontas fetch water, haul wood, do laundry, make candles, gather food, cook, and perform all the other strenuous labor involved in caring for her husband and her home. These servants, who would have lived with the Rolfes, were, in all likelihood, native women or girls, perhaps including one or more of Pocahontas's many half sisters or numerous aunts.

By all accounts, both John and Pocahontas were happy in their marriage. Sir Thomas Dale, who likely visited the house on Hog Island often, described them as a happy couple. "She lives civilly and lovingly with him, and I trust will increase in goodnesse, as the knowledge of God increaseth in her."[2] The word *lovingly*, we may assume, meant to Dale what it means to us. At least in Dale's company, in other words, the Englishman and his Indian wife were tender with each other, solicitous and respectful. When he praised Pocahontas for living "civilly" with her husband, Dale certainly meant that she observed the rules of "civilized" society: she dressed and acted in accordance with the manners and customs of the English world of which the Indian princess now found herself a part.

Perhaps the happiness he saw in the young couple living on Hog Island led Dale to desire an Indian princess to share his house in Henrico. Or perhaps—though there's no evidence to support the supposition—Pocahontas herself suggested to the governor that he bring one of her many half sisters to the colony, as a companion for her and possibly a wife for one of the settlers, a move that would bring the Indians and her adopted *Tassantassas* closer. What is known is that Dale, hearing that Pocahontas had a comely younger sister, a girl who was much loved by her father, decided to make her his wife. On May 15, just a few weeks after Pocahontas and Rolfe married, Dale dispatched Ralph Hamor, the colony's secretary, along with the interpreter Thomas Savage, to visit Wahunsonacock and ask the old chief's permission to marry his daughter.[3]

After traveling the roughly sixty miles to the village of Matchut, on the York River, Hamor and Savage met with the paramount chief in his longhouse. After sharing a pipe of tobacco, Wahunsonacock asked after his friend Dale and, of course, inquired about Pocahontas. Hamor, speaking through Savage, told the old man that Dale was well and then said "his daughter was so well content that she would not change her life to returne and live with him."[4] Wahunsonacock and Savage knew each other well by this time, well enough that the young Englishman could twit the old chief without too much fear. Wahunsonacock laughed heartily when he heard of his daughter's happiness. Then, after giving the chief gifts including two large pieces of copper, five strings of white and blue beads, five wooden combs, several fish-hooks, and a pair of knives, Hamor, speaking through Savage, got down to business. Hamor told the chief that Dale, having heard of the perfection of the chief's youngest daughter, wanted to make the girl "his neerest companion, wife and bedfellow."[5] Such a marriage, he said, would further strengthen the bonds between the native people and the English and prove Wahunsonacock's friendship.

Dale's offer, on its face, was remarkable for several reasons. First, Rolfe's marriage to Pocahontas aside, it was virtually unheard of, certainly at that time, for a wellborn Englishman to wed an Indian maid. Then there was the age difference. Dale was at least forty years old, probably older, having served with distinction as a military leader in the Netherlands in 1588, and the girl he wanted to bring to his bed was only about eleven. Even at a time when older men routinely married young girls, the union between Dale and a girl-child would have raised more than a few eyebrows in Virginia and in England. What was truly remarkable, however, was Dale's desire to take a child bride even though he already had a wife and children in London. At the very least, if he had married Wahunsonacock's youngest daughter, the other settlers would have known he was a bigamist. Certainly Pocahontas, who undoubtedly knew Dale was married, would have looked askance at the marriage and, as a newly converted Christian, would have considered the relationship sinful.

In any case, Wahunsonacock was not interested in Dale's offer. He interrupted Hamor before he finished speaking, an action the Powhatan people viewed as intolerably rude, even on the part of a chieftain. He said he could not possibly bear to part with another daughter and, with some justification, added that he had proven his friendship to Dale and the other English by allowing Pocahontas to marry Rolfe and to live with the English. Obviously upset, Wahunsonacock threatened once again to move with his people so far away that the English would never see him again, but added that he hoped the peace would last. At the end of this meeting, Hamor and Savage knew that the old chief would not budge and had to report their lack of success to Dale.

While Sir Thomas was likely unhappy that his attempt to marry the chief's youngest daughter came to nothing, he had to be pleased at the peace that settled on the Tidewater in the wake of Rolfe's marriage to Pocahontas. Even the Chickahominy people, a nation perfectly happy to fight either the English and Powhatan—or both—sued for peace when they learned of the friendship between the Powhatan and the whites. "Ever since [the wedding],"

Hamor reported, "we have had friendly commerce and trade, not onely with Powhatan himselfe, but also with his subjects round about us."[6] Rolfe, who had struggled so mightily in making his decision to marry the Indian princess he loved, waxed rapturous in describing the aftermath of the marriage, a state of affairs that became known as the Peace of Pocahontas. "The great blessings of God have followed this peace," he said, adding that the peace "bredd our plentie—everie man sitting under his fig tree in safety, gathering and reaping the fruits of their labors with much joy and comfort."[7]

And so, in the weeks and months after the wedding, Rolfe sat happily under his fig tree. Pocahontas, too, was happy for the most part, though it is not hard to imagine her sometimes missing the relative freedom of her earlier life. As she sat at the table in Rolfe's house, in her house, her head bowed before eating a meal of food prepared in ways unfamiliar to her or listened to her new husband reading from the Bible, as he must have done with regularity, she must have wanted, at least on occasion, to be transported magically to Wahunsonacock's smoky lodge, where she would be surrounded once again by the family and friends of her childhood. Still, she was, by all accounts, contented enough in her marriage.

Pocahontas's happiness must only have increased when, within just a few months of the marriage, she realized that she was pregnant. Children represented wealth and security to the Powhatan people, even more so than to the English. They were treasures that guaranteed the health and well-being of not just the family but the whole tribe. They were also much loved and treated lovingly.

Sometime in 1615, Pocahontas gave birth to a son. She and her husband named him Thomas, almost certainly as a compliment to Sir Thomas Dale, the man they both must have considered something like an honorary uncle, and the man who could do great things for Rolfe in Virginia and in London.

It isn't hard to imagine how relieved John Rolfe felt when both his wife and baby not only survived the delivery but seemed to thrive. Given his experience in Bermuda and his religious bent, he must have spent hours in prayer as the time for the baby's birth neared. It is likely, or at least possible, that Pocahontas slipped out of the Hog Island house and made her way, along with a half sister and another companion or two, to some private place in the nearby forest to deliver her baby in the Indian fashion. It certainly would have been natural, when the time for delivery arrived, for Pocahontas to turn to her Indian friends and family members for help.

According to William Strachey, Powhatan women—and this was the case with many North American tribes—strictly separated themselves from men during childbirth, retreating to a "nursery" that could be an isolated hut or some hidden bower in the forest. Though Indian women seemed to experience little difficulty in childbirth—William Strachey claimed that native women "are easily delivered of childe," a statement that was echoed by Captain John Smith—giving birth in some hidden bower in the forest or in a cottage on Hog Island was a risky business.[8] And though Pocahontas was undoubtedly helped by an Indian woman experienced in such matters, the possibility of some serious emergency arising still loomed large. And so Pocahontas and the women with her must have offered up prayers of thanks—either to the God of Reverend Whitaker or to the Okee of Pocahontas's childhood—when the baby made its way into the world kicking and screaming and healthy.

Soon after the baby's birth, Pocahontas or the relative or friend who had served as midwife would have carried the newborn infant to the James River near the house and dipped the baby in the stream, "over Head and Ears, in cold Water," in the words of Robert Beverley, the first Virginia-born settler to write a history of the colony.[8] Having bathed the baby, the woman would then have dried him carefully with feathers, wrapped him in warm, soft skins, and attached him to a cradleboard with soft thongs. In the weeks and months after his birth, according to the Indian custom, Thomas Rolfe probably spent much of his time wrapped and secure, lashed to a cradleboard and carried on his mother's back or suspended from a tree limb or a rack as his mother worked. Several times each day, Pocahontas would unlash her son to nurse him, play with him, and clean him. Like other children born to Indian women, young Thomas was no doubt lovingly tended by his mother. William Stith, a Virginia historian who was familiar with the Rolfe family history and tradition, said, "She was ... delivered of a Son, of which she was extremely fond."[9]

Meanwhile, as Pocahontas and her Indian servants cared for young Thomas Rolfe, John Rolfe's prominence in the Virginia colony increased when, not long after the marriage, he was named the colony's secretary, replacing Ralph Hamor, who returned to England. As secretary, Rolfe became a man of real substance, earning not only respect, but also a yearly salary of £20, equal in value to almost two shares of Virginia Company stock. Of greater importance, to Virginia and to Rolfe's fortunes, he continued, in those months, his experiments with tobacco.

Rolfe's agricultural experiments began sometime in 1611, when he planted a few tobacco seeds in the rich, loamy soil around Henrico. It is romantic to think that he had carried the seeds he planted from England on board the *Sea Venture*, salvaged them from the shipwreck, jealously cared for them in Bermuda, then carried them on to Virginia. He may indeed have done just that, though it is not likely since the Spanish in 1606 decreed that any Spaniard who sold tobacco seeds like those Rolfe planted in Jamestown— they were *Nicotiana tabacum* seeds from Trinidad rather than the *Nicotiana rustica* that was native to Virginia—could be put to death. It is more likely that Rolfe obtained the seeds in Jamestown from some sailor who had visited the Caribbean. In any event, Rolfe, an inveterate smoker who dearly loved his pipe, planted his valuable seeds and tended them as carefully as if they were ailing children. He harvested a small crop in 1612 and enough the next year to export a small crop, not more than a sample. In 1614, the same year he and Pocahontas married, he shipped a few more pounds of weed to England as he continued experimenting with different planting and curing methods. Following his marriage, he perfected his methods of production, undoubtedly with his wife's help. Though tobacco was the one Indian crop that was, because of its religious significance, tended by men, Pocahontas certainly had plenty of opportunity to observe the Powhatan methods of planting, tending, and curing their tobacco and would have shared her knowledge with her husband. She must have told him where to plant the seeds he carried to Hog Island from Henrico, how to crop the tops of the plants so that the lower leaves grew larger. It was probably on her advice that Rolfe began harvesting his plants one leaf at a time and wrapping the leaves in fronds for transportation, and undoubtedly it was from her that he learned to cure his tobacco using the Indian method of hanging the leaves individually on drying racks rather than stacking them in the sun and covering them with dried grass.

With Pocahontas's help, Rolfe developed a tobacco much sweeter and milder than the native Virginia smoke. Ralph Hamor, in his 1615 report on the situation in the colony, gave credit to Rolfe as "the gentleman, worthie of much commendations, which first tooke the pains to make traill thereof." The new tobacco, Hamor said, was "answerable to west-Indio, Trinidado, or Cracus (tobacco from Caracas, or Venezuela)," the three most popular commercial varieties then known.[10] Hamor himself was convinced by Rolfe's experiments; he said, "No country under the Sunne, may, or doth, affoord more pleasant, sweet, and strong Tobacco" than Virginia.[11] Rolfe, in a letter to King James, couldn't help but brag a bit about the product he'd created. Virginia tobacco, he said, "thriveth so well that no doubt but after a little more triall and expense in the curing thereof it will compare with the best in the West Indies.[12]

In fact, while the Virginia tobacco was sweeter than the acrid native product, it still ran a poor second to tobacco produced in the Spanish colonies. It was, however, good enough to eventually capture a large part of the English market, where tobacco use was rampant after the habit was introduced by John Hawkins, a compatriot of Sir Francis Drake, in 1565. In this way, the English farmers in Virginia were able to break the monopolistic stranglehold the Spanish had maintained on European smokers. By 1615, Rolfe and a few other farmers who were producing tobacco in Virginia managed to ship about two thousand pounds of tobacco to England. By 1617, that amount grew to twenty thousand pounds, jumping to forty thousand pounds in 1620.

In the two years following the marriage, as tobacco grew to shape the economic underpinnings of the colony, the Peace of Pocahontas reigned in the lands of the Powhatan Confederacy. Relations between the natives and the *Tassantassas* were, for the most part, tranquil. Governor Sir Thomas Dale, though a harsh taskmaster, had managed to impose order on the colony. Thanks to the peace and relative prosperity of the colony, Dale had been able to put into action his plan to disperse colonists. By 1616, according to Rolfe, settlers were scattered across the lands the Powhatan people knew as *Tsenacommacah*. Roughly 50 settlers lived in Jamestown, 20 had established themselves at the old Kecoughtan village near Point Comfort, and an additional 18 men lived at the mouth of the Chesapeake near Point Charles, where they fished and produced salt for the colony. Thirty-eight men and boys lived and farmed at Henrico, the town Dale created up the James River, just south of the falls. An additional 119 male colonists lived at Bermuda Hundred, about six miles below Henrico, where they farmed and produced charcoal and potash for soap. Another 25 resided and farmed across the river at West Hundred and Shirley Hundred. All told, the colony's total population—using Rolfe's figures—included 205 officers and laborers. The first of these, those Rolfe called officers, were men who served the company and colony but provided for themselves and their servants; the second group comprised either men who worked solely for the company or tradesmen such as blacksmiths, brickmakers, and so on, who worked both for themselves and for the company. In addition there were 81 farmers—men who worked for themselves but who were required to serve as soldiers when needed and to pay a corn tax to the company each year. By this time, the colony included 65 women and children. Livestock included 144 cows (with 20 expecting calves), 6 horses, 216 goats, and more poultry and pigs than could be counted. Things had certainly improved since the Starving Time. With settlements scattered across the Tidewater, peace at hand, and a stable economic outlook, it seemed to colonists and to the adventurers in London as if the Virginia experiment had turned a corner and that some true prosperity just might be in the offing.

Still, while no one could deny that Dale had been fairly successful in making Virginia secure, the Virginia Company in London continued struggling for solvency. Given the paucity of company records for the years before 1619, it is impossible to determine how exactly many tens of thousands of pounds the company had spent to establish this toehold in Virginia, but it was a substantial amount. According to Virginia historian Wesley Frank Craven, after Sir Thomas Gates returned to London in late 1610 bearing bad news about the loss of the *Sea Venture,* and somehow managed to convince the adventurers to continue supporting the colony, the company attempted to raise £30,000. They fell far short of their goal, managing to raise somewhere between £10,000 and £18,000. And that type of disappointment had been largely the history of the entire Virginia venture since 1607. Far more was spent than was ever realized, and losses amounted to much more than could be recouped by a few short years of tobacco production. Matters were only exacerbated by the fact that many of the early subscribers, individuals who bought shares on credit, refused to pay what was owed as soon as they heard or read bad news about the colony.

In 1612 the company, beset by financial woes, announced it would hold a lottery to raise cash. This lottery, with a grand prize of £1,000, was a success. Other lotteries that followed were, however, less favorably received. Sir Thomas Dale, of course, was aware of the company's financial problems and knew that a propaganda coup might be just what was needed to bring money flowing into the Virginia Company's treasury. In late 1615 or early 1616, as Dale prepared to return to England after a strenuous five-year tour of duty in Virginia, he determined to bring Pocahontas, her husband, and their baby—the first English-Indian family in Virginia—to promote the Virginia enterprise in England. Pocahontas, in the flesh, would represent that "savage" land, tamed and converted by the English colonists; John Rolfe, by this time a successful planter, was the living embodiment of what was possible in the New World; and little Thomas Rolfe, the half-English, half-Indian baby, was the flesh-and-blood representative of the future, a future in which native and English would live in harmony in the wonderful world of Virginia. It was a propagandist's dream come true.

In the spring of 1616, the *Treasurer*, the same vessel that had carried Pocahontas to Jamestown in the days following her kidnapping, began taking on commodities for the voyage from Virginia to London. Captain Samuel Argall, now one of the most experienced of all the Virginia Company's captains, with a half dozen transatlantic voyages under his belt, watched as the crewmen loaded the ship with cargo, perhaps a few lengths of clapboard, barrels of sassafras, and possibly some salted fish. At some point, Rolfe must have appeared to superintend the work as valuable bales and tightly packed hogsheads of his choicest tobacco were stowed below, bound for the smokers of England.

It was probably sometime in early April when the ship took on passengers. Among those who boarded were two unwilling voyagers—the Spanish spy Don Diego de Molina and Francis Lembry (or Lymbry), the pilot of Molina's Spanish caravel that had come calling in the Chesapeake in 1610. The two men had been held in Jamestown for six years. Now they were bound for London, where they were supposed to be paroled or freed.

Sometime after the boat took on its supplies and cargo, Pocahontas appeared with her baby and her retinue, a retinue that befitted her as the daughter of a king. The princess traveled with about a dozen Indians, including Matachanna, her half sister, and Matachanna's husband, sometimes referred to as Tomocomo but also known as Tomakin, Uttamatomakkin, or Tomo. The party included several other young native women, traveling like ladies-in-waiting with the princess. While Pocahontas would have been dressed as a young English woman, in her starched, tightly bound undergarments and dress, complete with a ruff and perhaps slashed sleeves, the other Indians were dressed in native garb. Pocahontas was, of course, familiar with the *Treasurer*, but as soon as she and her companions boarded the ship and saw the hustle and bustle of activity as sailors stowed supplies and cargo, she would soon have recognized that this voyage would be much different from the river journey she had made after she was abducted by Argall.

Pocahontas probably took quarters in the gunner's room, perhaps with Rolfe and the baby, perhaps with a few of her servant women. This was the same room, small but dry since it was used to store gunpowder, that she had occupied with Iopassus and his wife shortly after her kidnapping. It is natural to wonder what Pocahontas thought and felt as she stood in the room again, about to set sail with her English husband and half-English child, bound for a country she could not begin to conceive of, no matter how much she had been told by John Smith and Rolfe and Dale and the Reverend Alexander Whitaker. She must have been frightened—after all, she was still a young woman, barely out of her teens—bound on a voyage that was itself frightening to a place as foreign to her as the moon. She must have been excited, too, at the thought of experiencing a new world, a world she was perceptive enough to realize represented the inexorable future.

While the Rolfe family, including young Thomas, would have been relatively comfortable in their quarters, the other members of her party had to make do as best they could, bunking down wherever they found a slice of open deck. Perhaps they were assigned space in the forecastle with the seamen or in the dark, dank, and airless belowdeck. Given the nastiness of the quarters below, the Indians probably slept on deck. Of course, all would have been seasick and miserable within hours of leaving the shelter of the Chesapeake. Tomocomo did not like the voyage at all, expecting—as he did on long water voyages on the rivers and streams in *Tsenacommacah*—to tie up near land at night, to sleep and eat on land and relieve himself in the privacy of the forest and not while dangling over the ocean's waters in the beakhead of a rolling, rocking, plunging ship. Somehow, Tomocomo survived the voyage as, apparently, did all the Indians, since no mention is made of any dying in midocean. Francis Lembry, the pilot captured along with the Spanish spy Molina, was not so fortunate.

It seems that after the *Treasurer* set sail, Dale somehow got proof positive that Lembry was a traitor, an Englishmen in the employ of the hated Spanish. Perhaps he discovered for sure what some in Virginia supposed—that Lembry had traitorously guided the ships of the Spanish Armada into the English Channel in 1588. Perhaps Dale just got bored in midocean and saw no reason not to execute a man he considered a traitor. What is known is that someplace in the middle of the Atlantic Lembry was hanged from the yardarm over the deck. Given Dale's military background and nature, he undoubtedly called together the entire ship's company, including Pocahontas and Tomocomo and the other Powhatans, to witness the execution. It would be fascinating to know what the Indians thought as they saw Dale's version of English justice at work. Sadly, all we can do is try to imagine their reactions to an execution they would have found brutal.

On the voyage, Rolfe worked on his *True Relation*, a long letter addressed to King James. This letter, like similar writings produced by other company men, is largely a publicity broadside touting conditions in Virginia. In it he describes "a countrey spacious and wide, capable of many hundred thousands of inhabitants," with soil "most fertile" and "ayre fresh and temperate."[13] Crops being raised included "Indian wheate, called mays [maize] in the West Indies, pease and beanes, English wheate, peas, barley, turnips, cabbages, pumpions [pumpkins] . . . , carretts, parsnips, and such like, besides hearbs and flowers."[14] Rolfe told King James that two men working with a spade and shovel could raise crops worth £50 in a single year, a goodly amount of money. The situation in the colony had changed so that the native people, all living in friendship now with the English, routinely came to settlements to trade skins and even land for food. Of course, Rolfe wrote about tobacco— what he called "the principall commoditie the colony for the presenteth yieldeth"—and lauded the government control of tobacco production put in place by Sir Thomas Dale, who had decreed that "no farmor or other—who must maintayne themselves—shall plant any tobacco, unless he shaell yearely manure, set and maintayne for himself and every man servant two acres of ground with corne."[15] Without those controls, Rolfe warned, settlers would forego planting edible crops and focus all their attention on the labor-intensive business of planting and tending and harvesting their tobacco fields.

On its face, it seems strange that Rolfe would sing the praises of tobacco to James I, an open and ardent hater of what he called the "vile custom" of smoking. Though James had a weakness for young men and wine and happily tolerated drunkenness and debauchery among his courtiers, he was a prude when it came to tobacco. In 1604 he wrote, anonymously, a venomous diatribe against tobacco in which he railed against "the stinking suffumigation" of tobacco, castigated its users as beasts who were willing to bankrupt themselves, spending £300 or £400 per year to feed their filthy habit.[16] Smoking, he said, is a custom "loathsome to the eye, hateful to the nose, harmful to the brain, dangerous to the lungs, and in the black stinking fumes thereof, nearest resembling the horrible Stygian smoke of the pit that is bottomless."[17] Though published anonymously, there was no doubt who wrote "A Counter-

Blaste to Tobacco" since his views were well known and, by that time, he had published several other pamphlets and books.

Certainly, Rolfe knew of the king's views. Perhaps, when he wrote his letter to James I expressing his views on the need to establish quotas for tobacco in Virginia, Rolfe was staging a preemptive strike, hoping that by advocating limited action to curb tobacco production, he could convince the king not to ban production entirely. In any event, Rolfe's letter had little impact on the tobacco-hating monarch. Not surprisingly, though, while James I tried to control and even ban the production of tobacco in Virginia, he was no more able to convince Virginians not to grow tobacco than he was able to convince Englishmen, and a few women, too, not to smoke.

While Rolfe worked on his letter—it seems he completed it soon after his arrival in England—the *Treasurer* made her steady way across the Atlantic. Sometime in early June, the vessel passed Land's End and the Lizard and made her way into Plymouth Harbour. Dale sent word of his arrival in a letter carried by rider to the king's first secretary of state, Sir Ralph Winwood. In his letter, dated June 3, 1616, Sir Thomas promised to present himself to Winwood "with the greatest speed the wind will suffer me." He went on to praise Virginia as "one of the goodliest and richest kingdoms of the world" and to urge the continued support of the colonists he'd left behind.[18] Curiously, given Dale's pride in the role he claimed in Pocahontas's conversion, he did not bother to mention that the princess had accompanied him on his return to England. By June 22, though, word of her arrival had reached London, for, on that date, John Chamberlain, the inveterate gossipmonger, wrote in a letter to a friend that Dale had come to England with "ten or twelve old and young of that country [Virginia], among whom the most remarkable person is Pocahontas, daughter of Powhatan, a king or cacique of that country, married to one Rolfe, an Englishman."[19] By that time, in fact, Pocahontas, Rolfe, and their child, along with her Indian companions, were almost certainly in the city since they had debarked in Plymouth and traveled overland while Argall and Dale had sailed the *Treasurer* up the Thames.

The Powhatan princess and her Indian companions would have looked in amazement at the bustling port of Plymouth, filled with boats and ships and people, more people than Pocahontas or Wahunsonacock or any of the Virginia natives knew lived in the world. Then they would have ridden by coach for almost two hundred miles to London, along a coach road flanked by cleared fields filled with cattle and thick woodlands. Then they would have seen London itself, the noisy, smoky, smelly city with its narrow, crooked streets, its houses and shops all cheek to jowl, and its 200,000 residents, so many people that Tomocomo, who tried to keep count of the number of people he saw by cutting notches in a stick, gave up counting.

Pocahontas and the other Powhatans were not the first Indians to visit England, of course. In 1535 William Hawkins, one of the sea dogs from the west of England, brought a native he'd kidnapped in South America to London, where the no doubt completely bewildered native was presented to the court of Henry VIII. Over the years, several dozen natives from the Roanoke region as well as from Virginia had come to the English capital—willingly or not—to be gawked at and looked down upon. They usually died of illness before they were able to return to their homes. Still, the Indians must have created quite a stir when they arrived. Tomocomo surely attracted attention with his red-painted face and body, long scalp lock, fur mantle, and a revealing breechcloth that was his normal garb.

In London, Pocahontas and John Rolfe along with other members of their party were lodged at the Belle Savage Inn, just off Fleet Street. At first glance, it seems the choice of lodgings might have been made by some wag in the employ of the Virginia Company as a way to play a sly joke on Pocahontas. Instead, the choice appears to have been purely happenstance. The inn was owned by a family named Savage, and "Belle" probably derived from "bail," meaning boundary, since the Belle Savage sat just outside the old city wall, near Ludgate. The inn was well known long before Pocahontas and her party arrived. Built in 1529, the Belle Savage had hosted thousands of travelers over the years, providing not just beds but also food and drink, stables and a coach depot, and a friendly meeting place. The inn's courtyard even served as a theater—at least one performance of Christopher Marlowe's *Doctor Faustus* was staged there—as well as a setting for animal acts and juggling and professional swordplay. What Pocahontas and the other Powhatan people thought as they found themselves surrounded by the noise and rowdiness and smells and sights of a crowded London tavern can only be surmised.

Reasonably enough, given her role as a propaganda tool, Pocahontas and her entourage were supported by the Virginia Company while in England, to the tune of £4 per week. While this was not a fortune, to be sure, it was sufficient to maintain the princess and the rest of her party and, no doubt, to furnish Lady Rebecca Rolfe with the high-necked dresses and other finery she would need if she was to cut the proper figure in London society. Not long after her arrival, she—along with her husband and Tomocomo and perhaps some others in her Powhatan entourage—would have been welcomed by Sir Thomas Smythe and Lady Dale, Sir Thomas Dale's wife, and perhaps Ben Jonson, who would later write about the inappropriateness of housing Wahunsonacock's daughter in a tavern, a place "unfit too for a princess."[20] Not long after her arrival, she met the Reverend Samuel Purchas, the scholar and cheerleader for England's colonial ventures who was busily collecting as many tales from English settlers and adventurers as he could. Long before he knew of Pocahontas, Purchas had described Virginia as a maiden ripe for the plucking and the colonists as suitors who wished to turn her into an honorable Christian wife. When Purchas met the Indian princess in his house on the Thames, she must have appeared to him as the embodiment of his dreams of marriage between the Old World and the New.

Purchas was obviously taken with Pocahontas. In his *Purchas his Pilgrimes,* the churchman said the princess "did not only accustome her selfe to civilitie, but still carried her selfe as the Daughter of a King, and was accordingly respected."[21] Through Purchas, or maybe through Smythe, Pocahontas met some of London's leading lights, including the bishop of London. According to Purchas, the bishop "entertained her with festival state and pomp, beyond what I have seen in his great hospitality offered to other ladies."[22]

Sometime not long after the Rolfes arrived in London, Captain John Smith, the bearded Englishman whose life Pocahontas had saved in Virginia almost a decade earlier, learned of her presence. For some reason, perhaps because he was busy making arrangements for a voyage to the land he would come to name New England, perhaps because he was unsure of his welcome by the maiden who was now married to a successful planter, Smith did not rush to see the woman who had been such a great friend and protector when he was the leader of Jamestown. He did, however, make time to write a letter of introduction for the Powhatan princess to Queen Anne. While the letter itself has been lost, Smith later published in his *Generall Historie* a summary of the letter, as he remembered it. Addressed to the "Most Admired Queen," Smith's letter reviewed all that the Indian princess had done for him and for the English settlers in Jamestown. He described her "extraordinary affection to our Nation" and called her the "instrument to preserve this colony from death, famine and utter confusion," adding that without her help "Virginia might have [lain] as it was at our first arrivall to this day." He then went on to tell of her kidnapping and how she had "rejected her barbarous condition" after which "she was married to an English Gentleman, with whom at this present she is in England, the first Christian ever of that Nation, the first Virginian ever spake English, or had a childe in mariage by an Englishman."[23]

Smith, never one to exhibit fear, then went on to warn Queen Anne that "if she [Pocahontas] should not be well received, seeing this Kingdome may rightly have a Kingdome by her meanes; her present love to us and Christianitie might turn to such scorne and furie, as to divert all this good to the worst of evill: where[as] finding so great a Queene should doe her some honour more than she can imagine . . . would so ravish her with content, as endeare her dearest bloud to effect that [which] your Majestie and all the Kings honest subjects most earnestly desire. And so I humbly kisse your gracious hands."[24]

Smith's letter worked. The Indian princess and Tomocomo and perhaps others in their party, apparently accompanied and guided by Lord De La Warre (he was still in England but waiting to return to Virginia) and his wife, Lady De La Warre, were presented to the king and queen at Whitehall Palace. Smith, reporting what he had heard, said it "pleased both the King and Queenes Majestie hourably to esteeme her . . . both publikely at the maskes and otherwise, to her great satisfaction and content."[25] And Robert Beverley, the author of a history of Virginia written much after the fact, said the Indian princess was "carried to many plays, balls, and other public entertainments," where she was "repectfully receiv'd" by all the ladies of the court. Beverley went so far as to say, a bit patronizingly, that she "behaved her self with so much Decency" that "the poor Gentleman her Husband" was in peril of being "call'd to an Account" by the king for "having dared to marry a Princess Royal without the King's Consent"—a capital offense if he had been charged and found guilty.[26] In fact, there is no firm evidence to back up the story that Rolfe was in danger of punishment for marrying above himself, though it certainly was possible.

During all this social activity, Pocahontas managed to find time to sit for a portrait, a sketch made by Simon van de Passe, a Dutch-German engraver working in London. When he met Pocahontas, van de Passe was only about twenty-one years of age, still perfecting his craft. Eventually, he would create portraits of other famous individuals, including Captain John Smith and King James. His engraving of James I was included as the frontispiece in a collection of the king's writings, *The Workes of James*, published in 1616; his portrait of Smith, done at about the same time as that of Pocahontas, was used to illustrate Smith's map of New England, published in England after he explored and named the region in 1614. The portrait of Pocahontas was almost certainly commissioned by the Virginia Company for use in promoting the colony. Two years earlier, to promote one of its lotteries, the company had used the rather fanciful image of an Indian dressed in skins, armed with a bow and arrows, in St. James's Park. Now the company wanted the portrait of a "civilized" Indian lady, dressed in Jacobean splendor, to help flush investors out of the English woodwork.

Van de Passe's portrait depicts Pocahontas as a decidedly exotic-looking young woman. The artist made no attempt to anglicize her face; her features are decidedly those of an Indian. The cheekbones are high and pronounced, the eyes are exotic, the brows clearly defined and as dark as if they were inked on her face. The woman in the picture is dressed as if she is on her way to a soirée at Whitehall Palace: layers of fine cloth open to reveal layers beneath just as fine; a carefully worked lace ruff rises so high it tickles the bottoms of the lady's ears; a high-crowned hat, of a style made popular by Queen Anne herself, sits, decorated with a plume, on Pocahontas's proudly held head; her slender fingers hold an ostrich-feather fan; pearl earrings, perhaps made in England from pearls found in the Chesapeake, depend from her ears. What is most remarkable about the van de Passe portrait, though, is the look that Pocahontas casts out at the world that is looking back at her. Her eyes are piercing; her gaze appears so steady as to be challenging, daring the observer to question her right to be or to do anything she wished. Her jaw, too, is set, perhaps the way she set it when she left the Belle Savage to face and face down a world that could be, even at its best, harsh. She is every inch a princess.

John Chamberlain was one of many in London who purchased at least one copy of the van de Passe portrait when it was released as an engraving. He sent a copy on to a friend in early 1617 with a note: "Here is a fine picture of no fair Lady!" he wrote, a comment that says much more about him than it does about Lady Rebecca Rolfe.[27]

Perhaps the gown that Pocahontas wore in the portrait was the dress she wore when, on January 6, 1617, she and Tomocomo attended the annual Twelfth Night Masque at Whitehall. The performance that night would have baffled the Indian princess and her brother-in-law—it seems John Rolfe was not invited—and, indeed, would have baffled anyone not familiar with the conventions of the court masque. Ben Jonson, a favorite of Queen Anne, wrote a special script for Twelfth Night of 1617, as had been the custom in the court of James I. *The Vision of Delight,* as the masque was called, featured the model of a monster that disgorged six Italian dancers; the cast of characters included Delight and Wonder and Fantasy singing and emoting amid smoke and strewn flowers, all at a huge cost and to the delight of King James and Queen Anne and the invited guests who crowded into the long, narrow Banqueting Hall at Whitehall—all except, perhaps, Pocahontas and Tomocomo, who would not have understood the goings-on any more than the English in Virginia understood the real meaning of the Indian dances and songs of the Powhatan people.

According to Chamberlain, those at the masque treated Pocahontas kindly. Still, they—some of the highest born and most privileged in the kingdom—may well have snickered at her in her English finery and at Tomocomo in his skins and beads and paint. "The Virginian woman Pocahuntas, with her father-counsellor (Tomocomo), hath been with the King and graciously used, and both she and her assistant well placed at the masque," Chamberlain wrote.[28] Again, Chamberlain could not seem to refer to Pocahontas without a sneer. "The Virginian woman," he called her, not deigning to refer to her as a lady, despite her rank.

By that time, according to Chamberlain, John Rolfe was making plans to depart from England with his wife and child, to set sail before the start of the season of summer storms like the one that had sent the *Sea Venture* crashing into the Bermudan reef. Pocahontas, at least according to Chamberlain, was unhappy about the thought of returning home, though it is difficult to credit that idea, given the lack of any real documentation. Of course, she would have enjoyed the attention she received in London, but she must have missed her father and the land and rivers she had known so intimately since she was a child. Chamberlain's claim that she was loathe to leave England was almost certainly more the product of his Anglocentric way of thinking than any real desire on Pocahontas's part to be an exile from her native land and people.

By that time, however, Pocahontas must have been ailing, probably coughing, perhaps even spitting up blood. England's climate, even under the best of circumstances, was hard on the Native Americans who visited London. Of the dozen or so who traveled with Pocahontas in 1616, three died in the course of just a few months in England, and several others would not live to see Virginia again. Historian Robert Beverley claimed the "Smoak of the City" began to bother the princess.[29] That may well be true since London's air was thick with coal smoke. At the same time, while the weather in 1616 was, for England, pleasant, there was a great deal of sickness in the land. "We have a new ague or sickness that begins to spread itself in many places," Chamberlain reported on August 24 of that year. The illness, he said, "hath taken away diverse of good note, and upon short warning."[30] Whatever Pocahontas's ailment was, either some "new ague" or simply pulmonary or bronchial difficulty caused by the noxious coal smoke that was thicker over the city than the smoke of any campfire inside a Powhatan dwelling, sometime soon after the masque, a decision was made to move Pocahontas and her retinue out of London, to the village of Brentford, about nine miles up the Thames.

While the Rolfes were at Brentford, perhaps living in lodgings provided by the Percy family, which had property in the region, Captain John Smith, in the midst of his preparations for a voyage to New England, finally found the time to visit the Indian princess who had saved his life in Virginia. When Smith arrived at the house across the Thames from the site of modern Kew Gardens, he was accompanied by several friends, probably men who simply wanted to meet the famous Indian. If Smith expected Pocahontas to greet him warmly, he was disappointed. When the captain, then about thirty-seven years of age, walked into the room where Pocahontas stood waiting, she turned away, obviously distraught. What was going through her mind? Smith, for one, at first thought she was embarrassed that she no longer spoke English as she once had, a wrongheaded idea if there ever was one, since she had been living with her English husband for almost three years by that time. Perhaps Smith had changed so much in the years since she had last seen him—it had been nearly a decade—that she found her emotions difficult to hide. Or maybe she was simply angry that the man she had served and helped so much in Virginia had waited so long before coming to visit her. In any case, Pocahontas was so distraught that Smith, John Rolfe, and the others left her alone for a time, "as," in Smith's words, "not seeming well contented."[31]

For several hours, Rolfe, Smith, and the men who had accompanied the captain to Brentford may well have talked about Virginia. Smith must have been anxious to hear Rolfe's tale of the *Sea Venture* shipwreck and of Rolfe's time in Bermuda and Virginia. He would later write extensively about events that Rolfe would have described. Smith, too, would have wanted to take his own measure of the man Pocahontas had married, while Rolfe must have been fascinated to meet the man who had known his wife when she was a girl.

Eventually, Smith and the others returned to a reproachful Pocahontas,

who was ready to talk. She reminded Smith of what they had experienced together in her homeland. "You did promise Powhatan what was yours should
bee his, and he the like to you; you called him father being in his land a
stranger, and by the same reason so must I doe you," she said. In Smith's
mind, she was treading on thin ice. He knew English society would not allow
her to call him father because, as he told her, she was a king's daughter.

Pocahontas, the girl who risked her father's anger to help the English, was
a woman who would not allow Smith such an easy out. Words came tumbling
out, her disdain and disappointment palpable:

> "[You] were . . . not afraid to come into my fathers Countrie, and caused feare
> in him and all his people (but mee), and [yet you] feare . . . here I should call
> you father. I tell you then I will, and you shall call mee childe, and so I will
> bee for ever and ever your Countrieman."

Then, almost certainly with as much sorrow as anger, Pocahontas talked
of what seemed to be at the bottom of her discontent. "They did tell us alwaies you were dead, and I knew no other till I came to Plimoth," she said.
"Yet Powhatan did command [Tomocomo] to seeke you, and know the truth,
because your Countriemen will lie much."[32]

John Rolfe may well have listened amazed to his wife's words as she accused not just Smith but all the English, including Rolfe himself and Sir
Thomas Dale and Reverend Whitaker, all those who most certainly had told
her that Smith was dead, knowing full well he was alive, of being liars. Perhaps it was the cry of a young wife who realized that she had married a man
she would never have married had she known that the man she truly loved was
alive.

The meeting of these two friends must have been tinged with a great deal
of sadness for Smith and Rolfe as well. If nothing else, Smith would have realized the inexorable passage of time as he saw how much the princess had
changed in the years since she had served as a shield against the Indian war
clubs that had been raised to smash his skull. Rolfe must have felt a certain
sad jealousy as he saw the obvious bond between his wife and the red-
bearded man—perhaps a much deeper bond than that between himself and
Pocahontas.

In the months that the Rolfe family lived at Brentford, *Sea Venture* survivor
John Rolfe was busy promoting himself and the Virginia colony to leaders of

the company in London. Eventually, Sir Edwin Sandys, one of the company's leading investors and guiding lights, convinced Rolfe to lend his name, and his wife's, to a plan to convert the Virginia Indians to the Christian faith. The company had collected a goodly sum of money for the effort and gave Rolfe £100—five times his annual salary as colonial secretary—to finance the effort. In a letter to Sir Thomas Smythe, Sandys said the money was given to "Mr. Rolfe and his Ladye, partely in doing honor to that good example of her conversion . . . And partely upon promise made by the said Mr. Rolfe on behalfe of him selfe and the said Ladye, that bothe by their godlye and vertuous example . . . as also by all other good means of perswasions and inducements, they wuoud employe their best endevours to the winning of that People [the Indians] to the knowledge of God."[33] While Rolfe must have been happy to sign on to the plan, given his religiousity, Pocahontas must have been distraught to learn the company expected her to become a Christian missionary, especially in light of the fact that the company plan included removing Indian children from their homes to be educated in a kind of Christian boarding school to be established in Virginia.

In any event, by February 1617, the Rolfe family and the native people who had survived the winter were ready to depart for Virginia. Once again, Samuel Argall would serve as captain of the ship transporting Pocahontas to Jamestown. This time, though, Argall was returning to a position of power in the colony, having been named deputy governor of Virginia, since Lord de La Warre was in no hurry to return to the place where he'd fallen ill. Sometime that month, Argall's flagship, the *George*, along with the *Treasurer* (the ship on which Pocahontas had been kidnapped), and a small pinnace, took on supplies and passengers. Contrary winds, though, delayed the fleet's departure, and the passengers and crew were forced back ashore. Unfriendly winds held the ships in port for several weeks, until mid-March, when the winds finally abated. Rolfe, Pocahontas, little Thomas Rolfe, and the other passengers boarded and she weighed anchor.

By that time, Pocahontas must have been failing. Thomas Rolfe, Pocahontas's half sister, Matachanna, and several other Indians in the party were also ill. Still, the fleet pressed on until it reached the town of Gravesend, about twenty miles downriver from London. There, Rolfe told Argall they needed to stop because his wife and son were too sick to continue what was sure to be a difficult sea voyage. Again, no one knows today what illness struck Pocahontas or the others on the ship. It seems likely, given the windy, undoubtedly cold weather of February and early March, that the princess contracted pneumonia in addition to the chronic lung ailment she had suffered from for months. Whatever the sickness, she was simply too ill to survive an ocean crossing.

In Gravesend, Pocahontas was carried to an inn. No doubt a doctor was called and a minister as well. She would have been purged and bled, the most common treatments for any ailments. Tomocomo may well have tried his tribal remedies. Neither English remedies nor Powhatan cures worked.

According to Rolfe, who had already buried one wife and a daughter in Virginia, Pocahontas knew she was dying and bravely tried to reconcile him to her passing. "All must die," she said, then pointed to young Thomas as his father's best consolation, with the words, " 'Tis enough that her childe liveth."[34]

Pocahontas died on March 19 or March 20, and was buried on March 21 in the chancel of the ancient parish church of St. George's in Gravesend. When the church was destroyed by fire in 1727, the Indian princess's bones were lost, never to be recovered.

Even as Pocahontas was slipping away—Reverend Samuel Purchas later said with a macabre if waggish turn of phrase that she "came to Gravesend to her end and grave"[35]—at least one of her Indian companions died, three others grew too sick to make the voyage, and Thomas Rolfe continued ill. Finally, Captain Argall said the fleet had to resume its voyage or run the risk of missing favorable winds. He urged Rolfe, who must have wanted nothing more by that time than to return to his lush tobacco fields in Virginia, to leave his son behind. Rolfe refused and, in late March or very early April, the *George*, the *Treasurer*, and the pinnace sailed downriver from Gravesend. Sometime in the first week of April, the ships reached Plymouth and Rolfe could see that his son was not sufficiently healthy to make the Atlantic crossing. "In our short passage to Plymouth in smooth water I found such fear and hazard of his health, being not fully recovered of his sickness," Rolfe wrote, he had no choice but to leave his son behind. Not only was his son sick, he explained, "they who looked to him"—the boy's caretakers—"had need of nurses themselves." Rolfe spoke to Sir Louis Stukely, the vice admiral for Devonshire, and made arrangements for Stukely to care for the child until Rolfe's brother, Henry, could travel from London to take the child in his custody. "I know not how I may be censured for leaving my child behind me," Rolfe said.[36]

On April 10, 1617, the fleet bearing John Rolfe back to Jamestown set sail from Plymouth. It certainly would have been natural for Rolfe to stand on deck, looking at Plymouth Harbour as his ship moved into the open ocean and to think back to the day, almost exactly eight years earlier, when he and his first wife had set sail from the same port aboard the *Sea Venture* bound for a future beyond his wildest—or most terrifying—imaginings. He must have thought of his baby daughter, buried in Bermuda, and his wife who lay interred in Virginia and, of course, of Pocahontas and little Thomas. But he knew, he must have known, that the Bermudas were no longer the uninhabited place where he and the other *Sea Venture* survivors had struggled ashore in July 1609. He knew, as well, that the colony he was sailing to was no longer the terrifying and terrible place he had first seen when he and the other survivors—including Sir Thomas Gates, Sir George Somers, and William Strachey—had arrived at the end of the Starving Time. Unlike on that earlier voyage, when Rolfe set sail for the unknown, he now was on his way home.

15

"A Faire and Perfect Common Weale"

By mid-1617, when the newly widowed John Rolfe returned to the Chesapeake, most of the men and women who had boarded the *Sea Venture* when she took on passengers in England in 1609 were dead. Sir George Somers, admiral of the fleet of 1609, had, of course, died on his mission to obtain food for the starving Jamestown settlement. Rolfe's first wife was dead and buried in Virginia's soil. Henry Ravens and the six men who sailed with him to advise the Jamestown settlers of the wreck of the *Sea Venture* were dead, either lost at sea or, more likely, killed by Wahunsonacock's people after reaching the Chesapeake. The mutineer Henry Paine had been executed and the mariner Edward Samuell had been murdered by his shipmate, Edward Waters. Dozens or scores of others, as unremarked in death as they were when they boarded the *Sea Venture* bound for what they believed was a paradise on earth, had also perished in Virginia, victims of Indian attack, illness, or starvation, without leaving any historical record that can be found today.

By that time, too, the vast majority of the *Sea Venture* survivors who were still alive when Rolfe returned to Virginia had faded from public notice to become every bit as unknown, in historical terms, as the anonymous dead. Most of these survivors lived and worked in Jamestown or Henrico or down-river at Point Comfort. They woke at sunrise and toiled in the fields and hunted and fished and cleaned and cooked and laughed and cried without leaving any record of their passage. Even the major events of their lives—their marriages and the births of their children and their deaths—were, it seems, unrecorded.

Of the *Sea Venture* survivors in Virginia in 1617, none played a more important or more visible role than Rolfe. Over the course of the next few years, the tobacco he introduced to the colony made him a relatively wealthy man and one of the colony's most successful landowners, with servants and fields around Henrico and on Mulberry Island, downriver from Jamestown. An important man with connections in England thanks to his marriage to Pocahontas and his own self-promotion, Rolfe eventually served on the colony's governing council.

Between 1617 and 1622, the Virginia colony enjoyed a period of détente that had settled on the Tsenacommacah in the wake of Rolfe's marriage to the now-dead Indian princess. There were still sparks of trouble between the native people and the *Tassantassas,* but there was, in those years, little of the savage and brutal warfare that had marked the colony's earliest days. Rolfe and others who reported on the relations between the whites and the Indians had a tendency to speak glowingly of the amity that ruled where once there had been so much killing.

Thanks to the Peace of Pocahontas, the English were able to occupy ever more Indian land, land the natives were willing to trade for imported goods or, as often happened in those years thanks to the displacement of the Indians, for food when the natives' own supplies were short. And land was what the settlers wanted, acreage to plant profitable but land-devouring tobacco crops. Slowly at first, then faster, the colony took lands along the James from just below the falls to the river's mouth at Point Comfort and then crept inland. Settlements and townships were established and plantations, backed by wealthy investors in England, hacked from the woodlands. The tobacco introduced to the colony by Rolfe became the colony's prime crop and furnished the settlers and the Virginia Company with at least some of the profits they had so long dreamed of. The two thousand pounds of tobacco shipped to England by Rolfe and a few other farmers in 1615 became twenty thousand pounds in 1617. In 1620, the tobacco farms and plantations of Virginia shipped an estimated forty thousand pounds of weed to the ports of England.

As early as 1616, Rolfe—in his letter to James I—had preached to the Virginia Company that the only thing lacking to make Virginia a thriving and profitable colony were hard workers, more than the "small nomber" that had been sent to "advance so great a worke."[1] What were needed, Rolfe explained, were

> good and sufficient men, as well of birth and qualitie to command soldiers, to march, discover and defend the countrey from invasions: as also artificers, laborers and husbandmen, with whom, were the colony well provided, then might tryall be made what lyeth hidden in the wombe of the ground. The land might yearlie abound with corne and other provisions for man's sustentation—buildings, fortifications and shipping might be reared, wrought and framed—commodities of divers kinds might be yearly reaped and sought after, and many things (God's blessing contynuing,) might come with ease to establish a faire and perfect common weale.[2]

Even before Rolfe wrote those words, the leadership of the Virginia Company, prodded by a handful of more aggressive adventurers, including the Earl of Southampton and Sir Edwin Sandys, the wealthy and powerful son of the archbishop of York, knew that changes had to be made if Virginia was ever to be successful. Ten years into its history, the colony had lived up to no one's expectations. Hundreds of lives had been lost and thousands of pounds spent with virtually no return. Many of these company men—including Smythe, Sandys, and Southampton—were also, by that time, investors in the Somers Islands Company and, thus, intimately connected with its struggles and successes. They knew that Bermuda, despite all its problems, was thriving—the colony had six hundred settlers in 1616, just six years after its establishment—while the Virginia colony had fewer than four hundred. What was the difference between the two colonies? The answer was clear. Bermuda's investors were given large grants of land in exchange for the use of their capital, offering them the potential, at least, of profits from commodities raised on their lands in the islands. It had worked in the island colony; surely it would work in Virginia.

At that time, the leaders of the Virginia Company may well have breathed a prayer of thanks that John Rolfe had married his Indian princess, for the Peace of Pocahontas gave them an opportunity to offer generous land grants to adventurers and settlers. And the company had vast amounts of land under its control. In 1616 the company voted to offer fifty acres of land—either along the James or near one of the inland townships—to any colonist who paid his own way to Virginia or who purchased a full share of stock for £12 10s. Total grants could be as large as two hundred acres—a huge holding for all but the wealthiest of Englishmen in Stuart times. Investors of moderate means could take advantage of this offer if they were able to pay half the cost immediately and the balance in six months. Apparently the response to this offer was disappointing because in 1617 the company sweetened the pot, promising fifty acres of land for every person sent to the colony, with the payment in land going to the individual who bore the cost of transportation. This so-called Virginia headright enabled adventurers in England to send settlers to Virginia as indentured servants: they would do the necessary work of producing crops and other commodities, typically for seven years, at which time the indentured servants would be released from servitude with a land grant of their own, not of fifty acres, but of thirty.

In an even better offer, new investors (singly or in groups) could assemble a number of new settlers, pay their passage to Virginia, and start a "particular plantation" away from Jamestown. These plantations, called hundreds, were allowed a measure of self-government as an added inducement for investors to risk their capital. The response to these offers of precious land was everything the company could have hoped for. In the three years between 1618 and 1621, the company dispatched fifty ships and almost 4,000 men and women to the Virginia colony. This is in comparison to roughly 1,600 settlers sent to the colony in the years between 1607 and 1616.

By early 1618, the great Wahunsonacock knew that the only way of life he had ever known, the way of life he had enjoyed for almost eight decades, was coming to an end. He knew the confederacy of tribes he had created by dint of his strength of will, charisma, and political skill was being torn asunder by the bearded *Tassantassas*. His lands were no longer his own, his people were scattered, his daughter Pocahontas was dead. He must have been ill and tired. Sometime in April 1617, he died, somewhere in the forest. Before his death, he had named one of his younger brothers, Opitchapam (also called Itoyatan), as his heir, to be followed by Opechancanough, the Powhatan war chief who had captured Captain John Smith before his rescue by Pocahontas. Opitchapam, it seems, was soon relegated to a secondary position as Opechancanough took the point as the leader of the native people.

For a time, this change in Powhatan leadership did not seem to make much difference in Indian-English relations, which remained strained but, for the most part, friendly. Not much headway was made in establishing the schools for native children—one of the goals the Virginia Company had set out when Rolfe and Pocahontas were in London—but natives regularly visited plantations and townships, worked side by side with settlers in Jamestown and Henrico and in fields along the James. On the surface, at least, it seemed as if the wars between the Indians and the English were over, that the two people had found a means of accommodating each other.

In these years, the company hoped to obtain commodities from Virginia other than tobacco. Planting, growing, harvesting, and curing tobacco was a labor-intensive proposition, requiring a great deal of land. If tobacco was the colony's only crop, it was feared, farms would be scattered, making it difficult to provide protection to settlers and equally difficult for settlers to gather for church services, something that just could not be tolerated.

In attempts to wean the settlers off their tobacco dependency, the company dispatched vintners and experts in silk production, to no avail. Six Italian experts were dispatched to establish a glass furnace to produce beads, with disastrous results when one of the six murdered his wife not long after his arrival in Jamestown. Nothing worked. Tobacco continued as king of Virginia's economy despite the fact that its production required massive amounts of often backbreaking labor.

The labor problems were mitigated somewhat in 1619 when the *White Lion,* a Dutch trading ship, dropped anchor off Jamestown with a cargo of, among other things, twenty African slaves. By that time, the *Sea Venture* survivor George Yeardley was serving as Virginia's governor. Apparently, Yeardley was not put off at the idea of slave labor, for he promptly "bought" the human cargo in exchange for supplies needed by the Dutch ship. A few days later, a second vessel traveling in consort with the *White Lion* anchored off the English settlement. This ship was the *Treasurer,* the same vessel that had been the scene of Pocahontas's kidnapping, now under the command of Captain Daniel Elfrith, the same piratical Englishman who had delivered wheat and rats to Bermuda. Elfrith, too, had a ship full of captured slaves and he, too, attempted to barter for food. While Yeardley was willing to do business with a Dutch slave trader, he apparently drew the line at trucking with an English slaver. Perhaps he had heard of Elfrith's piratical exploits and found them distasteful or maybe he simply did not like the man. In any case, Elfrith soon sailed away without selling any of his human cargo.

It seems these unfortunate Africans, about evenly divided between men and women, were not slaves in the true sense. Instead, they were probably legally viewed as indentured servants, like so many of the earliest white settlers in Virginia. Like their white counterparts, then, they would have been eligible to earn their freedom after a period of service to a master. In fact, there is no record of hereditary chattel slavery in Virginia until the 1640s. Of course, as several historians have noted, this may be more a matter of a lack of records than proof that slavery was not condoned or practiced in Virginia as early as 1619.

In any event, whether they were slaves or indentured servants, their time in Virginia surely wasn't pleasant. Richard Frethorne, an indentured servant who came to the Chesapeake a few years later, wrote a pleading letter to his parents, describing terrible conditions in Virginia and begging that he might be "freed out of this Egipt, or els that it would please yow to send over some beife & some Cheese and butter."

Frethorne, who lived and worked at Martin's Hundred, a plantation about ten miles from Jamestown, went on to paint a wrenching picture of Virginia, a picture vastly different from the Edenic descriptions presented by colonial promoters:

> This is to let you understand that I your Child am in a most heavie Case by reason of the nature of the Country is such that it Causeth much sicknes, as the scurvie and bloody flix, and divers other diseases, wch maketh the bodie very poore, and Weake, and when wee are sicke there is nothing to Comfort us; for since I came out of the ship, I never at anie thing but pease, and loblollie (that is water gruell) as for deare or venison I never saw anie since I came into this land, there is indeed some foule, but Wee are not allowed to goe, and get yt, but must Worke hard both earelie, and late for a messe of water gruell, and a mouthfull of bread, and beife . . . people crie out day, and night, Oh that they were in England without their lymbes and would not care to loose anie lymbe to bee in England again, yea though they beg from doore to doore.

He ends his letter with a mournful request for his parents to help him. "O that you did see [my] daylie and hourelie sighes, grones, and teares, and thumpes that I afford mine owne brest, and rue and Curse the time of my birth with holy Job. I thought no head had beene able to hold so much water as hath and doth dailie flow from mine eyes."[3]

Still, despite all the illness and all the hunger and the dying that continued even as the colony's economy grew stronger—so much dying that of an estimated 6,500 settlers sent to Virginia in the years between 1607 and 1622, only about 1,200 survived—despite all these very real problems, the English colony in Virginia was firmly entrenched by 1619. The seeds that had been planted on Jamestown Island a dozen years earlier had taken root and, nourished by Gates and Strachey and Rolfe and the other survivors of the *Sea Venture* shipwreck, those roots had spread north and south along the James River, resulting in a flowering of plantations and townships.

By 1619, the company had changed its thinking about Virginia. No longer was the colony viewed as a purely commercial outpost or—as had been the case in at least a few minds in London—as a staging area for raids against Spanish treasure ships. Instead, Virginia was to be a lasting English outpost, modeled on Spanish colonial outposts in the West Indies. Sir Edwin Sandys, who along with Southampton financed the transportation of hundreds of settlers to Virginia, including more than three hundred in 1618 alone, took the lead in reorganizing the colony's politics along with its land distribution. This work climaxed in the breathtaking (for the time) decision that a "general assembly" of elective officers comprised of "Tow [two] Burgesses out of every towne, hunder [hundred] and other particuler planta[ti]on" had to meet at least once each year in Virginia.[4]

Thus it was that on July 30, 1619, a landmark was reached when Governor Yeardley, six councilors, and two representatives from each of the small settlements that were scattered across the Tidewater region gathered in the choir of the church at Jamestown for the first meeting of a legislative assembly ever convened on the North American continent. Rolfe, by that time, was an important enough figure that he had been named to the governor's six-man council established in accordance with the document known as the "Great Charter," given to Yeardley before he departed from London to replace Argall.

Rolfe was not the only *Sea Venture* survivor in attendance in the summer of 1619 when the House of Burgesses met for the first time in the little church in Jamestown. Richard Bucke, the minister and *Sea Venture* survivor who had led Somers and Gates and Rolfe and the others in prayer on the beach in Bermuda following the loss of the ship, opened the proceedings with a prayer, asking the Lord to guide the governor and representatives in their important business.

This first legislative assembly on American soil, while limited in scope, set in place a new era of colonial government and a new form of representative government that would later evolve and expand to shape the United States of America. The golden age of peace and prosperity that saw the Virginia colony grow so rapidly, that saw peace between the Indians and English even as both slavery and representative government were introduced to America, came to an end in 1622. By that time, the Indians knew the English, if they were not stopped, would destroy them completely. More and more settlers seemed to step ashore by the day, taking land, moving the Indians away from the territories they had occupied for longer than memory. Opechancanough, the great Wahunsanacock's brother, knew that if the *Tassantassas* were ever to be stopped, he and the other Indian leaders would have to take action. Plans were laid to surprise the English.

Even as these plans were being made, Indians continued acting friendly, working in the fields alongside the English, entering their palisaded plantations and townships and even their homes at will. The settlers were lulled into complacency. Sir Francis Wyatt, who replaced Yeardley on the merry-go-round as colonial governor, happily reported when he arrived in Virginia at about this time that he "found the Countrey setled in such a firme peace, as most men there thought sure and unviolable."[5]

On the morning of Friday, March 22, 1622, as on most days in those times of seeming peace, many natives came to the scattered English plantations to trade furs and corn for imported goods. Others went to farms, where they worked alongside settlers as the sun climbed into the sky over the Tidewater. More than a few completed their bartering or their chores and sat down with the English to enjoy breakfast. Then, at a predetermined time, the Indians, acting on orders of Opechancanough and the other local war chiefs, fell on the settlers, killing them and often mutilating their bodies. Even Englishmen and -women who had proven their good feelings for the native people were not spared.

At the end of the surprise attack, 347 English were dead. The toll would have been higher if friendly natives had not warned several communities, including Jamestown, just before the attack was launched. As it was, almost one-quarter of the English in Virginia were killed.

If Opechancanough thought the attack would achieve his dream of driving the *Tassantassas*, whom he had hated and mistrusted from their first landing in Virginia, out of his lands, he soon discovered he was wrong. Settlers were, for a time, forced to seek refuge in Jamestown and other palisaded towns. Soon, though the English were wreaking vengeance, now with the certainty that their actions were justified since the natives had proved, at least to English minds, that they were indeed savages and no more worthy of consideration than animals.

Over the next two decades, the native people of the Tidewater and the *Tassantassas* waged sporadic war punctuated by brief periods of détente. The Indians, though, were fighting a losing battle. In 1644 Opechancanough—then thought to be ninety years of age or older—mounted one more attack on the English. Though a number of settlers were killed, the attack was staged more as a symbolic gesture than for any strategic gain. Within six decades, Robert Beverley, the early Virginian historian, was able to write that "the Indians of Virginia are almost wasted."⁶ While that seems to have been an overstatment, it is surely true that by the mid-1600s the age of the Powhatan had come to an end. A proud people were driven from their lands and a centuries-old way of life eradicated. Virginia was secure in the hands of the English. The "faire and perfect common weale" that John Rolfe had envisioned in 1616 may not have been realized, but the first English colony in America, the colony that predated Plymouth Colony by thirteen years and that gave birth to the English colony in the Bermudas, was firmly on the path to success, thanks, in large part, to the men and women who took ship on the *Sea Venture* in 1609.

16

Aftermath

The *Sea Venture*

By 1644, when Opechancanough led his last attack on the English settlers in Jamestown, the once proud *Sea Venture*, admiral of the fleet of 1609, had been on the bottom of the ocean about half a mile off the northeast coast of St. George's Island for almost thirty-five years. In those long years, the ship's remains, locked in the grip of the coral reef about thirty feet below the ocean's surface, were worn by the tides, battered by storm-roiled waters, and attacked by sea life until all that remained was a ghostly shadow of the vessel that carried the Virginia-bound settlers across the Atlantic. The ship sat keel down in a sand hole between two coral jaws, surrounded by a scattering of ballast stones, cannonballs, and shards of pottery, along with other odds and ends. A cannon was wedged mouth down in the coral about twenty-five feet from what remained of this ship's worm-eaten keel. All the ship's bones and the scattered artifacts were crusted with barnacles that turned the ship into a seeming extension of the reef itself.

With the passage of time, as the vessel became one with the sea bottom, the men and women who lived on St. George's and the other Bermuda islands lost track of the remains of the ship that had wrecked on the reef just off St.

Catherine's Beach. Local fishermen and a few others had an idea that the wreck lay just to one side of a narrow cut in the reef, known as Sea Venture Channel, in a spot known as Sea Venture Flatt, but no one, it seems, could pinpoint the wreck site with accuracy. And centuries passed.

In 1958, Edmund Dowling, an amateur skin diver and a direct descendant of the *Sea Venture* survivor Sir George Yeardley, set out to find the wreck. Dowling, who was employed at the U.S. Naval Operating Base in Southampton, Bermuda, started his search using a grid system just inside the Sea Venture Channel, but had no success. After talking to local fishermen, he shifted his search to the seaward side of the channel. In October of that year, with the idea of duplicating the *Sea Venture*'s course, he headed from the open ocean toward Fort St. Catherine until he was able to anchor over a cut in the reef. He slipped on his diving gear and dropped into the blue-green water over the reef. At a depth of roughly thirty feet, he saw ballast stones and the remains of ship's timbers.

Over the next year or so, Dowling, who was only able to work part-time on the project, was helped by local divers, working in consultation with museums in the United States and the United Kingdom, to excavate the wreck site and recover artifacts. The artifacts recovered were found to be of the right period to identify the wreck as the *Sea Venture*, with the exception of a cannon that was mistakenly identified by experts at the Tower of London as a cannon from the eighteenth century, rather than a piece of armament from the early seventeenth. At that, interest in the project died and work did not resume until 1978, when divers working under the auspices of the Bermuda Maritime Museum resumed work on the wreck site. Artifacts recovered to date include the cannon (now believed to be from the early seventeenth century), about eighty cannonballs of varying sizes, some ceramics, a few household items, shot for small arms, and a cast-iron grenade. Perhaps the most interesting artifact discovered was a pewter candlestick, with a lump of candle still stuck in the candleholder. Maybe, just maybe, this was one of the candles William Strachey referred to when he wrote his description of passengers and crew searching with candles, at the height of the storm, to find where the *Sea Venture* was taking on water.

Today, the *Sea Venture* wreck site is protected, the ship's bones are undisturbed except by the ceaselessly moving ocean's waters. Not far from the site, a collection of the artifacts recovered from the wreck is on display at the Bermuda Maritime Museum.

Sir Samuel Argall

Upon his return to Virginia with John Rolfe in mid-1617, Argall assumed the post of deputy governor and admiral of Virginia. He came under attack for self-serving behavior in 1618 and was accused, in that year, of piracy by the Spanish, who claimed he dispatched a ship to the West Indies with a commission to attack and take Spanish shipping. In early 1619, he learned that Lord De La Warre was en route to Virginia to relieve him of his command. Fearing arrest, he left the colony for England. Able to avoid legal difficulties, Argall was knighted for his services in 1622 and died in 1625.

Reverend Richard Bucke

The long-serving and long-suffering minister who served on the *Sea Venture* and in both Bermuda and Virginia continued to meet the spiritual needs of the colonists in Jamestown until early 1624, when he died.

Christopher Carter, Edward Chard, and Edward Waters— the Three Kings of Bermuda

Edward Chard and Edward Waters, the *Sea Venture* survivors who were ready to fight to the death over the ambergris discovered in Bermuda, left Bermuda bound for some piratical adventures in the West Indies in 1615 or 1616. At that point, Chard fades into oblivion. Waters, however, ultimately made it back to Bermuda and then on to Virginia, where he became a successful planter. Though there's no record of his death, it is believed he may have been one of the settlers who perished in the Powhatan uprising of 1622. Christopher Carter, named along with Waters to the governing council in Bermuda after Governor Richard Moore departed from the islands for England in 1615, went on to become one of Bermuda's leading citizens.

Sir Thomas Dale

After leaving Virginia in May 1616, the hard-bitten soldier who imposed his hard rule on Jamestown was named a fleet commander by the East India Company. In 1620, while in Java, Dale fell ill and died.

Sir Thomas Gates

After his departure from Virginia in April 1614, Gates returned to his soldierly duties in Holland. By 1619, Gates was back in London, where he served as an officer of the Virginia Company, winning praise from other company officers, including Sir Edwin Sandys. In November 1620, he was appointed by James I to serve as one of the members of the council to oversee the settlement of New England. He died the next year.

Ralph Hamor

After leaving the colony in 1614, Hamor spent three years in England managing his family's extensive affairs. During that time, he became a heavy investor in the Virginia venture and returned to the colony in May 1617, perhaps as a passenger in the same vessel that carried John Rolfe back to the Chesapeake following the death of Pocahontas. Eventually, he became one of the colony's leaders. He died in Virginia in 1626.

Stephen Hopkins

The preachy man who served as an assistant to the Reverend Richard Bucke on board the *Sea Venture*, and who was sentenced to death for mutiny and then reprieved in Bermuda, returned to England sometime around 1612. His first wife—her name is thought to be Mary—died in 1613 and he married for a second time, in 1618, to a woman named Elizabeth Fisher.

In 1620, Hopkins took ship for the New World for a second time, sailing

with the nonconformist Pilgrims on the *Mayflower*. Eventually, Hopkins—
who was one of the signers of the Mayflower Compact—became a man of
some consequence in Plymouth Colony, acting as an emissary to the native
people of the region. Still, he managed to get in trouble with the somewhat
stodgy Pilgrim fathers several times, being charged with assault, price goug-
ing, and failure to properly regulate the amount of alcohol consumed in his
dwelling. Hopkins died in June or early July 1644. His wife, Elizabeth, died
in Plymouth in 1649.

Sylvester Jourdain

Nothing is known of Jourdain's career after he wrote his brief account of the
loss of the *Sea Venture*. A man of his name died in the parish of St. Sepulcher,
near Newgate, London, in 1650.

Captain Christopher Newport

After growing disenchanted with the Virginia Company's policies by 1612,
Newport joined the East India Company, where he served with distinction as
the leader on several voyages of trade and exploration. Eventually, he reached
the rank of admiral in the East India Company before dying on a voyage to
Java in 1617. For his service to the Virginia colony, Newport's widow was
granted 3,500 acres in 1621, including lands near present-day Newport News.

Opechancanough

The fierce warrior who became leader of the Powhatan people following the
death of his brother, Wahunsonacock, never stopped fighting the English. After the attacks on the colonists in 1644, Opechancanough—then almost a
hundred years of age—was captured by his enemies. According to witnesses,
at the time of his capture, he had suffered a stroke and was carried into a jail
cell on a litter, unable to open his eyes. One of his guards, "resenting the Ca-

sulities the Colony had suffer'd by [Opechancanough's] Means," murdered the old man in his cell.

George Percy

After his departure from Virginia in April 1612, Percy returned to his family's extensive estates in England and, perhaps because he was still in disfavor with James I, largely faded into obscurity. By 1625 he was in Holland for a second tour of duty in the seemingly endless war with the Spanish. His service was apparently notable since he was made the captain of a company. It was at this time that Percy lost a finger in battle. He never married and died in 1632.

John Rolfe

Perhaps the man most responsible for the first Virginia colony's ultimate survival, Rolfe became one of its leading citizens in the years between 1617 and 1622. In 1619, at about the same time as he served in Virginia's first General Assembly, he married again, taking for his third wife Jane Pierce, the daughter of William Pierce. Like Rolfe, Pierce was one of the *Sea Venture* survivors. The couple had one child, a daughter, Elizabeth, born in 1620 or 1621.

John Rolfe died some time in March 1622. It is surmised that he was a victim of the attack mounted by Pocahontas's uncle. At the time of his death, Rolfe was about thirty-seven years of age.

Thomas Rolfe

The son of John Rolfe and Pocahontas, Thomas, remained in England where he was raised by an uncle, until sometime between 1635 and 1640, when he returned to Virginia as a young man. After his return, he established contact with his uncle, Opechancanough, the man most responsible for the Massacre of 1622, visiting the old man at his headquarters on the Pamunkey River. If the younger Rolfe had any desire to live as an Indian, however, that desire seems to have died by 1646, when he was commissioned a lieutenant in the Virginia Colonial Militia and given the task of guarding Jamestown against Indian attack. As a colonial officer, he took part in raids against his mother's people in the wake of Opechancanough's last-gasp attack on the settlements in 1644. He eventually rose to the rank of colonel in the militia and became one of Virginia's planter-aristocrats, thanks in large part to extensive land-holdings he inherited from his father.

John Smith

Smith, who left Virginia wounded and discouraged in late 1609, never did return to the Chesapeake. In 1612 he published his "Map of Virginia," recognized as one of the most important works of early colonial literature. By 1614, he obtained backing for a voyage to north Virginia, where he prepared a detailed map of the region he named "New England." Other than a failed attempt to return to New England several years later, Smith never again went to sea. His remaining years were spent writing and publishing several books, including *The General History of Virginia, New England, & the Summer Isles*, published in 1624. Smith died broke and alone in 1631. He never married.

William Strachey

When William Strachey returned to England in 1616, he was filled with hope that his service to the Virginia Company, including his *True Reportory* of the wreck of the *Sea Venture*, would gain him the financial security and high position he hungered for. To boost his chances, he hurried to complete his history of the Virginia colony (*The Historie of Travaile into Virginia Britannia*) and sent a manuscript, complete with dedication, to the Earl of Northumberland, George Percy's older brother, hoping that his friendship with George would convince the earl, still being held in the Tower of London, to lend his name to the project. When he was unable to obtain patronage from Northumberland, he tried Sir Allen Apsley, a lesser-known man who also withheld patronage, and finally attempted to gain favor with Sir Francis Bacon. Sadly, at the same time Strachey was attempting to find success, Captain John Smith, an expert self-promoter, had already published his "Map of Virginia," stealing Strachey's thunder.

In 1621, Strachey married a woman known to history only as Dorothy. He never did escape poverty and died a pauper on June 21, 1621, so poor he had nothing to bequeath his widow.

Thomas West, Lord De La Warre

After departing from Jamestown in ill health in June 1611, fully planning to return, West spent roughly eight years in England attempting, unsuccessfully, to recover his health. He died of sickness while on a voyage back to Virginia in June 1618.

Reverend Alexander Whitaker

The man who was so instrumental in converting Pocahontas drowned in Virginia in March 1617, at about the same time that the Indian princess died in Gravesend.

NOTES

1: "Preparations Most Urgent"

1. Michael Drayton, "Ode to the Virginian Voyage," reprinted in Edward Wright Haile, ed., *Jamestown Narratives: Eyewitness Accounts of the Virginia Colony; The First Decade: 1607–1617* (Champlain, Va.: RoundHouse, 1998), p. xxi; hereafter Haile, *Jamestown Narratives*. This is the best, most complete collection of surviving accounts by and about Jamestown's first settlers. It should be required reading for any student of the history of early Virginia.
2. William Strachey is at best a shadowy figure, one of those actors who runs on history's stage to take a brief but important role and then runs off without leaving much in the way of solid biographical information. It is only thanks to the work of S. G. Culliford, who wrote his doctoral dissertation about Strachey, that even the bare bones of his story are readily available to the general reader. This dissertation was published in 1965 as *William Strachey, 1572–1621.*
3. S. G. Culliford, *William Strachey, 1572–1621* (Charlottesville, Va.: University Press of Virginia, 1965), p. 5.
4. In 1605 Sir Thomas Lowe, lord mayor of London, was named governor of the Levant Company, the joint stock company that oversaw English trade in Turkey. Lowe's family was related to Strachey by marriage, and it seems very probable that Strachey was able to use that relationship to land what should have been a lucrative job.
5. Culliford, *William Strachey*, p. 94.
6. Ibid., p. 61.
7. Ibid., p. 94.
8. Ibid., p. 55.

9. The play took its title from the cry of Thames wherrymen who would shout "Eastward ho!" or "Westward ho!" to let passengers know where they were headed.

10. Quoted in Ivor Noël Hume, *The Virginia Adventure* (Charlottesville, Va.: University Press of Virginia, 1997), p. 4.

11. Gilbert's ship, the *Squirrel*, was the smallest in the fleet and was dangerously overloaded during the voyage home. As the storm approached, other vessels approached *Squirrel* to rescue Gilbert, who refused to abandon his ship. He was seen sitting on deck with a copy of Thomas More's *Utopia* in his hands. A few hours later, the *Squirrel* was devoured by the sea.

12. Philip Barbour, *The Jamestown Voyages Under the First Charter* (Cambridge, England: Cambridge University Press, 1969), vol. I, p. 49ff.

13. In the years since the first English landed at Jamestown, the narrow neck of land that joined the Jamestown peninsula to the mainland washed away. Today, Jamestown is an island.

14. At different times in its history, the place we know today as Jamestown was known by a variety of names: James Fort, James Towne, James Cittie, and so on. For ease, I have decided to refer to it by its more modern and better-known appellation.

15. Edward Arber, ed., *Travels and Works of John Smith* (Westminster, England, 1895), vol. 2, p. 396; hereafter *Works of John Smith*.

16. George Percy, *Observations*, included in *Works of John Smith*, vol. I, p. lxi.

17. Ibid., p. lxxii.

18. John Smith's famous rescue by Pocahontas—the stuff of legend—has been called into question by several respected historians. Part of the problem in determining the truth of the story derives from Smith himself. A proud, headstrong man, Smith was given to self-promotion. It did not help matters that he did not mention the rescue in his first "history" of the colony, published in 1608. In fact, he did not tell the story until 1624, in a more complete recounting of Jamestown's history. It seems, however, that the 1608 version was a letter that was edited, perhaps heavily edited, by a reader in London before its publication. Also, in 1608, Smith was in Virginia, a good "Company man" trying to convince other settlers to come to the colony. The story of an Englishman's capture and near execution by Indians was hardly the kind of publicity to inspire confidence. By 1624, Smith's situation—and the situation in Jamestown—had changed. Smith, back in England, would have felt free to tell even the embarrassing truth that he, a soldier, had been saved by a mere girl! Other historians say that Smith embellished the truth and that what he had faced was not a real execution but, rather, an adoption ceremony. Of course, it would have been impossible for Smith to know that Wahunsonacock was role-playing when he seemed prepared to kill him.

19. Prince Henry, the son of James I and Princess Anne of Denmark, was an immensely popular young man, viewed by many in England as the potential savior of a nation being ill served by his father. He died in 1612 at the age of eighteen, opening the way for his ill-fated younger brother, Prince Charles, to assume the throne as Charles I.

20. The Reverend Crashaw could have been faulted for spiritual conflict of interest since he

was an investor in the company's plans, but less attention was paid to such niceties in 1609 than today.

21. Robert Gray, *A Good Speed to Virginia* (1609; reprint, New York, 1937), unpaginated.

22. Robert Latham, ed., *The Shorter Pepys* (Berkeley, Calif.: University of California Press, 1985), pp. 665–66.

23. Unlike the reserved and somewhat stodgy English of later times, the English in the sixteenth and seventeenth centuries—men and women both—were known throughout Europe as a warmly demonstrative people who unabashedly hugged and kissed in public.

24. David B. Quinn, "Notes by a Pious Colonial Investor," *William and Mary College Quarterly Magazine* (October 1959), p. 553.

25. Virginia 350th Anniversary Celebration Corporation, *The Second Virginia Charter, 23 May 1609*, 1957, p. 27ff.

26. Robert Johnson, *Nova Britannia* (1609; republished in *First Hand Accounts of Virginia, 1575–1705*, etext.lib.virginia.edu).

27. Barbour, *The Jamestown Voyages Under the First Charter* (Cambridge, England: Cambridge University Press, 1969), vol. 2, p. 255.

28. Ibid., p. 259.

29. Ibid., p. 260.

30. Lyme today is known as Lyme (or Lime) Regis, having been given its new name during the English Civil War when townspeople, loyal to King Charles I, mounted a spirited but doomed defense against the rebel forces of Oliver Cromwell.

31. Privateering was little more than legalized piracy. In times of war, private vessels were given the right to attack and capture enemy ships, stealing the ships and cargo as prizes of war.

32. Haile, *Jamestown Narratives*, p. 361.

2: Sailing in Friendly Consort

1. These weights were listed by John Smith in *An Accidence for Young Seamen*, a short book believed to be the first manual for mariners. It is included in Arber, *Works of John Smith*.

2. In 1571 the Protestant Inquisition held trials for thirty English seamen who had been captured in Captain John Hawkins's abortive raid on the port of San Juan de Ulloa. Eleven of these seamen, considered not just pirates but heretics, were given light sentences because they had been sixteen years of age or younger when their crimes were committed. It seems to be a safe bet that the percentage of very young sailors in 1609 was about the same as in the heyday of the Elizabethan sea dogs.

3. The full title of this work was *A True Relation of Such Occurrences and Accidents of Noate as Hath Hapned in Virginia since the first planting of that Collony, which is now resident in the South part therof, till the last returne from thence.* For obvious reasons, it is typically referred to by its shorter and more manageable moniker.

4. Arber, *Works of John Smith*, vol. I, p. 8.

5. Ibid., vol. I, p. 40.

6. Ibid., vol. 2, p. 479.
7. Quinn, "Notes by a Pious Colonial Investor," *William and Mary College Quarterly Magazine* (October 1959), p. 554. Powle was wrong about the number of settlers on board the six vessels. It is unlikely that many more than five hundred boarded in London.
8. Arber, *Works of John Smith*, vol. 2, p. 804.
9. William Strachey, *A True Reportory of the Wreck and Redemption of Sir Thomas Gates, Knight, upon and from the Islands of the Bermudas: His Coming to Virginia and the Estate of that Colony Then and After, under the Government of the Lord La Warr, July 15, 1610, Written by William Strachey*, included in Louis B. Wright, ed., *A Voyage to Virginia in 1609—Two Narratives* (Charlottesville, Va.: University Press of Virginia, 1993), p. 3.
10. Barbour, *The Jamestown Voyages Under the First Charter*, vol. 2, p. 263.
11. Gabriel Archer, one of the settlers, writing later of these instructions, confuses Bermuda with Barbuda. Some historians have made the same mistake and written that the officers of the fleet were instructed to rendezvous in Bermuda if they were separated by bad weather. In fact, as historian Philip Barbour noted in his *Jamestown Voyages Under the First Charter*, English mariners avoided Bermuda until after 1609.
12. Strachey, *A True Reportory*, p. 3.
13. A "knot" is a unit of measurement equal to one nautical mile per hour. A nautical mile is equal to one minute of longitude at the equator, or 1.15 statute miles. Hence, a ship making six knots would be traveling through the water at roughly seven miles per hour.

3: "A Dreadful Storm and Hideous"

1. Jan de Hartog, *The Call of the Sea* (New York: Atheneum, 1966), p. 417.
2. Strachey, *A True Reportory*, p. 4.
3. Ibid.
4. Ibid., p. 5.
5. Ibid., p. 6.
6. Ibid. Strachey's description of the rain flooding the air is not an exaggeration. Animals and birds have been known to drown during a hurricane, their lungs filled with wind-driven water.
7. Strachey, *A True Reportory*, pp. 7–8.
8. Ibid., p. 8.
9. Ibid., p. 9.
10. Ibid.
11. Ibid., p. 10.
12. Ibid., pp. 10–11.
13. Ibid., p. 11.
14. Ibid., p. 12.
15. Ibid.
16. Ibid., p. 14.

17. Sylvester Jourdain, *A Discovery of the Bermudas, Otherwise Called the Isle of Devils*, quoted in Louis B. Wright, ed., *A Voyage to Virginia in 1609—Two Narratives* (Charlottesville, Va.: University Press of Virginia, 1973), p. 106.

18. Jourdain, *Discovery*, pp. 106–7.

19. Archaeological studies of the wreck in the 1980s showed that the *Sea Venture*'s scant remains sit at a depth of about thirty feet in a cleft in the reef about a half mile roughly east-southeast of Fort St. Catherine. This opening is shaped like a V—or an arrowhead—pointing to shore. Sir George Somers, on the poop and conning the vessel, may well have seen what he thought was a blue-water channel leading to the beach and sailed into the cleft hoping it would lead to the beach.

20. According to legend, the tradition of allowing women and children aboard a sinking ship into lifeboats first did not start until 1852 with the loss of the HMS *Birkenhead* off the coast of Africa. Certainly none of the officers on board the *Sea Venture* would have considered not being among the first to flee the doomed ship. Given the importance of social rank in Jacobean England, highborn passengers would have considered it their right to be first in the ship's boats.

4: The Isle of Devils

1. *The First and Second Prayer Books of Edward VI* (London: Everyman's Library, 1968), p. 358.
2. Jeremiah 5:22 (King James Bible).
3. Sylvester Jourdain, *Discovery*, p. 108.
4. Edward Arber, *Works of John Smith*, vol. I, p. 303.
5. Henry Wilkinson, *Adventurers of Bermuda* (London: Oxford University Press, 1933), p. 23.
6. Ibid., p. 24.
7. Ibid., p. 37.
8. Quoted in Jean Kennedy, *Isle of Devils* (Glasgow: William Collins Sons, 1971), p. 22.
9. Ibid.
10. Ibid., p. 23.
11. Jourdain, *Discovery*, p. 109.
12. Ibid., p. 108.
13. Strachey, *A True Reportory*, p. 28.
14. Jourdain, *Discovery*, p. 110.
15. Strachey, *A True Reportory*, pp. 32–33. These wild pigs—tasty treats for the survivors—eventually were memorialized on "hogge money." These coins, believed to be the first ever minted specifically for use in an English colony, were probably originated in London and were first sent to the islands in February 1616. Specifically minted for use in the Bermudas, they are extremely rare. They were made of a mixed metal called "brasse" and featured a ship on one side—almost certainly a depiction of the *Sea Venture*—with a picture of a wild boar on the obverse.
16. Strachey, *A True Reportory*, pp. 30–31.

17. Jourdain, *Discovery*, p. 111.
18. Strachey, *A True Reportory*, p. 33.
19. Jourdain, *Discovery*, pp. 111–12.
20. Strachey, *A True Reportory*, pp. 25–26.
21. Ibid., p. 23.
22. Ibid., p. 39.
23. Ibid., p. 35.
24. A diorama on display at Fort St. Catherine shows William Strachey sitting by a fire, staring out to sea.
25. It is believed that Ravens and his shipmates made it to the Chesapeake, where they were captured and killed by Indians. It is just as likely that their little boat sank somewhere between Bermuda and Virginia.

5: "That Disorderlie Company"

1. George Percy, *Observations gathered out of a discourse of the plantation of the southern colony in Virginia by the English, 1606. Written by that honorable gentleman, Master George Percy*, reprinted in Haile, *Jamestown Narratives*, p. 96.
2. Ibid., p. 90.
3. The records say some six hundred passengers embarked for Virginia. Of those, 150 (the *Sea Venture* passengers) were in Bermuda. It is safe to assume twenty or so passengers were included in the thirty-two who died on board *Diamond* and *Swallow*. Another twenty or so were lost when the unnamed ketch was lost with all hands. That leaves roughly 410 passengers arriving in Jamestown, assuming—and it's not a safe assumption at all—that no one else died in the crossing.
4. Arber, *Works of John Smith*, vol. 2, p. 480.
5. Ibid., vol. 1, p. xcv.
6. Ibid.
7. Ibid., p. xciv. Some historians take Archer's letter at face value. However, the noted historian Philip Barbour is of the opinion that Archer meant Barbuda and not Bermuda. This makes sense for the reasons already stated.
8. Ibid., vol. 2, p. 480.
9. George Percy, *A Trewe Relacyon of the Proceedings and Ocurrentes of Momente which have Happened in Virginia from 1609, until 1612*, included in *Virginia: Four Personal Narratives* (New York: Arno Press, 1972), p. 262.
10. Arber, *Works of John Smith*, vol. 2, p. 482.
11. George Percy tells a different tale. He claims that Smith, for some unfathomable reason, incited the Indians to attack the settlement by telling them those inside had almost no gunpowder. This is simply unbelievable, though it is apparent that the little fort was easily overrun by a handful of attackers, so supplies of powder and shot may indeed have been low. See Percy, *A Trewe Relacyon*, pp. 263–64.
12. Arber, *Works of John Smith*, vol. 2, p. 482.

13. Ibid., p. 484.
14. Ibid.
15. Ibid., p. 485.

6: Mutinies

1. Strachey, *A True Reportory*, p. 39.
2. Ibid., p. 40.
3. See Arber, *Works of John Smith*, vol. 2, p. 638. John Smith says, "such a great difference fell amongst their Commanders [leaders], that they [the survivors] liued asunder in this distresse, rather as meere strangers then distressed friends." Their distress, of course, is the loss of their ship.
4. There were probably a few boys and girls young enough to be considered "children" by contemporary reckoning; however, no children are mentioned in any surviving accounts of the shipwreck or time in Bermuda. That may be because none sailed on the *Sea Venture* or—just as likely—because children old enough to walk were considered (and treated like) little adults.
5. Strachey, *A True Reportory*, p. 53.
6. Ibid., p. 39.
7. The cedar trees that grew in such profusion today are quite rare in Bermuda today. Almost all were killed by a blight within a few decades of the arrival of the English.
8. Strachey, *A True Reportory*, p. 41.
9. Ibid., p. 40.
10. Ibid., p. 43.
11. Ibid., pp. 43–44.
12. Ibid., p. 45. It is believed that Hopkins married a woman named Mary in 1604, when he was twenty-six or twenty-seven years of age, and that the couple had three children, Elizabeth, Constance, and Giles. When he took ship for Virginia in 1609, he left his wife and three small children in London.
13. Strachey, *A True Reportory*, p. 55.
14. Ibid., p. 56.
15. Ibid., p. 46.
16. Ibid., p. 47.
17. Ibid.
18. Ibid.
19. Ibid., p. 48.
20. Ibid., p. 49.
21. Ibid., pp. 49–50.
22. Ibid., p. 50.
23. Ibid., p. 52.
24. Ibid., p. 50ff.
25. Ibid., p. 53.

26. Ibid., p. 53.

27. John Smith, *Historye of the Bermudaes*, edited by Henry Lefroy (London, 1882), p. 14. This book, sometimes credited to Nathaniel Butler, one of the earliest governors of Bermuda, seems instead to have been the work of Captain John Smith. Much of it repeats, almost word for word, Smith's *General Historie of the Bermudas, Now Called the Summer Isles*, included in his *Works* and—at least as telling—the Bermuda historian General Sir J. Henry Lefroy states without reserve that the book is Smith's work. Because of that, quotes from the volume edited by Lefroy will be credited, when credit is given, to John Smith.

28. Strachey, *A True Reportory*, p. 55.

29. Ibid., pp. 56–57.

30. Ibid., p. 58.

31. Ibid., p. 60.

7: Famine Ghastly and Pale

1. Strachey, *A True Reportory*, p. 60.

2. Ibid.

3. The lead used to measure the water's depth was roughly conical, with an indentation or concavity in its base or heel. Typically, a mariner would place a gob of tallow or some other sticky substance in that concavity so that when the lead hit bottom it would pick up materials from the seabed. These materials would indicate proximity to shore and suitability for anchoring.

4. Strachey, *A True Reportory*, p. 60.

5. Arber, *Works of John Smith*, vol. 2, p. 533.

6. George Percy, *A Trewe Relacyon*, included in *Virginia: Four Personal Narratives* (New York: Arno Press, 1972), p. 264.

7. Actually, the location is on the Nansemond River where it branches off the James River.

8. Arber, *Works of John Smith*, vol. 2, p. 481.

9. Percy, *A Trewe Relacyon*, p. 264.

10. Arber, *Works of John Smith*, vol. 1, p. 132.

11. Percy, *A Trewe Relacyon*, p. 265.

12. Ibid.

13. Ibid., pp. 265–66.

14. Ibid.

15. Ibid.

16. Henry Spelman, *Relation of Virginea*, in Arber, *Works of John Smith*, vol. 1, p. civ.

17. Percy, *A Trewe Relacyon*, p. 266.

18. In 1607 a group of English colonists under the command of George Popham attempted to establish a settlement at the mouth of Maine's Kennebec River. After suffering a series of setbacks, the settlers, including Captain James Davies, abandoned their attempt and returned to England. While in Maine, however, they built the *Virginia*, the first ship

built by the English in North America. It is believed this is the same *Virginia* that sailed with the supply fleet of 1609.

19. Percy, *A Trewe Relacyon*, p. 266.
20. Ibid., p. 267.
21. Ibid., p. 266.
22. Ibid., p. 267.
23. Ibid., p. 269.
24. Ibid., p. 267.
25. Ibid. Percy's description of this event reads, in part, "And amongste the reste this was moste Lamentable Thatt one of our Colline murdered his wyfe . . . etc." Some historians have interpreted this as "one of our(s), (a man named) Colline(s). . . ." To me, this is a stretch, even though there were two men who might have fit the bill—a gentleman named Henry Collings, who arrived in the settlement in the fall of 1608, and Henrie Collins, who arrived on board one of the ships in the fleet of 1609. How much easier it is—and more logical—simply to accept Percy at face value and not to convict Collins or Collings on such flimsy evidence.
26. Arber, *Works of John Smith*, vol. 2, p. 499.
27. Percy, *A Trewe Relacyon*, p. 267.
28. The Council of Virginia, *A True Declaration* (1610, reprinted in Haile, *Jamestown Narratives*, p. 474).
29. Percy, *A Trewe Relacyon*, p. 267.
30. Ibid., p. 268.
31. Strachey, *A True Reportory*, p. 62.

8: "Misery and Misgovernment"

1. Strachey, *A True Reportory*, p. 63.
2. *Letter to the Virginia Company of London, 7 July 1610*, reprinted in Haile, *Jamestown Narratives*, p. 456.
3. Percy, *A Trewe Relacyon*, p. 269.
4. Strachey, *A True Reportory*, p. 63.
5. Arber, *Works of John Smith*, vol. 2, p. 444.
6. Strachey, *A True Reportory*, p. 65.
7. Ibid., p. 72.
8. Ibid., p. 74.
9. Ibid., p. 75.
10. Ibid., p. 76.
11. Ibid.
12. Percy, *A Trewe Relacyon*, p. 270.
13. Strachey, *A True Reportory*, p. 76.
14. Ibid., p. 77.

15. The Council of Virginia, *A True Declaration*, reprinted in Haile, *Jamestown Narratives*, p. 474.

9: The Buried Heart

1. Strachey, *A True Reportory*, p. 84.
2. Ibid.
3. Ibid., p. 85.
4. The Council of Virginia, *A True and Sincere Declaration*, reprinted in Haile, *Jamestown Narratives*, pp. 361, 363.
5. Ibid., p. 363.
6. Ibid., p. 371.
7. Susan Myra Kingsbury, *The Records of the Virginia Company of London*, (Westminster, Md.: Heritage Books, CD ROM), vol. 3, p. 25.
8. The Governor and Council in Virginia, *A Letter to the Virginia Company of London, 7 July 1610*, reprinted in Haile, *Jamestown Narratives*, p. 455.
9. Ibid.
10. Thomas West, Lord De La Warre, *Letter to Salisbury, rec'd September 1610*, reprinted in Haile, *Jamestown Narratives*, p. 466.
11. Ibid.
12. Ibid.
13. Jamestown expert and archaeologist William Kelso reported the recovery of artifacts including scrap copper, jettons (small copper coinlike objects that may have been used as Indian trade items or perhaps as substitute currency), armor, discarded weapons, and food remains in a trench or cellar within the palisade walls. While it is not certain— these artifacts can only be said to date from after 1610, not necessarily in 1610, as Dr. Kelso has pointed out on several occasions—it is at least possible or even likely that they provide evidence of Lord De La Warre's clean-up campaign. See William Kelso, *Jamestown Rediscovery*, vols. 1–7 (Jamestown, Va.: Association for the Preservation of Virginia Antiquities, 1995 and annually thereafter).
14. The Ancient Planters of Virginia, *A Brief Declaration of the Plantation of Virginia*, reprinted in Haile, *Jamestown Narratives*, p. 897.
15. Jourdain, *A Discovery of the Bermudas*, pp. 115, 116.
16. George Somers, *Letter to [the Earl of] Salisbury, 15 June 1610*, reprinted in Haile, *Jamestown Narratives*, p. 446.
17. From Argall's account, published in Samuel Purchas, *Purchase his Pilgrimes*, quoted in Philip Barbour, *Pocahontas and Her World* (Boston: Houghton Mifflin, 1970), p. 83.
18. Quoted in Barbour, *Pocahontas*, p. 83.
19. Smith, *Historye of the Bermudaes or Summer Islands*, p. 15.
20. There is today a memorial to Admiral Somers in a charming fenced garden in downtown St. George's. There is no guarantee, however, that the memorial marks the resting place of the admiral's heart.

10: Violent Proceedings and Villainy

1. Strachey, *A True Reportory*, pp. 79, 80.
2. William Strachey, *The Historie of Travaile into Virginia Britannia*, reprinted in Haile, *Jamestown Narratives*, p. 615.
3. Strachey, *A True Reportory*, pp. 88, 89.
4. Percy, *A Trewe Relacyon*, p. 270.
5. Strachey, *A True Reportory*, p. 89.
6. In his biography of Strachey (*William Strachey, 1572–1621*), S. G. Culliford allows the possibility that the *True Reportory* might have been addressed to Elizabeth Howard, the wife of Baron Howard of Walden, since the Strachey family had lived on Howard lands through much of the sixteenth century. However, he makes a compelling case that the letter was instead addressed to Lady Sara Smythe. Since Strachey did want the letter to circulate quickly among the members of the Virginia Company's governing council and since Smythe attended every meeting of the council, it just makes sense that Strachey's "Excellent Lady" was none other than Smythe's wife.
7. Strachey, *A True Reportory*, pp. 90, 91.
8. Ibid., p. 91.
9. Ibid., p. 90.
10. In late 1608, in accordance with instructions forwarded to Jamestown by the Virginia Company, John Smith and Captain Christopher Newport presented Wahunsonacock with presents including a fancy bed, a basin and ewer, and fine red robes along with a copper crown the chief was urged to don in a gesture that the Indian could not possibly have understood and that was meant to signify he was swearing loyalty to the English. The "coronation" quickly became a ludicrous example of the English lack of understanding of the chief and his people: Wahunsonacock refused to kneel to receive his crown until several Englishmen leaned on his shoulders, forcing him into something like a crouch. No fool, Wahunsonacock was not impressed by the ritual. In exchange for his fine presents, he gave Newport an old tattered robe, his worn shoes, and a few baskets of unshucked corn.
11. Strachey, *A True Reportory*, p. 92.
12. Several contemporary authorities asserted that Wahunsonacock was responsible for the eradication of the 114 colonists left alive on Roanoke Island in 1587. William Strachey, in his *Historie of Travaile into Virginia Britannia*, laid the responsibility squarely at the paramount chief's feet, saying that the "men, women, and children of the first plantation at Roanoak were by practice and commandment of Powhatan . . . miserably slaughtered" (William Strachey, quoted in Haile, *Jamestown Narratives*, p. 648). Several modern historians, however, call Powhatan's guilt into question. As far as the English in Jamestown and London were concerned, though, Wahunsonacock was clearly responsible for the murder of the English of the Lost Colony.
13. Virginia 350th Anniversary Celebration Corporation, *The Three Charters of the Virginia Company of London* (Williamsburg, Va., 1957), p. 60.
14. Ibid., p. 62.

15. Percy, *A Trewe Relacyon*, p. 271.

16. Ibid.

17. Ibid., p. 272.

18. Ibid.

19. Ibid.

20. Ibid., p. 273.

21. Ibid.

22. Ibid., pp. 273, 274.

23. Ralph Hamor, *A True Discourse of the Present State of Virginia and the Success of the Affairs there till the 18 of June, 1614,* reprinted in *Virginia: Four Personal Narratives* (New York: Arno Press, 1972), p. 26. According to a story that may well be apocryphal, Dale was so enraged by what he viewed as misrepresentations by Captain Christopher Newport and other experienced Jamestown hands who returned to England full of good news about the colony, that when he spied conditions at Point Comfort, he grabbed Newport's beard and gave it a mighty tug. If he did, he was lucky not to have experienced firsthand the old privateer's wrath.

24. Thomas Dale, *Letter to the Council of Virginia, 25 May 1611,* reprinted in Haile, *Jamestown Narratives,* p. 523.

25. Hamor, *True Discourse,* p. 26.

26. Dale, *Letter to the Council of Virginia.*

27. Hamor, *True Discourse,* p. 26.

28. William Strachey, comp., *For the Colony in Virginea Britannia. Laws Divine, Morall and Martiall, etc.* (1610; reprint, Charlottesville, Va.: University Press of Virginia, 1969), p. 19.

29. Percy, *A Trewe Relacyon*, p. 280.

30. Alexander Whitaker, *Letter to the Reverend William Crashaw, 9 August 1611,* reprinted in Haile, *Jamestown Narratives,* p. 549.

31. Don Diego de Molina, *Letter, 28 May 1613,* reprinted in Haile, *Jamestown Narratives,* p. 746.

32. This number—two thousand of those sentenced to death in England in a single nine-month period—gives us an idea of the popularity of the death penalty in Jacobean England.

33. Thomas Dale, *Letter to Salisbury, 17 August 1611,* reprinted in Haile, *Jamestown Narratives,* p. 554.

34. John Shirley, "George Percy at Jamestown, 1607–1612," *The Virginia Magazine of History and Biography* 57, no. 3, pp. 239, 240.

35. Percy, *A Trewe Relacyon*, p. 280.

36. Ibid., p. 281.

11: To Populate and Plant the Islands

1. William Crashaw, *Epistle Dedicatory to Alexander Whitaker's Good Newes from Virginia,* 1612, reprinted in Haile, *Jamestown Narratives,* pp. 701–2.

2. Smythe's house was large enough that it provided, in 1619, lodgings for the Marquis de

Tremouille, a special envoy of the French king, and for 120 French retainers who accompanied the marquis to England.

3. Strachey, *A True Reportory*, p. 100.
4. Edward Arber, *Works of John Smith*, vol. I, p. I.
5. The group of Essex conspirators included the brother of Jamestown colonist George Percy, Sir Charles Percy (not to be confused with Lord Henry, the Earl of Northumberland, who would be implicated in the treasonous Gunpowder Plot of 1605).
6. Quoted in Elizabeth Jenkins, *Elizabeth the Great* (New York: Coward-McCann, 1959), p. 315.
7. John Smith, *Historye of the Bermudaes*, p. 16.
8. Ibid., p. 17.
9. Robert Johnson, *The New Life of Virginea*, reprinted in Haile, *Jamestown Narratives*, p. 560.
10. *The Tempest*, I.1 (New York: Washington Square Press, 1994).
11. Strachey, *A True Reportory*, pp. 12–13.
12. *The Tempest*, I.2. 231–236.
13. Strachey, *A True Reportory*, p. 6.
14. *The Tempest*, I.2. 37–38.
15. Strachey, *A True Reportory*, p. 7.
16. *The Tempest*, I.2. 252.
17. *The Tempest*, I.2. 272.
18. In fairness, it must be noted that not everyone agrees that Shakespeare used the *True Reportory* as the basis for his play. The general belief, however, is that there is a link between the *True Reportory* and *The Tempest*. It seems logical.
19. Virginia 350th Anniversary Celebration Corporation, *The Three Charters of the Virginia Company of London* (Williamsburg, Va., 1957), p. 77.
20. Smith, *Historye of the Bermudaes*, p. 17.

12: A Most Pious and Noble End

1. Ralph Hamor, *True Discourse*, p. 33.
2. Ibid., p. 23.
3. Ibid., p. 28. Hamor said there were six ships in the fleet, while Percy said there were nine. It was this small armada that struck such terror into the colonists who believed—in the wake of the capture of the Spanish spy, Don Diego de Molina—that the fleet was a Spanish expedition come to eradicate Jamestown.
4. Letter from Samuel Argall to Nicholas Hawes, quoted in Philip Barbour, *Pocahontas and Her World* (Boston: Houghton Mifflin, 1970), p. 101.
5. Virginia 350th Anniversary Celebration Corporation, *The Three Charters*, pp. 57, 73.
6. Ibid., p. 63.
7. Hamor, *True Discourse*, p. 5.
8. Hamor, a bit of a sexist, included a side note in his narrative reminding readers that women, to get what they want, "can command teares." See Hamor, *True Discourse*, p. 5.
9. Ibid.

10. Ibid., p. 6.

11. Ibid., p. 5.

12. William Strachey, *The Historie of Travaile into Virginia Britannia*, reprinted in Haile, *Jamestown Narratives*, p. 620.

13. Ibid., p. 631.

14. Hamor, *True Discourse*, p. 6.

15. Ibid., pp. 6, 7.

16. Elizabeth Thomson, ed., *The Chamberlain Letters* (New York: Capricorn Books, 1966), p. 210.

17. Hamor, *True Discourse*, pp. 29, 30.

18. Crashaw, *Epistle Dedicatory to Alexander Whitaker's Good Newes from Virginia*, reprinted in Haile, *Jamestown Narratives*, p. 700.

19. Alexander Whitaker, *Good Newes from Virginia*, reprinted in Haile, *Jamestown Narratives*, p. 729.

20. Ibid., p. 731, 732.

21. Sir Thomas Dale, *Letter to D.M.*, included in *Virginia: Four Personal Narratives* (New York: Arno Press, 1972), p. 55.

22. The King James Bible was being written while Alexander Whitaker was a student at Cambridge and was published about the time he set sail for Virginia. While it is possible he had one of the new Bibles in his possesion, it is much more likely he had his own copy of the Geneva Bible, published in 1560.

23. For a discussion of the Powhatan religious beliefs, see Margaret Williamson, *Powhatan Lords of Life and Death* (Lincoln: University of Nebraska Press, 2003), pp. 174–75.

24. Quoted in Philip Barbour, *Pocahontas and Her World*, p. 113.

25. The Stockholm Syndrome got its name during a bank robbery in that city in 1973. The hostages defended their captors in legal proceedings. The term was coined by psychologist and criminologist Nils Bejerot to describe the behavior of hostages who, it is believed, relate to their captors as a way to guarantee their own safety.

26. John Rolfe, *Letter to Sir Thomas Dale*, included in *Virginia: Four Personal Narratives*, p. 64.

27. Ibid.

28. Sir Thomas Dale, *Letter to D.M*, included in *Virginia: Four Personal Narratives*, p. 52.

29. Ibid., p. 53.

30. Ibid.

31. Ibid., pp. 53, 54.

32. Hamor, *True Discourse*, p. 10.

33. Rolfe, *Letter to Sir Thomas Dale*, p. 67.

34. Ibid., p. 63.

35. Ibid., p. 61.

36. Dale, *Letter to Sir Thomas Dale*, p. 54.

37. Genesis 25:23 (King James Bible).

13: "Our Hoped and Desired Ilands"

1. Edward Neill, *History of the Virginia Company of London* (New York: Burt Franklin, 1968), p. 55.
2. Arber, *Works of John Smith*, vol. 2, p. 641.
3. *Letter from a Bermuda colonist*, reprinted in *Memorials of the Bermudas* (Toronto: Bermuda Historical Society, University of Toronto Press, 1981), vol. I, p. 66.
4. Rev. Lewis Hughes, *A letter sent in to England from the Summer Islands Written by Mr. Lewis Hughes, Preacher of God's Word There, 1615*, reprinted in *Memorials of the Bermudas* (Toronto: Bermuda Historical Society, University of Toronto Press, 1981), vol. 2, p. 577.
5. Ibid., vol. I, p. 67.
6. Ibid., p. 66.
7. Ibid.
8. Ibid., p. 67.
9. Ibid., p. 68.
10. Ibid., p. 71.
11. Virginia Company, *A Commission granted by us the undertakers for the Plantacon of Somer Islands*, reprinted in Lefroy, *Memorials of the Bermudas,* vol. I, p. 58ff.
12. Ibid., p. 61.
13. This church was eventually replaced by a cedar structure with a thatched roof. In 1715 this original church was replaced by a stone structure that still stands in downtown St. George's. St. Peter's is believed to be the oldest continuously used Anglican Church in the Western Hemisphere. The church's altar was crafted by Governor Richard Moore in 1615.
14. Lefroy, *A Commission*, p. 60.
15. Arber, *Works of John Smith*, vol. 2, p. 642.
16. Ibid.
17. Ibid.
18. Ibid., p. 643.
19. Ibid.
20. Ibid.
21. Smith, *Historye of the Bermudaes*, p. 23.
22. Arber, *Works of John Smith*, vol. 2, p. 644.
23. We don't know for sure when the *Plough* departed from the Bermudas. However, the so-called First Supply—about thirty settlers and some food and other supplies on board the *Elizabeth* (the second English ship sent by the Virginia Company to Bermuda)—departed from England in February 1613 bearing orders for Moore to send the ambergris on to the company without delay. Since it would have taken at least two months for the *Plough*, which arrived in the Bermudas in July 1612, to make the return voyage to England, and it would have taken the company a few weeks at least to learn about the ambergris and prepare orders for the *Elizabeth* to carry to the settlement on St. George's, it seems likely that the *Plough* would only have spent a few weeks in the islands before heading back to England.
24. Arber, *Works of John Smith*, vol. 2, p. 643.

25. Quoted in Wilkinson, *Adventurers of Bermuda*, p. 71.

26. Arber, *Works of John Smith*, vol. 2, p. 645.

27. Ibid.

28. Hogge money coins were, for the most part, used to purchase supplies, including liquor, from passing vessels. As a consequence, few remained in Bermuda. Today, hogge money is extremely rare, with only some forty coins known to be in existence.

29. Arber, *Works of John Smith*, vol. 2, p. 644.

30. Ibid.

31. Ibid.

32. Ibid., vol. 2, p. 645.

33. For an account of Ramirez's shipwreck, see Chapter 4.

34. Arber, *Works of John Smtih*, vol. 2, p. 646.

35. Ibid.

36. Ibid., p. 647.

37. Ibid.

38. Quoted in Jean Kennedy, *Isle of Devils* (London: Willam Collins Sons, 1971), p. 80.

39. Smith, *Historye of the Bermudaes*, p. 31.

40. Ibid., p. 32.

41. Arber, *Works of John Smith*, vol. 2, p. 646.

42. Quoted in Kennedy, *Isle of Devils*, p. 81.

43. Lewis Hughes, *A Plaine and true relation of the Goodnes of God towards the Sommer Ilands*, reprinted in Lefroy, *Memorials of the Bermudas*, vol. 2, p. 582.

44. Ibid.

45. Ibid., p. 583.

14: The Virginian Woman

1. Brickmakers, bricklayers, and masons were included among the settlers from the colony's earliest days and by 1614, when Rolfe and Pocahontas married, were contributing their skills to the construction of many homes and other dwellings.

2. Sir Thomas Dale, *Letter to D.M.*, reprinted in *Virginia: Four Personal Narratives*, p. 55.

3. Thomas Savage was about fourteen years of age in 1608 when he was "given" to Wahunsonacock by Captain Christopher Newport to learn the Indian language and customs. For the next three decades he served as a translator and intermediary between the English and the Powhatan. He was a favorite of Wahunsonacock, who addressed him as "my childe." See Hamor, *True Discourse*, in *Four Personal Narratives*, p. 38.

4. Ralph Hamor, *True Discourse*, reprinted in *Four Personal Narratives*, p. 40.

5. Ibid., p. 41.

6. Ibid., p. 11.

7. John Rolfe, *A True Relation*, included in *Virginia: Four Personal Narratives*, p. 105.

8. Robert Beverley, *The History and Present State of Virginia* (1705; reprint, Charlottesville, Va.: Dominion Books, 1968), p. 171.

9. Quoted in Frances Mossiker, *Pocahontas: The Life and Legend* (New York: Da Capo Press, 1996), p. 205.

10. Hamor, *True Discourse,* p. 24.

11. Ibid., p. 34.

12. Rolfe, *A True Relation,* p. 105.

13. Ibid., p. 103.

14. Ibid., p. 105.

15. Ibid., p. 108.

16. Quoted in Iain Gately, *Tobacco* (New York: Grove Press, 2001), pp. 67, 68.

17. Otto J. Scott, *James I* (New York: Mason/Charter, 1976), p. 290.

18. Thomas Dale, *Letter to Winwood, 3 June 1616,* reprinted in Haile, *Jamestown Narratives,* pp. 878, 879.

19. Thomson, ed., *The Chamberlain Letters,* p. 214.

20. Quoted in Mossiker, *Pocahontas: The Life and Legend,* p. 225.

21. Ibid., p. 227.

22. Quoted in Helen Rountree, *Pocahontas, Powhatan, Opechancanough* (Charlottesville Va.: University Press of Virginia, 2005), p. 177.

23. Arber, *Works of John Smith,* vol. 2, pp. 531, 532.

24. Ibid., p. 533.

25. Ibid., p. 534.

26. Beverley, *The History and Present State of Virginia* (Charlottesville, Va.: Dominion Books, 1947), pp. 43, 44.

27. Thomson, *The Chamberlain Letters,* p. 216.

28. Ibid., p. 215.

29. Beverley, *The History and Present State of Virginia,* p. 43.

30. Thomson, *The Chamberlain Letters,* p. 136.

31. Arber, *Works of John Smith,* vol. 2, p. 533.

32. Ibid.

33. Quoted in Camilla Townsend, *Pocahontas* (New York: Hill and Wang, 2004), p. 156.

34. John Rolfe, *Letter to Sandys, 8 June 1617,* reprinted in Haile, *Jamestown Narratives,* p. 889.

35. Quoted in Mossiker, *Pocahontas: The Life and Legend,* p. 280.

36. John Rolfe, *Letter to Sandys, 8 June 1617,* p. 889.

15: "A Faire and Perfect Common Weale"

1. Rolfe, *A True Relation,* included in *Virginia: Four Personal Narratives,* p. 110.

2. Ibid., p. 104.

3. Kingsbury, *The Records of the Virginia Company of London,* vol. 4, p. 58ff.

4. Ibid., vol. 3, p. 483.

5. Edward Arber, *Works of John Smith,* vol. 2, p. 573.

6. Beverley, *The History and Present State of Virginia,* p. 232.

BIBLIOGRAPHY

Ackroyd, Peter. *London: The Biography.* New York: Doubleday, 2000.

Adams, Stephen. *The Best and Worst Country in the World.* Charlottesville: University Press of Virginia, 2001.

Akrigg, G. P. V. *Jacobean Pageant: The Court of King James I.* Cambridge: Harvard University Press, 1962.

Andrews, K. R. "Christopher Newport of Limehouse, Mariner." *William and Mary College Quarterly Historical Magazine* (January 1954): 28–41.

Arber, Edward, ed. *Travels and Works of John Smith.* 2 vols. Westminster: Constable, 1895.

Arents, George. "The Seed from Which Virginia Grew." *William and Mary College Quarterly Historical Magazine* (April 1939): 123–129.

Barbour, Philip L., ed. *The Jamestown Voyages Under the First Charter.* 2 vols. Cambridge, England: The Hakluyt Society, 1969.

———. *Pocahontas and Her World.* Boston: Houghton Mifflin, 1970.

———. *The Three Worlds of Captain John Smith.* Boston: Houghton Mifflin, 1964.

Beverley, Robert. *The History and Present State of Virginia.* Charlottesville: Dominion Books, 1968.

Chute, Margaret. *Shakespeare of London.* New York: Dutton, 1949.

Culliford, S. G. *William Strachey, 1572–1621.* Charlottesville: University Press of Virginia, 1965.

De Hartog, Jan. *The Call of the Sea.* New York: Atheneum, 1966.

Emerson, Everett H. *Captain John Smith.* New York: Twayne, 1971.

Fausz, J. Frederic. "Middlemen in Peace and War: Virginia's Earliest Indian Interpreters, 1608–1632." *The Virginia Magazine of History and Biography* (January 1987): 41–64.

———. "An Abundance of Blood Shed on Both Sides." *The Virginia Magazine of History and Biography* (January 1990): 3–56.

First and Second Prayer Books of Edward VI. London: Everyman's Library, 1968.

Gately, Iain. *Tobacco.* New York: Grove Press, 2001.

Gayley, Charles M. *Shakespeare and the Founders of Liberty in America.* New York: Macmillan, 1917.

Gleach, Frederick. *Powhatan's World and Colonial Virginia.* Lincoln: University of Nebraska Press, 2000.

Gray, Robert. *A Good Speed to Virginia.* New York: Scholars' Facsimiles and Reprints, 1937.

Greenblatt, Stephen. *Will in the World.* New York: Norton, 2004.

Haile, Edward W., ed. *Jamestown Narratives: Eyewitness Accounts of the Virginia Colony.* Champlain, Va.: RoundHouse, 1998.

Hamor, Ralph. *A True Discourse on the Present State of Virginia.* London: 1615. Reprinted in *Virginia: Four Personal Narratives.* New York: Arno Press, 1972.

Hatch, Charles. *The First Seventeen Years: Virginia, 1607–1624.* Charlottesville: University of Virginia Press, 1957.

Herman, Arthur. *To Rule the Waves.* New York: HarperCollins, 2004.

Horn, James. *A Land As God Made It: Jamestown and the Birth of America.* New York: Basic Books, 2005.

Jenkins, Elizabeth. *Elizabeth the Great.* New York: Coward-McCann, 1959.

Jourdain, Sylvester. *A Discovery of the Bermudas, Otherwise Called the Isle of Devils,* in Louis B. Wright, ed., *A Voyage to Virginia in 1609—Two Narratives.* Charlottesville: University Press of Virginia, 1993.

Kennedy, Jean. *Isle of Devils.* Hamilton, Bermuda: William Collins Sons, 1971.

King James Bible. New York: World Publishing.

Kingsbury, Susan Myra. *The Records of the Virginia Company of London.* 4 vols. Washington, D.C.: GPO, 1933.

Latham, Robert, ed. *The Shorter Pepys.* Berkeley: University of California Press, 1985.

Lee, Christopher. *1603.* New York: St. Martin's, 2004.

Lefroy, J. H. *Memorials of the Discovery and Early Settlement of the Bermudas or Somers Islands.* 2 vols. Toronto: Bermuda Historical Society, 1981.

McCary, Ben C. *Indians in Seventeenth-Century Virginia.* Charlottesville: University Press of Virginia, 1995.

Miller, Helen Hill. *Passage to America.* Raleigh: America's Four Hundreth Anniversary Committee, North Carolina Department of Cultural Resources, 1983.

Morison, Samuel Eliot. *The European Discovery of America, The Northern Voyages.* New York: Oxford University Press, 1971.

Morrill, John, ed. *The Oxford Illustrated History of Tudor and Stuart Britain.* New York: Oxford University Press, 1996.

Mossiker, Frances. *Pocahontas.* New York: Da Capo, 1996.

National Park Service, U.S. Department of the Interior. *Jamestown Archeological Assessment.* Washington, D.C.: GPO, 2001.

Neill, Edward. *History of the Virginia Company of London.* New York: Burt Franklin, 1968.

Percy, George. *A Trewe Relation of the Proceedings and Ocurrentes of Moment.* Reprinted in *Virginia: Four Personal Narratives.* New York: Arno Press, 1972.

Porter, Roy. *London: A Social History.* Cambridge: Harvard University Press, 1995.

Powell, William S. "Aftermath of the Massacre: The First Indian War, 1622–1632." *The Virginia Magazine of History and Biography* (January 1958): 44–75.

Price, David A. *Love and Hate in Jamestown.* New York: Knopf, 2003.

Quinn, David Beers. "Advice for Investors in Virginia, Bermuda, and Newfoundland, 1611." *William and Mary College Quarterly Historical Magazine* (January 1966): 136–145.

———. *England and the Discovery of America.* New York: Knopf, 1974.

———. *Set Fair for Roanoke.* Chapel Hill: University of North Carolina Press, 1985.

———. "Notes by a Pious Colonial Investor." *William and Mary College Quarterly Magazine* (October 1959): 551–555.

Raine, David F. *Sir George Somers: A Man and His Times.* Bermuda: Pompano Press, 1986.

Rich, R. *News from Virginia.* New York: Scholars' Facsimiles and Reprints, 1937.

Rolfe, John. *Virginia in 1616.* Reprinted in *Virginia: Four Personal Narratives.* New York: Arno Press, 1972.

Rountree, Helen C. *Pocahontas, Powhatan, Opechancanough.* Charlottesville: University of Virginia Press, 2005.

———. *The Powhatan Indians of Virginia.* Norman: University of Oklahoma Press, 1989.

Rountree, Helen C., and Turner E. Randolph III. *Before and After Jamestown.* Gainesville: University Press of Florida, 2005.

Rowse, A.L. *The Elizabethans and America.* New York: Harper Colophon Books, 1959.

———. *Shakespeare's Southampton.* New York: Harper and Row, 1965.

Shakespeare, William. *The Tempest.* New York: Washington Square Press, 1994.

Shirley, John W. "George Percy at Jamestown, 1607–1612." *The Virginia Magazine of History and Biography* (July 1949): 227–243.

Smith, John. *Historye of the Bermudaes.* London, 1882.

Stern, Virginia F. *Sir Stephen Powle of Court and Country.* Selinsgrove, Pa.: Susquehanna University Press, 1992.

Stewart, Alan. *The Cradle King.* New York: St. Martin's, 2003.

Stow, John. *The Survey of London.* London: J. M. Dent & Sons, 1970.

Strachey, William. *Laws Divine, Morall and Martiall, etc.* Charlottesville: University Press of Virginia, 1969.

———. *A True Reportory of the Wreck and Redemption of Sir Thomas Gates, Knight, upon and from the Islands of the Bermudas: His Coming to Virginia and the Estate of that Colony Then and After, under the Government of the Lord La Warr, July 15, 1610, Written by William Strachey,* in Louis B. Wright, ed., *A Voyage to Virginia in 1609—Two Narratives.* Charlottesville: University Press of Virginia, 1973.

Thomson, Elizabeth, ed. *The Chamberlain Letters.* New York: Capricorn Books, 1965.

Townsend, Camilla. *Pocahontas and the Powhatan Dilemma.* New York: Hill and Wang, 2004.

Vaughan, Alden T. *American Genesis.* New York: HarperCollins, 1975.

Virginia 350th Anniverary Celebration Corporation. *The Three Charters of the Virginia Company of London.* Williamsburg, 1957.

Wilkinson, Henry. *The Adventurers of Bermuda.* London: Oxford University Press, 1933.

Williamson, Margaret Holmes. *Powhatan Lords of Life and Death.* Lincoln: University of Nebraska Press, 2003.

Wingood, Allan, J. "Sea Venture: An Interim Report on an Early 17th Century Shipwreck Lost in 1609." *The International Journal of Nautical Archeology* (November 1982): 334–347.

———. "Sea Venture: Second Interim Report—Part 2: the Artifacts." *The International Journal of Nautical Archeology* (May 1986): 149–159.

Woodward, Grace Steel. *Pocahontas.* Norman: University of Oklahoma Press, 1969.

Wright, Louis B., ed. *A Voyage to Virginia in 1609—Two Narratives.* Charlottesville: University Press of Virginia, 1973.

Zuill, William. *The Wreck of the Sea Venture, 1609.* Bermuda: Globe Press, 1981.